Shoals to Sand Dunes: Your Alabama Travel Guide

by Lynn Edge

**Seacoast Books
Publisher
Birmingham, Alabama**

DEDICATION

For my high school English teacher, J. Wilburn Holmes, who told me I was wasting my time writing, and my college English professor, Samuel Mitchell, who told me I wasn't. I guess the success of this book will prove who was right. Mr. Mitchell, I hope you win.

Edge, Lynn
Shoals to Sand Dunes: Your Alabama Travel Guide
Book design by Chris Roberts

ISBN: 1-878561-03-0

Printed in the U.S.A.
First edition

Table of Contents

Alabama: Much more than Cotton and Steel

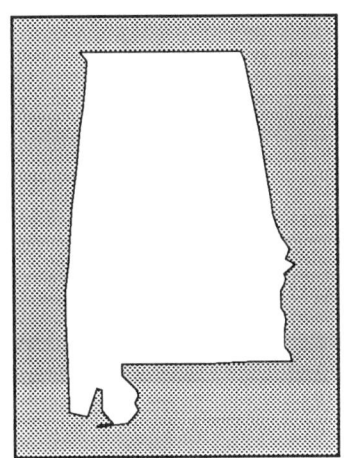

For too long, people have thought of Alabama as a state with only two features - steel mills and cotton fields. Those who aren't familiar with the state are surprised to learn that there are mountains in Alabama and many of them aren't sure the state reaches all the way to the seashore. Fortunately for we who live here, Alabama isn't just a lump of land designed to keep Georgia and Mississippi from bumping into one another.

When the states are listed alphabetically, Alabama comes first. When they are listed by diversity of natural resources, Alabama is second only to California. In this almost-rectangular state called Alabama, the Appalachian foothills meet the Gulf Coastal Plains. In the north, the mountains roll gently, covered with kudzu, pine trees and hardwoods. In the south, the land slopes toward the Gulf and the pines hold sandy soil near the breaking waves.

In Alabama, there are places to snow ski and places to waterski. The elevation in the state ranges from almost 2,500 feet in the north to sea level at the coast.

Water covers about one million acres in Alabama. This state has more miles of navigable waterways than any other in the nation. Alabama, literally, is wrapped in rivers and streams with the Tennessee River on the north, the Warrior-Tombigbee and Tennessee-Tombigbee system on the west, the Tri-River system combining with the Chattahoochee on the east and the Alabama River running through the central and southwest parts of the state.

Alabama is either home to or a migration resting place for more than 350 species of birds. The state has more than 200 species of freshwater fish and about 300 species of salt water fish.

The state park system - with 21 parks - is among the best in the nation. Alabama also has 24 public lakes and four national forests.

But Alabama is more than just her lush forests, tumbling rivers and white sand. It is a state with a delightful mix of rural, urban and suburban cultures. There are more than 20 colleges and an entire junior college system in Alabama. The state has more than 100 museums. It is crisscrossed with a system of interstate, federal, state and county highways that circle large cities and cut through small towns.

To greet people coming to Alabama, eight Welcome Centers are scattered around the state's borders. The centers have maps, brochures and people to give visitors information. But what makes them different from the ones in other states is that most have porches with rockers, pine trees and picnic tables. A stop at one of Alabama's welcome centers sort of slows vacationers down and sets the tone for a relaxing trip through the state. More than 200,000 people each year are welcomed to Alabama at one of the centers.

Alabama also is her people. The state has given birth to musicians, political dynasties, writers, performers, statesmen, civil rights leaders, sports stars, scientists, and at least one astronaut. Among her children are W.C. Handy, Nat King Cole, the Bankheads, Harper Lee, Fannie Flagg, Nell Carter, Kate Jackson, Bo Jackson, Willie Mays, the Wallaces, Jenni Chandler, Johnny Mack Brown, Jim Nabors, George Lindsey, Wayne Rogers, William Gorgas, Lister Hill, Hugo Black, Willie McCovey, William Rufus King, Helen Keller, Hank Williams, Teddy Gentry, Randy Owen, Jeff Cook, Jesse Owens, Walker Percy, Rosa Parks and Henry Hartsfield.

And Alabama is her people whose names may not be so well known. These are the people who still say "Y'all" even if they've gone to some big college "up north." Southern hospitality is a way of life to them, no matter if they live in Birmingham or Branchville.

The travel brochures call Alabama "The State of Surprises." That's a good slogan. It's also the truth. Alabama constantly surprises not only her visitors, but her citizens as well. There's something new to be discovered at every turn, some new treat in store in every county. This book was written to help you be pleasantly surprised at the treasures the state of Alabama holds. Y'all have fun with it.

Things to Know
About Alabama

Alabama, the 22nd state to join the Union, sits cozily amid its neighbors in the South with Mississippi to the west, Georgia to the east, Florida to the south and Tennessee to the north. The foothills of the Appalachian Mountains reach into the state and the Gulf of Mexico makes up part of its southern border.

These physical features make Alabama a place of both breathtaking mountain views and sundrenched seashores. Alabama is the 29th largest state in the United States and the fifth largest state in the 15 states considered to be "Southern States." It became a state on December 14, 1819.

Alabama seceded from the Union on January 11, 1861 and was readmitted on June 25, 1868.

For visitors and residents alike, here is a quick overview of the state:

Population: 4,040,587 (1990 Census)
Land area: 51,705 square miles
Greatest distance east to west: 210 miles
Greatest distance north to south: 329 miles
Coastline: 53 miles
Acres of forest land: 21,361,100
Water resources: 504,336 acres of ponds, lakes and reservoirs. Nineteen rivers measuring a combined distance of 3,074 miles. Major creeks with a combined distance of 10,837 miles. Freshwater wetlands cover 400,000 acres, tidal wetlands cover 2.6 million acres. There are 625 square miles of estuaries, harbors and bays.

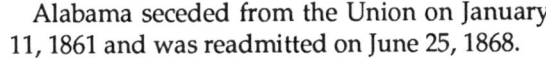

Quick Facts

Climate: Spring temperatures usually arrive early in Alabama, with temperatures in the 60s daily by March. During the summer, temperatures usually reach into the 90s and sometimes even into the 100s. In North Alabama, the first killing frost usually comes in October or November and ends by late March or early April. The Southern portion of the state usually doesn't get a killing frost until late November or early December. January temperatures in the state average about 52 degrees Fahrenheit in the south and about 46 degrees in the north. Temperatures can drop to 0 or below periodically during the winter and freezing temperatures are not uncommon, especially in the northern portion of the state.

Precipitation: Annual precipitation from rain, melted snow and other moisture averages about 65 inches on Alabama's coast and about 53 inches in the north. Most of the state rarely experiences snow, but the higher elevations of North Alabama do have snowfall during the winter.

Capital: Montgomery

Time Zone: Central

Area Code: 205 (Must be used for all in-state long-distance calls.)

Speed limit: Maximum speed limit generally is 55 miles per hour, with the exception of rural interstates, where a 65 mile per hour limit is posted. Slower speed limits often apply and are posted.

Seat belt laws: Children under six must be in approved passenger restraints anywhere in the vehicle. Ages 4 and 5 may use a regulation seat belt. Age 3 and under must use an approved safety seat. At the present, there is no mandatory seat belt law for adults.

Other traffic information: Right turn after a stop on red is permitted throughout Alabama unless otherwise posted. Minimum driver's license age is 16. Learner's permit at 15. Motorist may report highway emergencies by calling the toll-free Highway Emergency Hotline, 1-800-525-5555.

Liquor laws: By the bottle at stores and facilities with liquor licenses 6 days a week until 2 a.m. on Sunday. Jefferson County and Huntsville (limited) permit Sunday liquor sales after 1 p.m. Minimum age is 21. Drivers are considered legally intoxicated and may be charged with driving under the influence of alcohol if the alcohol content in their blood is .10 percent or greater. Alabama has an implied-consent breath analysis law. If you are suspected of driving under the influence of alcohol, you are required to take a breath test. Refusal to do so can result in a 90-day suspension of your driver's license.

Interstate System: There are 829 miles of interstate highway in Alabama. The state has more than 10,000 miles of state highways and more than 58,000 miles of county highways.

Sales Tax: The State of Alabama charges a 4 percent sales tax on almost all retail purchases. Most cities and counties add their own sales taxes. Total sales taxes, therefore, range from 4 to 10 percent.

Welcome Centers: Alabama provides some of the nation's nicest and friendliest welcome centers. If you are entering the state on one of the interstates, be sure and stop by for a free soft drink, tourism information and a friendly welcome. Welcome Centers are on I-65 South, coming from Tennessee, in Limestone County near Ardmore; on I-10 West, coming from Florida, in Baldwin County; on I-59 South, coming from Georgia and Tennessee, in DeKalb County; on I-10 East, coming from Mississippi, in Mobile County, near Grand Bay; on I-85 South, coming from Georgia, in Chambers County near Lanett; on I-59/20 North, coming from Mississippi, in Sumter County; on I-20 West, coming from Georgia, in Cleburne County. There is one Welcome Center not located on an interstate. It is the Houston Welcome Center, on U.S. 231, just north of the Florida line near Dothan.

Visitor information: Alabama Bureau of Travel and Tourism, 1-800-ALABAMA (Nationwide). Hearing impaired travelers may get information about the state by either using their TDD or the Alabama Relay Service. TDD users should call 205-240-3150; those using ARC may call toll-free, 1-800-548-2546 and then give the operator Alabama's toll-free tourism number.

The Shoals: Florence to Ivy Green

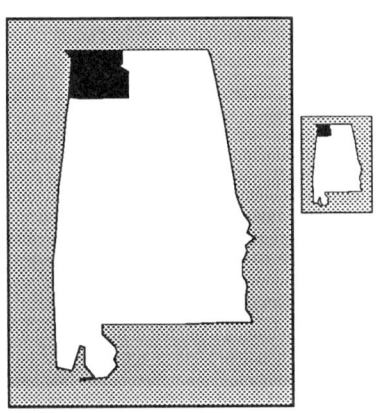

The Tennessee River, winding and splashing its way through the northwest corner of Alabama, almost seems to have reached out and gathered cities around it. Many of the cities in this part of the state are set cheek-by-jowl, their borders defined by the twists and turns of the river. Across this corner of the state, about 10 miles east of the Mississippi border, the Natchez Trace Parkway cuts a path northeast about 50 miles to the Tennessee line. From the first buffalo trampling through the wilderness, to the Indians, settlers, soldiers, ministers and bandits who followed, the Natchez Trace has provided a pathway for a colorful procession of America's frontier history.

The first national highway of the Old Southwest, the Natchez Trace served as a buffalo and Indian trail until French and Spanish settlers arrived in the 18th century and began using the crude path. By 1801, the U.S. government had ordered that the Trace be cleared and improved. The route quickly became the most important thoroughfare from Nashville to Natchez and remained so for the next two decades. To aid travelers, the government sanctioned inns - known as "stands" - at one-day intervals along the Trace.

The Natchez Trace has served as a military road many times, most notably in 1813 when General Andrew Jackson's army marched to the Battle of Horseshoe Bend and again in 1815 when Jackson took the route on his return from the Battle of New Orleans. By the early 1820's, the steady stream of travelers who had followed the Natchez Trace for decades vanished as steamboats offered safer and faster transportation. By the late 1820's, the once busy Trace was used only as a path between small communities, but in the early 1900's interest in the historic route was renewed. A garden club in Mississippi began marking the path in 1909 and 50 years ago, the modern parkway was born - a project of Tennessee, Alabama and Mississippi.

The road today closely follows the old Trace with markers and exhibits depicting the hardships of early travelers. A highlight of any journey along the Trace is the chance to stop and walk the original portions that have been

5

preserved. The old Trace leads away from the sounds of passing cars to places where sunlight pierces deep forests.

Many of those stops along the way are in Alabama. One of the nicest is Rock Spring, where the trail takes you back to the spring itself.

No doubt because the Tennessee River and the Natchez Trace cross this four-county "square" at the top of the state, many important events in the state's history have taken place here. And from this part of the state have come many of Alabama's most famous native sons and daughters.

FLORENCE

Florence, the area's largest city, has an impressive genealogy. The town was established in 1818 by a group of land developers - a group that include General John Coffee, surveyor general of the Alabama Territory; John McKinley, who later became a U.S. Supreme Court justice, and James Jackson, a wealthy planter and horse breeder. A young Italian surveyor laid out the town and, in his honor, the city got the name of an Italian city. One of the first people who bought a lot in the newly established town was Andrew Jackson.

Even though the city of Florence appealed to the rich and famous, it didn't sit on the best spot along the river. Nearby were dangerous shoals where the river was impassable by

Alabama's NW Corner

Much of the land in this region, sitting in the northwestern corner of Alabama, lies in the valley of the Tennessee River. Near the four largest cities in this region - the Quad Cities of Florence, Muscle Shoals, Sheffield and Tuscumbia - the river tumbles over the rocky shoals that once made it impossible to navigate. Farmlands and hydroelectric plants both flourish here, where about 200,000 of Alabama's citizens make their home.

barge. So, with the help of Secretary of War John Calhoun and President James Monroe, citizens of Florence persuaded the federal government to help finance the construction of a canal around the shoals. The canal was finished in 1836, but within a year became inoperable. Fortunately, a railroad came soon after that to aid with the transportation problem. Florence's impressive list of founders didn't save the city from disrespect during the Civil War. The city was invaded several times by Federal troops and was threatened by Union gunboats on the river. Fortunately, the city escaped much of the heavy damage suffered by a number of other cities. And after the war, the city came back, carrying on its heritage and providing a hometown for four Alabama governors - Hugh McVay, Robert M. Patton,

Edward A. O'Neal and Emmet O'Neal. Another governor, George Houston, was reared on his father's plantation about 15 miles west of Florence. It also gave birth to the "Father of the Blues," W.C. Handy. The log cabin where Handy was born in 1873 today houses the W.C. Handy Home and Museum. The museum pieces include Handy's trumpet as well as the piano upon which he composed the "St. Louis Blues." Also in the museum is Handy's library and mementos from his musical career. Handy's home - at 620 West College Street - is open from 9 a.m. to noon and from 1 to 4 p.m., Tuesday through Saturday and is closed on major holidays. Admission is $2 for adults, $.50 for children.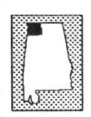

Another part of Handy's life history is found at St. Paul AME Zion Church on Cherokee Street. Founded in 1860, the church was moved to this site several years ago. Handy's grandfather and father were pastors at the church where visitors can see the stained glass window donated by Handy's father. Handy's father, by the way, didn't encourage his son's career. As a Methodist preacher, the elder Handy believed that nonreligious music was the work of the devil. Despite this, Handy learned dance tunes from a country fiddler and he and his friends used home-made instruments to play this "sinful" music.

Each August, Florence honors this native son with the W.C. Handy Music Festival. The celebration spans not only a week but almost an entire corner of the state. Events are scheduled in Florence, Sheffield, Tuscumbia and Muscle Shoals to honor Handy. Festival events include tours of the Handy Home, concerts, jam sessions, children's programs, a "Hallelujah Picnic," dances and a "Street Strut."

Pope's Tavern in Florence may not have been the birthplace of a famous person, but it certainly played host to a number of them. It was built by slave labor in 1811 as a stage stop and tavern. Among its guests was Andrew Jackson, who was quartered there. The tavern, at 203 Hermitage Drive, also served as a hospital for both sides during the Civil War. Today the structure houses a historical museum. A visit to the museum wouldn't be complete without seeing the "Florence Light Running Wagon," which came from the Florence Wagon Factory. Between 1889 and 1930, the factory was the world's second-largest builder of wagons. Pope's Tavern is open Tuesday through Saturday from 10 a.m. t0 4 p.m. and closed major holidays. Admission is $2 for adults and $.50 for children.

Also on this end of town is the University of North Alabama, the south's first co-educational college. Wesleyan Hall, one of the few Gothic Revival-style buildings in the Tennessee Valley, played unwilling host to General William Tecumseh Sherman in 1865. He headquartered there while on his way to reinforce Union troops in Tennessee.

Florence is a city filled with historic houses and structures. In fact, there are four districts which include almost 100 buildings. Among the houses in the districts are the Price Homestead, which had the first residential telephone in Florence; the Shepard-Kerr House, built in Steamboat Gothic

style; the Carter House, one of Lauderdale County's first pre-fabs and the Rogers-Rosenbaum House, the first house in Florence to have an elevator.

A brochure detailing walking tours of the historic districts is available from the Chamber of Commerce of the Shoals at 104 South Pine Street in Florence or 1105-A Highway 72 West in Tuscumbia.

In the heart of Florence is an Indian Mound and Museum. The mound is the largest ceremonial mound in the Tennessee Valley and the museum has a large collection of Indian artifacts dating back 10,000 years. The Indian Mound and Museum is open Tuesday through Saturday from 10 a.m. to 4 p.m. and closed major holidays. Admission is $2 for adults, $.50 for children.

WILSON DAM

The state's tallest official tourist attraction is rising in Florence, near Wilson Dam. Renaissance Tower, a 300-foot high structure, will include a restaurant, observation area and information center. The tower is scheduled to open in May, 1991.

Wilson Dam, about three miles west of Florence off U.S. 72 on Alabama 133 South, helped to tame the shoals that made navigation on the Tennessee so difficult in this area. The dam towers 137 feet high and is 4,541 feet long. Its power plant has a generating capacity of more than 600,000 kilowatts. But once the dam was capable of generating more controversy than energy.

When the United States entered World War I in 1917, one of the first priorities was to begin large-scale production of munitions. A key ingredient in making the munitions was large quantities of synthetic nitrates. To meet this need, President Woodrow Wilson initiated a crash program to build a

Alabama Bureau of Tourism and Travel

Wilson Lock and Dam, Tuscumbia.

hydroelectric dam and nitrate plant on the Tennessee River in Northwest Alabama.

Construction began in February, 1918, with a work force that quickly swelled to more than 18,000 people. In late November, the first nitrates were produced. But the war had ended two weeks earlier and controversy soon developed over what to do with the facilities, which included the still-unfinished dam.  Some members of Congress wanted to sell the complex to private industry, but the move was vigorously opposed by Senator George Norris of Nebraska and by other congressmen who recognized an opportunity to develop the natural resources of the entire Tennessee River basin, a region that includes seven states and about 40,000 square miles.

The issue remained unresolved until Franklin D. Roosevelt was elected president in 1932. One of the first acts of his New Deal was the creation of the Tennessee Valley Authority, with Wilson Dam - which finally had been completed in the mid-1920s - as its nucleus.

Flood control, improvement of river navigation and the production of hydroelectric power to promote economic development were all made part of the plans for TVA. Today, Wilson is one of nine mainstream dams forming a stairway of lakes on the Tennessee River, beginning above Knoxville and descending to Paducah, Kentucky.

Wilson's main navigation lock (as long as two football fields) can raise and lower barges as much as 100 feet as they make their way down the river. The lock here is the world's highest single lift lock. The largest hydroelectric installation in the TVA system, Wilson Dam also is the heart of the Wilson Dam/Muscle Shoals Reservation Area, a tract of about 2,400 acres that includes a visitor center, scenic overlooks, walking and cycling trails, camping and boating facilities and fishing.

Reading a sign telling you that the lock at Wilson holds 50 million gallons of water and empties in only 12 minutes may mean little. Seeing the lock in action is awe-inspiring. Until you've seen that much water move that rapidly, you can't imagine the force it generates. The powerhouse lobby is open to visitors and there is a visitors' overlook on the lockmaster's control building at the dam. The public areas of the dam are open daily for tours and admission is free.

Wilson Lake extends upstream to Wheeler Dam, off U.S. 72 East on Alabama 101 South. Wheeler Dam, 72 feet high and more than 6,000 feet long, impounds a 74-mile-long lake. Farther east - about 25 miles from Florence along U.S. 72 - is Rogersville and Joe Wheeler State Park, named for the Confederate general. This 2,550-acre park has several separate areas - the Wheeler Dam area, First Creek and Joe Wheeler State Resort and Elk River.

Joe Wheeler Resort has a lodge, which overlooks the river, as well as camping facilities. The recreation facilities here - like those at any Alabama resort park - are many and varied. There are hiking trails, an 18-hole golf course, putting greens, a driving range, lighted tennis courts, basketball courts, a pool, a private beach and a marina.

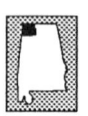 Elk River State Park, just over the county line in Limestone County, is considered part of this state park as well. The 55-acre area has facilities for fishing, boating and picnicking. The lodge here, which sleeps 26, often is used for family reunions and church groups. Elk River Park is 15 miles west of Athens on U.S. 72.

HEADING SOUTH...

If you choose a southward rather than an eastward path out of Florence, you won't feel that you've cheated yourself. There's just as much to see in this direction. In fact, it just makes sense to plot a course that lets you double back and take in all the sights in the area.

Almost directly across the river from Florence is Sheffield, where Alabama's first railroad was chartered in 1830. That first rail ran between Sheffield and Tuscumbia, barely two miles away. Still, it was a start and that heritage is honored at The Sheffield Depot.

Located at 1001 Shop Pike, the depot was built in the 1940s. Today it houses the Right Track Restaurant-Museum. The museum includes railroad memorabilia and replicas. The restaurant houses independence. The food is prepared and served by mentally handicapped citizens of the area. The restaurant is part of a program designed to help the people who work there develop independent living skills. Don't leave without trying the cinnamon rolls.

IVY GREEN

Following the route of that first railroad will lead you to Tuscumbia and Ivy Green, the home of Helen Keller. Standing on the walk in front of the small white house in Tuscumbia, the first thing that comes to mind is that it's an unlikely place for a miracle. Still, it was here that the miracle of learning began for Helen Keller.

The house was built by Helen's grandfather David in 1820. David came from Maryland to the Tennessee Valley in 1813 and staked out a large plantation. When he built Ivy Green seven years later, Keller floated the family's treasured household goods down the river and hauled them by ox cart to the new home. David's son, Arthur, become a captain in the Confederate Army. After the war, Capt. Keller returned to Ivy Green and brought his bride Kate. Capt. Keller converted his father's small office on the plantation into a bridal suite. In this tiny two-room cottage near the main house, Helen was born on June 27, 1880.

The Kellers added a small playhouse onto their cottage and filled it with toys for Helen. Here, Helen took her first steps and lived life as a normal toddler. But all that ended when Helen was 19 months old. She became ill, so ill that the family doctor thought she would die. Though Helen survived, the fever had left her blind and deaf. When Helen was six, Capt. Keller and his wife decided that a teacher must be found for their daughter. Capt. Keller visited Alexander Graham Bell. That visit led to Keller's hiring 20-

year-old Anne Sullivan from Perkins Institution in Boston.

Anne and Helen made the house's small office their classroom and, without much cooperation from Helen, Anne began to teach the youngster. After two weeks, the child had learned 10 or 20 words, but that's all they were - just words. She had connected no meaning to them. One morning, after trying to teach Helen the words "mug" and "milk," Anne led the struggling, temperamental child to the pump house where she began to pump water over the girl's hand. As the water flowed over Helen's hand, Anne formed the letters "W-A-T-E-R" into Helen's other palm. Anne had found the link she needed to break Helen's barrier to learning. Now the word had meaning.

"That word startled my soul," Helen later wrote. "Until that day, my mind had been like a darkened chamber, waiting for words to enter and light the lamp, which is thought." Before the evening was over, Helen had learned - and comprehended - 30 words and Anne Sullivan had earned her nickname "The Miracle Worker." After that, Helen never stopped learning. She became a talented writer and speaker and an outspoken advocate for the rights of the handicapped. Helen died in 1968, but the miracle she found beside the plain water pump at Ivy Green still calls visitors to the city of Tuscumbia.

Touring Ivy Green, one can peek through the door of the cottage where Helen was born. Her cradle and a few of her toys still sit inside. In the main house, visitors can see the upstairs bedroom shared by Helen and Anne - the bedroom in which Helen once locked Anne. Downstairs is the parlor where Capt. Keller, a newspaper editor, would sit and read his paper. One of the downstairs rooms has been devoted to Helen's personal mementos, including her Braille typewriter. Also there are memorabilia from the making of the film "The Miracle Worker," starring Anne Bancroft as Anne Sullivan and Patty Duke as Helen. But one of the most popular places for visitors is the simple well pump where miracles began.

Ivy Green, two miles off U.S. 72 and U.S. 43 in Tuscumbia, is open Monday through Saturday from 8:30 a.m. until 4:30 p.m. and Sunday from 1 to 4:30 p.m. (The final tour begins each day at 4 p.m.). Admission to Ivy Green is $3 for adults and $1 for children. The Helen Keller Festival, Tuscumbia's weekend-long salute to Miss Keller each June, includes a tennis tournament, entertainment, arts exhibits, a marathon run and tours of many of the city's homes and his-

Belle Mont, Tuscumbia

toric sites. Each summer, "The Miracle Worker" is performed at Ivy Green, usually during parts of June and July. The play begins at 8:15 p.m. and the gates open at 7 p.m. Admission is $7 for adults and $6 for children for reserved seats; $5 for adults and $4 for children for general admission. The ticket price includes a tour of Ivy Green between 7 and 8 p.m.

BELLE MONT

Another home you need to see in Tuscumbia is Belle Mont, one of Alabama's most distinguished plantation houses. Belle Mont, just off Colbert County 43, was built in 1830 for Dr. Alexander Mitchell. Mitchell, a Virginia native, wore many hats - he was a physician, a planter, an early county official and one of the largest slaveholders in the area.

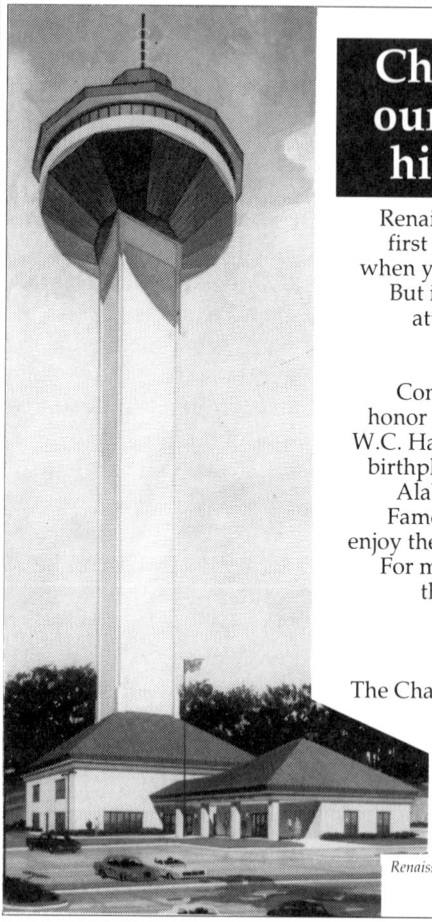

Recent research has turned up a story that says Mitchell's first wife died shortly after the construction of Belle Mont began. Mitchell's new wife, a Philadelphian, couldn't adjust to life in the South and the mansion was put on the market.

In 1833, Isaac Winston - uncle of Alabama's first native-born governor, John Anthony Winston - bought Belle Mont. In its prime, Belle Mont was a 1,680-acre estate, landscaped with summer flowers and fruit trees. It was the social center of the area. Around its U-shaped courtyard floated both casual conversation and talk of important business deals. Following the death of Catherine Winston in 1884, Belle Mont was used primarily as a retreat.

Belle Mont's history is a little hazy for a number of years after that, but it is known that J.C. Fennel and Gordon Preuit purchased it in 1941 and the Fennel family donated the house and about 35 surrounding acres to the state in 1983. Today, Belle Mont is being restored. Work on much of the house is finished and a comprehensive analysis has determined the chronology of its interior and exterior. Still to be done is such work as the replacement of marble mantelpieces removed by vandals several years ago.

Belle Mont currently is open on Sundays only from 1 to 5 p.m. Admission is $3 for adults, $2 for students and $.50 for children.

You'll Hear Music in Tuscumbia

Alabama Music Hall of Fame is off U.S. 72 near Tuscumbia. Honoring Alabama's contributions to the music industry, the Hall of Fame has on display everything from a Grammy award to a tour bus.

Set into the floor in the lobby of the building are bronze stars honoring the state's "Music Achievers." Near the lobby is the Hall of Fame Room, with portraits of those people who have been inducted into the hall. Also are are lifelike plaster casts of the group "Alabama," Lionel Richie and Hank Williams Jr. Leaving the Hall of Fame Room, visitors walk inside a giant jukebox, which plays tunes by Alabama performers. On display here, you'll see Elvis Presley's first contract - drawn up between Alabamian Sam Phillips and RCA - and some of the clothing worn by Jim Nabors when he played Gomer Pyle. The focal point of this part of the Hall of Fame is a life-size wax figure of Montgomery native Nat King Cole.

From the jukebox, visitors walk through a giant guitar and into the County Music Section of the Hall. Here there is a wax figure of Hank Williams Sr., dressed in one of Williams' stage costumes. Throughout this section, there are instruments and costumes from Alabama musical stars. The middle of the section is filled, literally, with the Southern Star tour bus that was the first to take the group "Alabama" from place to place. You can climb aboard and see what it is like to be "on the road."

The next section honors Alabama's Rhythm and Blues performers, such as W.C. Handy, Wilson Pickett and Percy Sledge. Among the items on display here are outfits some of the performers have worn as well as a number of gold records. In the section of the Hall that highlights the Muscle Shoals music industry, there are artifacts and instruments from a number of performers who have recorded at Muscle Shoals. You can become a performer

yourself here. There is a small recording studio, where you can choose a musical track and sing along, recording your voice on a cassette tape that you take home with you. Jake Hess' Grammy Award is on display in the Gospel Music section of the Hall along with costumes and clothing donated by Richie.

Hall of Fame hours are 10 a.m. to 6 p.m. Monday through Saturday and 1 to 5 p.m. Sunday. Admission is $6 for adults, $5 for senior citizens and students and $3 for children 6 to 12.

East of Tuscumbia, you can visit the site of LaGrange College, the first chartered college in the state. The college was burned by Union forces on April 28, 1863, but the city of Leighton, where it was located, celebrates an annual "Recall LaGrange Day" to honor the history of the college. Leighton is about 15 miles east of Tuscumbia off Alternate U.S. 72 East.

A little farther east on Alternate 72, near Wheeler, you'll find the home of Confederate Army hero General "Fighting" Joe Wheeler. Wheeler served in campaigns against the Indians before he joined the Confederate Army in 1861. During the Civil War, he earned a brilliant record as a cavalry general at the Battle of Shiloh and in battles in Tennessee and Georgia. Wheeler served in the U.S. Congress in the late 1800s and volunteered to fight in the Spanish-American War. At age 62, he was commissioned to command troops in Cuba.

The Joe Wheeler Plantation contains period antiques and rare china which was buried to protect it during the Civil War. The home is open year-round from 9 a.m. to 7 p.m., Monday through Saturday and from 12:30 to 7 p.m. on Sunday. Admission is $2 for adults, $1 for children under 12.

The hometown of Olympic great Jesse Owens is Oakville, in Lawrence County southwest of Wheeler. To get there, take Alternate U.S. 72 west from Wheeler two miles to Courtland. From Courtland, take Lawrence County 150 South to where it intersects with Alabama 157. Take 157 East to Oakville. The city recently has erected a monument dedicated to Owens' memory and honoring not only his athletic achievements, but also the inspiration he brought to "a world enslaved by tyranny" when he took four gold medals in "Hitler's Olympics."

Oakville is on the northern edge of the William Bankhead National Forest. About 22 miles inside the forest, off Alabama 33 South is the Old Pine Torch Church. They still hold Sunday services at this church, established in 1850.

Another side trip from Tuscumbia takes you southwest of the city to an attraction you won't want to miss as long as you're in the area. From Tuscumbia, take Business Route 72 South/43 West back to U.S. 72. It will take a little winding around, but it will be worth it to say you've seen a graveyard just for coon dogs. When you get to U.S. 72, take that road west to where it intersects with Alabama 247. Take Alabama 247 West about 12 miles, turn right and follow the signs to Key Underwood Coon Dog Memorial Graveyard.

When Underwood's favorite coon dog Troop died in 1937, his owner buried him here. Now more than 100 dogs are buried in the cemetery, which has become a traditional resting place for hunting dogs. The graves of these faithful companions are marked with touching tributes to the time they spent with their owners. The graveyard is open daily during daylight hours and there is no admission charge.

Near where the Trace crosses Colbert County a few miles north of Cherokee, there once was a ferry service operated by George Colbert. Colbert, who established the Colbert Ferry in 1790, is said to have made more than $20,000 each year ferrying people (at $1 a head) and livestock across the Tennessee. Colbert, once chief of the Chickasaw Nation, is supposed to have made about $75,000 ferrying Jackson's troops over the river.

The Dismals and other Natural Beauties

Southeast of Cherokee, you'll find some of the best natural beauty Alabama has to offer. Near Russellville, there are rock bridges, wilderness areas and reservoirs.

Magnolias, wild ferns, mountain blooming laurel and waterfalls provide the setting at Rock Bridge Canyon. Here, you can picnic near the natural bridges, formed of sandstone with quartz embedded in lines through it. Or you can explore Rockwall Springs. Take your comfortable shoes if you are going to spend some time enjoying the area - you'll have to do some walking. To reach Rock Bridge Canyon, go about 18 miles south of Russellville on U.S. 43, then west on Alabama 172. The canyon area is open daily from sunrise to sunset and admission is $3.

Alabama Mountain Lakes Tourist Association

Dismals Canyon, Phil Campbell

The Shoals 15

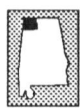

Another attraction you'll find in the area doesn't have a very inviting name. The Dismals Canyon is filled with boulders, incredible plant life and worms that glow in the dark. The 80-acre canyon was acquired by the United States in a treaty with the Chickasaws and then granted to private parties by President James Buchanan.

Naturalists who have visited the Dismals Canyon over the years say they have found ferns growing there that can't be found anywhere else. The trailing arbutus growing on sheer rock there usually is a plant that grows only on leaf mold. The Canadian Hemlock trees here tower more than 100 feet into the sky over the canyon's waterfalls and streams.

"Dismalites," the glow-in-the-dark worms, cling to moss growing here and, as far as is known, can be found at no other spot in the world.

There is evidence that the Indians used the Dismals Canyon as a home. "The Kitchen" is a rock shelter where they once cooked. And it is said that Aaron Burr hid out there in 1804 after shooting Alexander Hamilton.

The Dismals Canyon, 12 miles southwest of Russellville on U.S. 43, reopened to the public in late 1990 and hours vary. Check before you make the drive. Admission is $4 for adults and $3 for children.

Bear Creek Development Authority operates 15 public use areas around the four Bear Creek Lakes. In the Bear Creek complex, there are five camping areas with more than 200 campsites. From April until October 15, the gates to the camping areas are closed at 10 a.m. and open at 7 a.m. There is a $2 per day user fee for the public use areas and camping fees vary from $4 to $8.50 per night.

WHERE TO STAY

There are any number of chain motels and hotels in the area. Camping is available in the state parks, city-run parks and the recreation areas of the Shoals.

WHERE TO EAT

In addition to the chain restaurants, you'll find a number of local establishments that specialize in fish dishes as well as steaks. Among them are:

In Florence: Dale's, Princeton, C.C. and Company, Beau Weevils (set in an old house), Cloukies (breads and pastries here are homemade), Newbern's and The Court Street Cafe.

In Sheffield: The Southland, George's Steak Pit, Cafe Continental, Filling Station (in an old gas station), Cajun's.

In Muscle Shoals: The Chicago Connection and New Orleans Transfer.

In Tuscumbia: Colbert Grill (set in an old diner).

ANNUAL EVENTS

Annual events in this part of the state include:

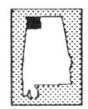

Muscle Shoals Birthday Celebration, April.
Jesse Owens Memorial Run, Moulton, May.

Recall LaGrange, Leighton, (Civil War re-enactments, music, history tales), May.
Mayfest, Rogersville, May.

The Miracle Worker, Tuscumbia, late June through late July.
Helen Keller Festival, Tuscumbia, late June.
Tour of Historic Homes, Tuscumbia, June.

Spirit of Freedom Celebration, Florence, July.

Summerfest Antique and Classic Car Show, Moulton, August.
W.C. Handy Music Festival, Florence, August.
U.S. Drag Boat Association Big River Finals, Florence, August.
Watermelon Festival, Russellville, August.

Northwest Alabama State Fair, Muscle Shoals, September.
Coon Dog Memorial Graveyard Labor Day Celebration, Cherokee, September.

Indian Corn Festival, Florence, October.
Shoals Fall Fest, Muscle Shoals (first weekend), Sheffield (Sheffield-fest, second or third weekend), Tuscumbia (Cold Water Fair, second or third weekend), Pumpkin Days (Florence, last weekend), October.
Renaissance Faire, Florence, October.

W.C. Handy Birthday Commemoration, Florence, November.

Wheeler Parade of Lights, Rogersville, December.
Rivermont Parade of Lights, Sheffield, December.
Edgemont Drive Parade of Lights, Sheffield, December.
Jackson Heights Parade of Lights, Muscle Shoals, December.
Wilson Parade of Lights, Florence, December.
NCAA Division II Football Championship, Florence, December.

Huntsville and Decatur: Past, Future

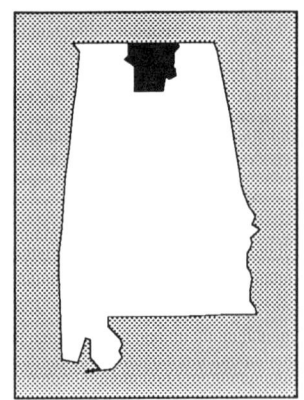

Alabama's past and future meet in this region. Within three counties here - Limestone, Madison and Morgan - are Mooresville, the state's oldest incorporated town; Somerville, a town where the 1800s still are in vogue, and Huntsville, the city that launched the United States into the Space Age.

Mooresville, in Limestone County, is an entire community on the National Register of Historic Places. Incorporated in November, 1818, the city is older than the state itself. When Mooresville became a town, it had 62 residents living in its one square mile area.

Today the city - surprisingly unchanged - is a living record of life in the 19th century. The streets and lots that visitors see as they stroll through Mooresville are the same ones that were laid out when the town came into being almost 200 years ago. The post office in Mooresville is the oldest in the state. The postmaster there places mail for today's residents in the wooden cubby holes that have been holding mail for Mooresville's citizens since 1819 and the mail still is hand stamped there.

Among the early settlers in Mooresville was Joseph Sloss, an Irish immigrant who first settled in Baltimore, then came to Huntsville. In 1819, Sloss, a tailor, set up shop in Mooresville. He was such a talented tailor that his reputation soon spread to other parts of the nation. A tailor in Tennessee, Andrew Johnson - who eventually would leave the tailor's trade and become the 17th president of the United States - was so impressed with what he heard about Sloss that he came to Mooresville as Sloss' apprentice. For several months during the 1840s, Johnson trained at Sloss' home in Mooresville. Sloss' house, now known as the Thatch-Hurn-Boozer-McNeal Home, still stands in Mooresville.

Among the other structures in Mooresville is the Community Church, built in 1820. The church, once abandoned, has been restored and one of the original chandeliers - which weathered the Civil War - still hangs there. The church had a slave balcony, which was boarded up after the war.

General James Garfield preached at the Church of Christ in Mooresville during the Civil War. The Bible he used is on display at the church. It is said that William McKinley also preached here.

To take yourself on this trip to Alabama's past, stop by the post office and get a copy of "A Walking Tour of Mooresville." The book costs less than $5 and is well worth the price. Mooresville is just off Alabama 20 about six miles northeast of Decatur.

ATHENS

Northwest of Mooresville is Athens, the county seat of Limestone County and the first city in Alabama to get electricity from the Tennessee Valley Authority. Athens, it seemed, was a natural choice for the county seat. It was in a central location and was - and still is - fortunate enough to be a traffic hub. Back in the early days of the county, that traffic was horses and stage coaches.

A number of the coach routes converged in Athens and provided easy access for the young ladies who came there to attend the Athens Female Academy, founded in 1822.

Huntsville & Decatur Area

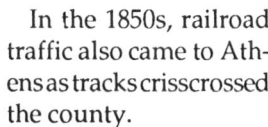

Almost 400,000 people live in the three counties in this region, a testament to the effect the Space Age had on Alabama's population. Rocket ships are just as common a sight as corn stalks and cotton fields here on the Tennessee border. The two largest population centers in Madison, Limestone and Morgan Counties are Decatur and Huntsville.

Alabama Mountain Lakes Tourist Association

Mooresville Post Office

In the 1850s, railroad traffic also came to Athens as tracks crisscrossed the county.

When the automobile came along, the city remained at the center of things. Both the Bee Line Highway (now U.S. 31), running from the Gulf Coast to the Great Lakes and Lee Highway (now U.S. 72), which linked the East Coast to the West, met in Athens. Today, Athens easily is accessible from Inter-

---

state 65.

If you're visiting Athens, you can enjoy everything from a corner drug store - complete with soda fountain - to shopping in a boutique.

The best way to see it all is to stop by the Athens-Limestone Chamber of Commerce and pick up copies of the driving tour brochure and the walking tour guide. The important stops are outlined and explained and the most convenient route through the city is charted for you. Among the buildings on the tour are the Beaty-Mason House, one of the oldest in the city; the Walker-Anderson-Patton House, which is said to have been purchased with gold paid to Walker as the defense lawyer in a spectacular murder trial; the Horton-Reynolds House, which belonged to Judge James E. Horton Jr., jurist in the "Scottsboro Boys" trial; the Rogers-Wolfe House, designed by Alfred Raney, who also designed the Grand Hotel in Point Clear, and the Martin-Malone-Johnson House, built by former Alabama Governor Joshua Martin.

The Richardson-Gordon House was used as a hospital during the Civil War. It seems to have been the site of more than a little excitement during that time. A soldier is said to have been shot while riding his horse through the hallway of the home.

Also on the tour is the Hendricks-Bailey House, which P.W. Hendricks started building before World War I. In 1905, an article in the "Alabama Courier" praised Hendricks and his brother for having "caused to be used more bricks and mortar than any man who ever lived in Athens, to them...is the town endebted (sic) for substantial growth and attractive appearance."

If those taking the tour of the city could have seen the Griffis-Pepper House in its heyday, they might have run into a knight in shining armor. The house stands in the middle of what was the Mason Racetrack, where thoroughbreds once raced and medieval jousting tournaments were played. The track was abandoned in the 1890s and the land was divided into building lots.

Although most of the homes in the historic district are private residences and can be viewed only from the outside, The Donnell House is being restored and is open by appointment.

In the heart of the city's historic downtown shopping district are a number of commercial buildings. The center of the district is the Courthouse, completed in 1919 and restored in 1975. From the Courthouse, visitors can walk around the city square and enjoy a malted at the corner drug store, which still has its soda fountain. Also in this area are the L&N Depot, which now houses a business. The 1933 Post Office Building is the home of the Limestone County Archives. Chapman's Quarters on Washington Street has a number of shops, restaurants and boutiques.

The Houston Memorial Library, built in 1835, was the home of former Alabama governor George S. Houston. Houston also was a U.S. Congressman and Senator. The home was donated to the city and today houses a library and museum outlining the history of Limestone County.

Brochures on walking/driving tours of the historic districts are available at the Athens/Limestone County Chamber of Commerce. Not far from the center of town is Athens State College. Founded as Athens Female Academy, it became Athens College in 1842. In 1931, the school became co-educational. In 1975, it became Athens State.

A walk across the campus is something like a history lesson in the growth of the city as well as the college. In 1820, Judge John McKinley gave 35 acres just east of what then was the city of Athens for a female academy and in 1822, classes started in a two-story frame building. In 1842, the Thomas Maclin family donated "the Maclin grove of stately oaks and flowering tulip poplars" - five acres of land - to the school and construction began on the Greek Revival style buildings there.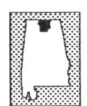

Founders Hall, the main building, is built of bricks made on the grounds of the college and Ionic columns support the front of the building. The bricks and columns are a testament to the master mason who did the work on them. That mason was a slave belonging to a Dr. Stith Malone. The outer walls of the building are 24 inches thick. The inner walls are only slightly slimmer - 15 inches thick.

Founders Hall is said to have been spared from the wrath of Union troops when someone presented the soldiers with a copy of a letter that was supposed to have been written by Abraham Lincoln.

Modifications and additions have been made to that original building, but the graceful lines still are there. At one time, the exterior of Founders Hall was unpainted brick with white or ivory trim. It and three other buildings on campus were painted white after World War II. The other three - Brown, McCandless and McCain - all have been restored to their original appearance. The bricks of Founders Hall now are almost 200 years old and might not withstand the sandblasting necessary to take all the white paint off. So Founders remains white and keeping it painted is an almost continuous job.

Today, Founders is the administration building. On the second floor is The Altar of the New Testament. Carved in tulip poplar wood by Eunice McDonnell Meadows, the altar depicts stories from the New Testament.

Brown Hall on the Athens State campus was named for 21-year-old Florence Brown. Miss Brown died of typhoid after caring for the college girls who had the disease during an epidemic in the early 1900s. The building, which has served as a dormitory and the President's Home, today houses administrative offices and conference rooms.

Naylor Hall, completed in 1948, was built as a dormitory for the school's short-lived football team. It was named for Dr. E.R. Naylor, a former president of the college who managed to keep it open during the Depression by admitting male students in 1931. He also negotiated the gift of a hosiery mill nearby to provide employment for those students.

Brochures on a walking tour of the campus are available at the Athens/Limestone County Chamber of Commerce and at the college.

About 10 miles north of Athens on U.S. 31 North is the town of Elkmont. Elkmont was the site of the Battle of Sulphur Creek Trestle on September 25, 1864. On that day, Union Colonel W.H. Lathrop and his 1,100 men were responsible for protecting a railroad trestle across Sulphur Creek from destruction by Confederate General Nathan Bedford Forrest and his 4,000 troops. The trestle, 71 feet high and 561 feet long, was an important link in the Union supply line that ran through North Alabama to Chattanooga, then south to General Sherman in Georgia.

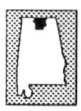

The Union troops had stationed themselves in a fort, where the Confederates confronted them and demanded their surrender. When Colonel Lathrop refused, the battle was on and Lathrop became one of the first casualties. Major Eli Lilly (of pharmaceutical fame) took over the command. As the battle went on, Lilly's men ran out of ammunition and resorted to whittling musket balls down to the size needed to fit into their guns.

At last, out of ammunition and having suffered 200 casualties, the Union forces surrendered. The Confederates took the fort and burned the trestle.

Among Lathrop's troops in this battle were two companies of black troops, members of the 11th U.S. Black Troops. The use of ex-slaves and free blacks was an experiment designed to allow use of the regular troops in front line duty.

Elkmont today is "Elkmont Rural Village," filled with energy-efficient homes and office buildings fueled by solar power. While many of the homes are of rough-hewn wood and horses and pastures still abound, about all that remains of the Elkmont that developed after the Civil War is the depot, constructed in 1887 to serve the Tennessee and Alabama Central Railroad. It now houses the town library, a history museum and a senior citizens center. The depot is open from 9 a.m. to 5 p.m. Monday through Friday.

Southwest of Athens, on Limestone County Road 24, Lucy's Branch Resort and Marina sits on the banks of the Tennessee River. Picnic areas, tennis courts, a swimming pool, hiking trails and a miniature golf course all are part of the 88-acre resort. There also are docks for the boat owner and boat rentals available for those who want to give boating a try. Forty cabins are available for rent and there are campsites as well.

On to Decatur

Traveling south from Athens on U.S. 31 will take you to Decatur. President James Monroe selected the site for this city in 1820, instructing the Surveyor General to reserve the land for a town to be named in honor of Steven F. Decatur, who died that year. (Decatur had been a hero of the Battle of Tripoli in 1804 and was a Commodore of the United States Navy during the War of 1812.)

During the Civil War, Decatur found itself on a constant seesaw, changing hands regularly as first the Union, then the Confederacy would hold power. The city constantly was attacked and abandoned. So unending was the fighting in the city that only five buildings were left standing at the end of the war.

Alabama Mountain Lakes Tourist Association

Old State Bank, Decatur

Three of the antebellum homes are in the Old Decatur and Albany Historic Districts. Also on the tour are almost 200 Victorian homes. The tour begins at the Old State Bank, which first opened its doors for business on July 29, 1833. Present at the opening was Martin Van Buren. The bank's first money, $2,000 in silver, was brought from New Orleans by steamboat to Florence and carried from there to Decatur on a wagon. Unfortunately, the bank system had failed by the mid-1840s and the bank closed its doors.

The building stood empty for a number of years, but was opened again in 1860 - not as a bank, but as a hospital and guardhouse for Union troops occupying Decatur. Periodic clashes between the Confederates and the Union forces left the bank building scarred from musket fire.

In 1881, the building became a bank again. This time, it was the First National Bank of Decatur. When First National constructed new offices, the building changed purposes once again. Over the next few years, it was a private residence, a boarding house, a saloon and an office. The building has belonged to individuals, to the City of Decatur and to the local American Legion Post.

It now seems to have found its true purpose - telling people about Decatur. It houses the Decatur Convention and Visitors Bureau. It is open for tours from 9:30 a.m. to noon and from 1 to 4:30 p.m. Monday through Friday, except holidays. There is no charge for the tour.

A brochure detailing a walking tour of Decatur's historic sites is available at the Convention and Visitors Bureau. The Old Decatur Courthouse was the scene of a trial that changed the course of American judicial history. In

1933, the "Scottsboro Boys" were retried there. This case led to the landmark U.S. Supreme Court decision that a defendant has the right to be judged by a jury of his peers. The ruling meant blacks no longer could be excluded from serving on juries.

WILD, WILD WILDLIFE

Besides historical sites, Decatur also offers visitors recreational opportunities as well as at least two different ways to look at wildlife.

America's first wave pool was built at Decatur's Point Mallard Park about 20 years ago. Four hydraulic fans send powerful bursts of air into individual tunnels of water below the pool. With the fans operating alternately every 1.5 seconds, waves are created. The fan-shaped pool is 180 feet long, 75 feet wide at the deep end (eight feet) and 150 feet wide at the beach area (where the water is only one inch deep). It holds 450,000 gallons of water.

The wave pool, with its three-foot man-made waves for splashing in and riding on still is the focal point of the park, but it's not the only thing there. It has become the centerpiece of a large Aquatic Center that includes three flume water slides, an Olympic 50-meter pool, a kiddie pool, a sand beach and a picnic area. At the Olympic pool is the Jenni Chandler Diving Well, named for Alabama's Olympic gold medalist who trained at the pool for her appearance in the Montreal Games.

The park also has an 18-hole championship golf course, three ballfields, a six-court tennis complex, a recreational center and an outdoor stage. A four-mile trail along the Tennessee River gives hikers and cyclists a chance to enjoy the natural beauty of the park. During the winter, the Deep South's only outdoor ice skating rink is open at Point Mallard.

People not only come to the park to enjoy the water and other recreational facilities, they also come to get married. A pyramid-shaped outdoor prayer chapel at Point Mallard is the setting for weddings year-round - with 30 or 40 being held during the summer.

The water park at Point Mallard is open from mid-May to Labor Day. Hours are 10 a.m. to 6 p.m. on Monday, Wednesday, Friday, Saturday and Sunday and 10 a.m. to 9 p.m. on Tuesday and Thursday. Admission is $7 for adults (12 and over) and $5 for children (5-11). The ice skating rink is open from mid-November to mid-March. General admission is $3. Skate rental is $1.

Water and wildlife abound at Wheeler National Wildlife Refuge. Wheeler, a 34,500-acre refuge, was begun in 1938 when President Franklin Roosevelt signed a bill that set aside a portion of the area impounded by TVA's Wheeler Dam as a protected area for wildlife. It was the first national wildlife refuge to be set along a reservoir and is the southernmost refuge in the United States.

Wheeler Wildlife spreads along 20 miles of the Tennessee River with about half of the area being backwaters and the rest covered in meadows and woodlands filled with oak, maple, pine, gum and black cherry trees.

At the refuge, migrating birds - hundreds of thousands of them - find a wintering ground. Human visitors find a spot for fishing, boating, picnicking and studying and photographing birds. Just as the humans who come to the refuge like to spread a picnic lunch, the birds like to get something to eat when they arrive. And they find plenty waiting for them. The water, of course, is loaded with things birds like to eat. Birds who winter at Wheeler have a varied menu, though. Land on the refuge is made available for farming, if the farmers will leave one-fourth of the harvest - usually corn and wheat - for the birds to have when they get there.

On an island at the edge of the refuge is the Givens Wildlife Interpretive Center, the South's largest educational center for waterfowl and animal study.

Wheeler Wildlife Refuge is about two miles east of Decatur on Alabama 67. The visitors center here is open daily from November through February from 10 a.m. to 5 p.m. From March through October, hours are 10 a.m. to 5 p.m. Wednesday through Saturday only.

Wildlife in a more controlled environment is offered at Cook's Natural Science Museum in Decatur. The museum has an extensive collection of insects, snakes, birds, animals, seashells and coral as well as rocks and minerals. Many of the exhibits are displayed in a hands-on setting. The museum, privately owned, was begun as part of an employee training program by Cook's Pest Control Company.

Admission to the museum is free. Hours are 9 a.m. to noon and 1 to 5 p.m. Monday through Saturday and 2 to 5 p.m. Sunday.

NEXT STOP IS SOMERVILLE

Somerville, about 14 miles southeast of Decatur on Alabama 67, is a city that only recently has made its way into the world of paved roads and tourists.

The asphalt roads running through the town were red clay until 1986 and, in many ways, the town has remained a community of the 1800s. Somerville was chosen as the county seat of Cotaco (Morgan) County in June, 1818, but the town wasn't incorporated and buildings didn't go up there until 1819. By 1825, land had been secured for a permanent town square with a courthouse, jail and town spring. In 1837, funds were available for the construction of the two-story Federal-style building on the square today - the state's oldest standing courthouse.

Somerville was the county seat of Morgan County until the incident known in the town as "the night Decatur stole the County Seat." County residents voted in the early 1890s to move the county seat to Decatur, but many people in Eastern Morgan County objected to the move. The residents there threatened to band together, separate from the rest of the county and form a new one with Somerville as the county seat. The people of Decatur, fearing violence from those who wanted to keep the county seat in Somerville, decided to move the county records at night.

Once Decatur had become the county seat, the Old Morgan County Courthouse was used as a girls academy and later became the Morgan

---

County College, a Presbyterian training school. Today the building has been partially renovated and serves as a nutrition center for senior citizens and as a site for the Municipal Court held here each month. The bell in the belfry, once used to call court to convene, now rings in each new year.

Another building still remaining in the city's center is The Jail, built as a replacement structure for Somerville's first jail, which burned sometime before the 1870s. Walls studded with nails to prevent prisoners from sawing through to freedom still can be seen.

During the 70 years that Somerville was the county seat, it flourished as a cotton town. What remains of that part of Somerville's history are the structures that reflect those times. The Rice House, built in 1835, is a brick Federal-style house once owned by Morgan County Judge Green Pryor Rice. It is one of Somerville's oldest structures and is un-

Alabama Mountain Lakes Tourist Association

Courthouse, Somerville

usual in the style in which the bricks are laid. Flemish bond style - in which the bricks are placed inward in an overlapping pattern - is used around the entire house, rather than just on the front as usually was done.

The Binford-Peck House served as the residence and office of two Somerville physicians and, during the 1930s, housed the telephone switchboard for the town.

Mixed with the old in Somerville is the new - there's a Town Hall now and the community has annexed some additional properties. The town has decided not to let the old get away, however. An extensive renovation and restoration program is under way to preserve the city's landmarks.

Huntsville's Rocketing Future

Alabama schoolchildren have grown up with a history book called "Mounds to Missiles" and Huntsville is where the missiles come in.

While Cape Canaveral and Houston may have gotten more attention during the Space Age, they really are the "crib" and "youth bed" of the Space Age. The cradle is Huntsville. In this city, Wernher von Braun and his colleagues developed the United States' first guided missiles and it was here that the space scientist and his team designed the rockets that took Americans to the moon. The "von Braun team" worked at Huntsville's Redstone Arsenal and Marshall Space Flight Center in the 1950s and 1960s, bringing America into the Space Age with the Jupiter and Saturn rockets.

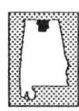

The Alabama Space and Rocket Center, a sprawling complex of hardware and hands-on experiments that sits on Alabama 20 just west of Huntsville, began as a smaller vision of von Braun's in the mid 1960s. In 1965, he addressed a joint session of the Legislature, asking them to support a bill allowing the state to build a Space Science Center in Huntsville. The dream began to take shape when Governor George Wallace signed the bill into law.

Ground was broken for the exhibit building in 1968 and by 1969 rockets and space vehicles were rumbling down the highway toward the center to take their place in a "Rocket Park" just out the door of the exhibition hall. The center opened on March 17, 1970.

Inside the exhibit hall that first day, visitors could see actual space capsules and simulations of other space travel vehicles. Outside, a 363-foot tall Saturn V rocket dominated the displays of missiles and space modules.

Later, the inside exhibits were expanded to include a home for Monkeynaut Baker, one of the two first animals in the United States to take a space flight, and a piece of Skylab that crashed back to Earth when that experimental station ended its stay in space in the 1970s. Miss Baker lived at the Space and Rocket Center from 1971 until her death in 1984. Skylab still is there and has

Alabama Bureau of Tourism and Travel

Space Shuttle at Space and Rocket Center, Huntsville

been joined by a number of hands-on exhibits that include computer games simulating space activities.

The outdoor displays grew along with the ones inside and soon visitors were experiencing G-forces and weightlessness. In 1972, a bus tour of NASA's Marshall Space Flight Center nearby was added. On the tour, visitors get to see "behind the scenes" at the center, where astronauts train and equipment is tested for America's missions into space.

A 288-seat theater was added to the center in 1982. The audience doesn't just watch the film there, though. With special film, projection and sound effects, members of the audience feel they've become part of the action.

In 1989, NASA's 30-ton Skylab engineering prototype became part of the museum exhibit. In the space station mock-up, visitors can walk inside the crew cabin and see the equipment - such as folding shower stalls and exercise machines - used by the astronauts in zero gravity.

As the U.S. Space Program moved into the age of the Space Shuttle, so did the park. The Shuttle Liner was installed near Rocket Park. Visitors climbing inside get to experience the rush of lift-off and carry out various duties of the astronauts during a shuttle mission.

In 1989, the world's only full-scale Space Shuttle exhibition went on display at the center. The shuttle orbiter seen at the Space Center was used to test equipment and procedures for assembling the Space Shuttles that took astronauts into space. The external tank was NASA's first. It was used for almost 10 years during tests of the main shuttle engine.

A new area, Shuttle Park, has been added to the outdoor display space. When you consider that the orbiter is 122 feet long and has a wingspan of 78 feet, it's easy to see why this new exhibit needed a spot of its own. The external tank is more than 150 feet long and 27 feet in diameter. It weighs about 30 tons. With the 90-ton orbiter mounted atop the external tank, the tail fin soars more than 80 feet above the ground. When the exhibit is completely installed, it will include solid rocket boosters and the engines from Columbia, the first Space Shuttle.

It's easy to spend a whole day just seeing everything the Space and Rocket Center has to offer. In fact, you need to plan carefully during peak months, especially during the summer, or you might miss something even during a day-long trip. Space Center officials recommend that you allot about 45 minutes for the movie at the Spacedome Theater. Usually there are a couple of different films showing at various times during the day. Choose the one you want to see early and be there at the time it's scheduled. Often during the summer, seats at the midday shows are filled early.

Set aside two to four hours for touring the museum and outdoor exhibits. You'll need another two hours for the bus tour of the Marshall Center. If your schedule doesn't allow you enough time to see everything, select the things you really want to do and buy individual tickets to those things. Remember, though, your best buy is a combination ticket for everything if you have the time.

The Space and Rocket Center is open from 8 a.m. to 7 p.m. from May through September. Hours from September through April are 9 a.m. to 5 p.m. Tickets are $10.95 for adults and $6.95 for children (11 and under) and senior citizens (60 and over). These prices are for the "package" tickets. If all of the displays whet your appetite for more space adventure, you can train at U.S. Space Camp or U.S. Space Academy, programs for young people and adults. Space Camp for students usually lasts a week. Adult Space Campers usually spend a long weekend at the camp. Space Campers  live and work the way the astronauts do and culminate their experience with simulated shuttle missions.

HUNTSVILLE BEFORE THE ROCKETS

Until Werner von Braun and his team of scientists arrived in Huntsville and made it "The Rocket City," cotton still was king in this part of the state. In the late 1800s, Madison County was one of the top cotton producing counties in the nation and well into the 1900s, the area still depended on cotton for its economic base. Cotton was grown throughout the county and made into cloth at several cotton mills. The last cotton mill in the county closed in 1989 and computers have taken the place of harvesters in the lives of most of Madison County's citizens.

Fortunately, the city has kept the best of the old to mix with the new. Historic districts and museums preserve the lifestyles of the past practically in the shadow of America's rockets of the future.

Big Spring, just west of Courthouse Square, literally is the heart of the city. Producing 24,000,000 gallons of natural spring water daily, it is the place where John Hunt founded the city in 1805. The park that surrounds it today is filled with gifts to the city from other nations and is the site of a number of outdoor festivals each year.

Across from the park is the Huntsville Museum of Art, ranked in 1987 as one of the top 100 art museums in the country by the Institute for Museum Services. Four galleries house the museum's growing permanent collection as well as traveling exhibitions from major art museums. An art research library here is open to the public. The museum is open from 10 a.m. to 9 p.m. on Tuesday, from 10 a.m. to 5 p.m. Wednesday through Friday, from 9 a.m. to 5 p.m. on Saturday and from 1 to 5 p.m. on Sunday. There is no admission charge.

You'll find plows, not paintings, at Harrison Brothers Hardware, a few blocks from the Museum of Art. Alabama's oldest operating hardware store, Harrison Brothers was opened in 1897. Little has changed since that time. There still are bare light bulbs hanging from the ceiling and floor-to-ceiling ladders roll along the walls so clerks can reach the merchandise stored there. Purchases made at the store still are rung up on the antique cash register and wrapped in brown paper that's tied with string. The last Harrison brother died in 1983, but the store remains open, operated by the Historic Huntsville Foundation.

Harrison Brothers Hardware is open weekdays from 9 a.m. to 5 p.m. and

Saturday from 10 a.m. to 2 p.m.

Huntsville not only cradled America's Space Age, the city also "birthed" the state of Alabama. In 1819, delegates met here for a Constitutional Convention and drew up the documents for Alabama's statehood. Understandably proud of its part in forming the state, Huntsville has frozen a small portion of the city in time. It's always 1819 at Constitution Hall Village.

Alabama Mountain Lakes Tourist Association

Constitution Hall Village, Huntsville

The village, a museum complex near the center of town, has four buildings from the 1805 to 1819 period of Alabama history, all reconstructed on their original sites.

Constitution Hall itself began life as a cabinet shop. When the delegates all got to Huntsville, they found the two-story frame building was the only one large enough to accommodate them. The cabinet shop became the delegates' meeting place.

Near Constitution Hall is the Clay Building, which housed the law offices of Clement Comer Clay, one of the delegates to the convention. Also in the building were the Post Office and the offices of the Federal survey team.

The "Alabama Republican," the newspaper people in 1819 relied on for word of the convention, was published by John Boardman from his office in the Boardman complex. Boardman not only reported on the proceedings at the convention, but issued the first complete printing of the Constitution of the State of Alabama. Also in the Boardman complex is the state's first incorporated library. In the early days of the lending library, patrons were allowed to check out books for one hour a day, two days a week.

Home life in the early 1800s is typified in the Neal House, home of Stephen Neal, Madison County's first sheriff. The house has all the amenities of the day - an adjoining kitchen, servants' quarters and a carriage house.

During a tour of Constitution Hall Village, visitors are greeted by costumed interpreter/guides who explain the significance of the various buildings as well as go about the daily work that might be seen on a typical street in 1819 Huntsville. Starch is made by boiling potatoes, clothes are pressed with irons heated in a fireplace, vineyards are tended and gardens are weeded

---

without modern machinery.

Constitution Hall Village is open from 9 a.m. to 5 p.m. Monday through Saturday (The last tour begins at 4 p.m.) and is closed on Sundays and major holidays. Admission is $5 for adults and $2 for students, children six to 12 and senior citizens. Children under six are admitted free.

Huntsville has two main historic districts. The Old Town Historic District is north and east of Courthouse Square and contains 19th and 20th century homes, some still in the process of restoration.

The Twickenham Historic District, south and east of Courthouse Square, is the state's largest district of antebellum homes. Among the homes in the district is the Moore-Rhett House, constructed of hand-pressed bricks made by slaves. A black craftsman, Charles Bell, from Charlottesville, Virginia, came to Huntsville to build the three spiral stairways in the home. Two of the stairways led to the second floor. The third, built around a large post, led to a tower that once was on the roof. This house was the scene of one of Huntsville's most famous social events - a formal party in 1892 honor "Lily Flagg," the world's champion butter-fat-producing cow.

Also in the district is the Cruse House, home of Mary Ann Cruse, an author of children's books who used the income from her writing to purchase stained glass windows for the Church of the Nativity. The church is another of the buildings in the district. A Union officer was ordered to stable horses in the church during the Civil War, but refused to do so after he read the words "Reverence My Sanctuary" engraved over the entrance to the building.

Federal Army General Ormsby Mitchel chose the McDowell-Levert House as his main headquarters during the Civil War. The United States flag flew over the Lane House during the Civil War. Its owner, George W. Lane, was a staunch Union man and passed along valuable information to the Union troops during the war. At the Thomas White House, Confederate soldiers were hidden in the basement until they could slip by the Union troops for brief visits at home.

Weeden House Museum in the historic district is the birthplace of 19th-century artist and poet Miss Howard Weeden. After the Civil War, Miss Weeden helped support her family by teaching art here. Later, the house was the home of John McKinley, Associate Justice of the U.S. Supreme Court. The house/museum, furnished with period antiques, is open Tuesday through Sunday from 1 to 4 p.m. Admission is $2 for adults and $1 for children.

Walking tour brochures of both historic districts are available at the Huntsville Convention and Visitors Bureau.

A few blocks from the historic districts is the Huntsville Depot Museum. The depot opened in 1860 as a "passenger house" and Eastern Division headquarters for the Memphis and Charleston Railroad Company. Captured by Union troops, it was used as a prison during the War. Much of the graffiti written by the soldiers held there still can be seen on the walls. Today, the depot houses a museum of regional transportation history. From September through April, the depot is open 11 a.m. to 4 p.m. From May through August, the hours are 10 a.m. to 5 p.m. The depot is closed on major holidays. Admission is $2.50 for adults and $1.50 for children (4-12) and senior citizens.

AN HISTORICAL TROLLEY RIDE

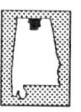

You can get an overall view of the historic sites in the downtown area by catching the trolley that leaves the depot for 30-minute round trips past the "old and new Huntsville." During the ride, which costs $.50, the conductor points out places of interest along the way and answers riders' questions. The route takes passengers past the Huntsville Museum of Art, the Von Braun Civic Center, the Historic Twickenham District, Constitution Hall Park, the Weeden House Museum and Harrison Brothers Hardware.

The trolley operates Tuesday through Sunday from 10 a.m. to 12:30 p.m. and from 1 to 4:30 p.m.

Just out of the downtown square area is Maple Hill Cemetery, one of Alabama's oldest. The graves of five Alabama governors are here.

Burritt Museum and Park is set on 167 acres atop 1,800-foot Monte Sano ("Mountain of Health") on the east side of Huntsville. The museum is in an 11-room house built in the shape of a Maltese Cross and houses exhibitions on the history of the city. On the grounds of the park are historic structures including log cabins, a blacksmith shop, a smokehouse and a church. Nature trails, gardens and picnic facilities complete the park setting, which offers a panoramic view of the city. The park is open daily 7 a.m. to 30 minutes before sunset. The museum is open from March through December, Tuesday through Sunday from noon to 5 p.m. The grounds are open during the same months from 7 a.m. to sunset.

JUST OUT OF TOWN...

Monte Sano State Park, four miles east of Huntsville off U.S. 431, is a 2,140-acre recreation area that offers hiking trails, picnic areas, a playground and a large amphitheater. There are camping sites and cabins here. The park is open all year long and fees are charged for use of some park areas.

The Huntsville-Madison County Botanical Gardens, set on 35 acres southwest of downtown near the Space and Rocket Center, were opened in 1990. The gardens are open form 9 a.m. to 5 p.m. Monday through Saturday and from 1 to 5 p.m. on Sunday.

On the Tennessee River south of town is Ditto Landing and Marina. Boating facilities, picnic areas, tennis courts and a softball diamond are part of the marina complex. At the landing are a playground and a bicycle motorcross course. Camp sites are available here.

Just 12 miles from downtown Huntsville are 72 acres of wooded paths and nature trails for getting away from the daily grind for a while. The Madison County Nature Trail is set around a 16-acre lake. Also in the trail area are a chapel, wooden bridges, a wildlife sanctuary, two outdoor schoolrooms and a Braille Trail. The nature trail is open daily from sunrise to sunset.

WHERE TO STAY

There are a number of chain hotels and motels in the area. In addition, there are several independent facilities. Among them are:

In Athens: Athens Motel, The Mark Motel and Welcome Inn Motel.
In Decatur: Point Mallard Inn.

Bed and Breakfasts in the area include:
In Decatur: the Dancy-Polk House and Hearts and Treasures Bed and Breakfast.
In Huntsville: Bed and Breakfast Huntsville (This B&B is located in an old slave barn, updated for its 1990s tenants.).

In addition to the camping facilities at state parks in the area, there are several privately owned campgrounds. Among them are:

In Athens: Hatfield Campgrounds.
In Decatur: Point Mallard Park.

WHERE TO EAT

Chain and fast food restaurants can be found throughout the area. In addition, there are independent restaurants, delis and cafes. Among them are:

In Athens: Carter's Barbeque, Catfish Inn, the Rebel Cafeteria and Jerry's.
In Decatur: Court Street, Big Bob Gibson Bar-B-Que and Shelley's Irongate Restaurant (located in a restored Victorian home).
In Huntsville: Bubba's and Twickenham Station (Part of the restaurant is in an old railroad car.).

ANNUAL EVENTS

Among the annual events taking place in this part of the state are:

Watercolor Society's Competition, Huntsville, January.

Hospice Chili Challenge, Athens, February.

Readying For Spring, Huntsville, March.
Youth Art Exhibition, Huntsville, March.
Spring Wild Plant Exhibition, Huntsville, March.
Musical Explosion, Athens, March.

Dairy Days, Huntsville, April.
Spring Pilgrimage Tour, Athens, April.
Pilgrimage of Homes, Huntsville, April.
Spring Fest, Huntsville, April.
Racking Horse Spring Celebration, Priceville, April.

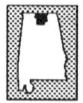

Homespun, Athens, May.
Preparing the Fleece, Huntsville, May.
Panoply, Huntsville, May.
Hot-air Balloon Races, Decatur, May.
Herbs in Thyme, Huntsville, May.
Alabama A&M Founders Day, Huntsville.

Summertime in The Village, Huntsville, June-August.
Alabama Sports Festival, Huntsville, June.
Twickenham Doll Show and Sale, Huntsville, June.
Folklife Festival, Huntsville, June.

Bama Barefooters Open, Huntsville, July.
Limestone County Fair, Athens, July.
Spirit Of America Festival, Decatur, July.
Space Celebration, Huntsville, July.

Old Time Train Excursion, Huntsville, August.

State Fiddling and Bluegrass Convention, Huntsville, September.
Mountain Dulcimer Festival, Huntsville, September.
Racking Horse World Celebration, Priceville, September.
Civil War Living History Encampment, Huntsville, September.

Tennessee Valley Old Time Fiddlers Convention, Athens, October.
Chautauqua, Huntsville, October.
Alabama Cotton Festival, Huntsville, October.
Indian Heritage Festival, Huntsville, October.
Harvest Festival, Huntsville, October.
Putting By for Winter, Huntsville, October.

Under the Christmas Tree, Huntsville, November.
Southern Wildlife Festival, Decatur, November.
Christmas Boat Parade, Decatur, November.

Christmas Parades, Decatur and Athens, December.
Parade of Lights, Huntsville, December.
Alabama's Birthday Celebration, Huntsville, December.
Christmas Tour of Homes, Decatur, December.

NE Alabama Mountains and Valleys

Those who don't know the state of Alabama always seem surprised when someone mentions "going to the mountains" here. People, it seems, tend to think of Alabama as flat and colorless. It only takes one trip to this part of the state to quickly dispel that myth.

Here, the mountain ranges line up beside one another and cut a diagonal path across the northeast corner of the state. The Talladega Mountains, the Appalachians, the Lookout Mountains and Sand Mountain give breathtaking vistas, dense forests and green valleys.

RANDOLPH, CLAY, TALLADEGA COUNTIES

Lakes and streams fill this part of Alabama as well. The people in the Randolph County town of Wedowee like to boast that their lake - Lake Wedowee - is among the cleanest in the state. The 10,000-acre lake offers fishing and boating to residents and visitors.

Also in Randolph County is the city of Roanoke, home of the "Ella Smith doll." In 1908, a Birmingham newspaper hailed Roanoke as the only city in the South where dolls were produced. The "Ella Smith Unbreakable Doll" industry is gone from Roanoke now, but the building where the dolls were produced still stands on Vaughn Street.

One more "must see" in Randolph is Butler's Mill, a functioning grist mill. The two-story frame structure was built in 1881 to combine a sawmill, a grist mill, a cotton gin and a feedmill in one operation.

Butler's Mill, between Alabama 48 and U.S. 431 four miles west of Graham on County Road 92, is open Saturday from 8 a.m. to 4 p.m. There is no admission charge.

To the west of Randolph County is Clay County, where U.S. Supreme Court Justice Hugo Black grew up. The Ashland home where Black spent much of his childhood is listed on the National Register.

Also in Clay County is the beginning of the Pinhoti National Recreation Trail System. The Pinhoti, the longest hiking trail in Alabama, runs 85 miles from the Friendship Community in Clay County to Dugger Mountain near

Piedmont. The trail, which gets its name from the Creek Indian words "pinwa" (turkey) and "huti" (home), has 25 more miles of side trails and loops.

There are numerous entries to the trail, including the Friendship Community, the Coleman Lake Recreation Area at the northernmost end and Cheaha State Park.

The trail runs through the Talladega National Forest which also reaches into Talladega County. Within the forest is the Lake Chinnabee Recreation Area, which offers fishing, swimming and boating. A network of hiking trails (part of the Pinhoti) winds through the area. The waterfalls in this section are worth the hike. Most of these trails lead north from Chinnabee through the mountainous terrain of Cheaha State Park.

To reach the recreation area, take Alabama 21 north from Talladega for seven miles, turn east on County Road 96 for 12 miles. Take Forest Service Road 646 two miles to Lake Chinnabee.

At the southern end of the National Forest is the city of Sylacauga, which bills itself as the "Home of the Hodges Meteorite and Jim Nabors."

The Jim Nabors part is fairly easy to understand. The singer/actor, star of "Gomer Pyle, USMC," was born and grew up in Sylacauga.

The Hodges Meteorite requires a little more explanation. On November 30, 1954, Mrs.

Northeast Alabama

The Cumberland Plateau, an area of gently rolling land and the Appalachian foothills cut across the northeast corner of Alabama and form a corridor that reaches into Georgia and Tennessee. Also in this 11-county region is part of Alabama's Piedmont, with its hills and sandy valleys. In this part of the state is Alabama's highest point, Cheaha Mountain, which rises 2,407 feet above sea level. More than 775,000 people live in this area of the state, which reaches from the northeastern corner of Alabama southward along the border with Georgia. Among the largest cities in the region are Gadsden, Anniston, Guntersville, Fort Payne, Jacksonville, Scottsboro and Talladega.

Hewlett Hodges stretched out on the sofa in her home in Sylacauga to take an afternoon nap. Just as she got comfortable, there was a loud crash and something hit Mrs. Hodges left arm.

Opening her eyes, Mrs. Hodges found herself staring at a large hole in the roof. Beside her on the couch was a big black rock. A quick look around the room told Mrs. Hodges that the rock had landed on a radio sitting at the end of the sofa and then hit her. Fortunately, the greater damage was to the radio.

Something of this nature is bound to cause a stir in any town and before long, the doctor, the police and a number of curious onlookers had arrived at Mrs. Hodges' house.

Among those who came to see what caused the excitement was George Swindle, a field representative with the U.S. Geological Survey who happened to be in the area conducting a water survey. Swindle identified the rock as a visitor from outer space, a meteorite. His records show that it weighed about nine pounds and was about six inches in diameter.

The crowds still were there when Mr. Hodges got home that night, but the meteor was gone. Of course, Hodges wanted to see this rock, but it had been taken away in a helicopter dispatched from Maxwell Air Force Base in Montgomery. The folks at Maxwell turned it over to the Air Defense Command, who sent it to Wright-Patterson Air Force Base in Dayton, Ohio, for tests.

After a great deal of legal negotiation, the meteorite was returned to Sylacauga, but the ownership of the chunk of heavenly body still was in doubt. The lady who owned the house where the Hodgeses were living claimed it was hers - it crashed through her roof. The Hodgeses said it was theirs - it had hit their radio, their sofa and Mrs. Hodges.

While all the legal hassling was going on, Mrs. Hodges was in the news spotlight. Her picture appeared in a number of newspapers and magazines and she made an appearance on "I've Got A Secret."

The Hodgeses and their landlady reached a settlement in late 1956 and the meteorite ended up at the Museum of Natural History in Tuscaloosa, where it still is on display today.

Besides being the home of a celebrity and a history-making rock, Sylacauga also is where you'll find the Isabel Anderson Comer Museum and Arts Center. Indian artifacts, archaeological finds and an excellent permanent collection make up the core of the museum's exhibits. In addition, traveling exhibits are booked regularly at the museum, giving each visit to the center a new look.

The museum is open Tuesday through Saturday from 1 to 4 p.m. and Sunday from 2 to 5 p.m. There is no admission charge.

DeSoto Caverns

Northwest of Sylacauga is Childersburg and DeSoto Caverns.

A Creek Indian legend says this is the birthplace of the Creeks. According to the legend, the Indian god Sawgee Putchehassee, the giver and taker of breath, lived in a great cavern surrounded by emerald woods. In that cavern, Sawgee Putchehassee is said to have given breath to the first Creek Indians.

But the god didn't want these people to live in the darkness of the cavern, so he sent them outside in the warmth of the sun and taught them to grow corn to sustain themselves. That, the story goes, is how the first men came to dwell in the area that now is Childersburg.

The Indians, it is known, lived in a village next to what we now know as DeSoto Caverns for many centuries. It is said that Hernando DeSoto, leading an expedition of 600 men, came upon the Indian village in 1540. The party, searching for gold, was welcomed by the chief.

DeSoto and his men weren't the perfect guests. They took the chief hostage, took some of the Indians as slaves and raided the storage bins for food.

Today's visitors to the Childersburg area and to the caverns that now bear DeSoto's name don't seem to be the type to take hostages as they search for gold, but more like the type to take pictures as they search for fun.

A visit to DeSoto Caverns is a lot like a living history lesson and cloud-watching all wrapped into one. The history of the cave's uses, told in a light-hearted fashion by young guides, extends from the prehistoric Indians, through the early days of settling America, on to the Civil War and through the days of Prohibition.

During the early 1700s, traders took a path through what now is Alabama that led very near DeSoto Caverns. One trader, I.W. Wright, today is known less for his trading ability than the fact that his name is said to be the oldest graffiti to be found in any cave in the United States. Apparently, Wright stopped off at DeSoto Caverns to rest during his travels and chiseled his name in a rock. When the Creeks caught him in their ancestral cave, they dispatched him to that Big Trading Post in the sky.

DeSoto Caverns became the first officially recorded cave in the United States in December, 1796, when Benjamin Hawkins, General Superintendent of all Indian tribes south of the Ohio River, wrote to President Washington describing the beauty of the cavern.

The cave has a spring-fed well, which made it the perfect spot for Confederate soldiers to mine calcium nitrate and gave the cave its next opportunity to step into the historic spotlight. The cavern became a gun-powder mining and refining center. A tour of the caverns gives visitors a look at the well and leaching trough the soldiers used.

When Prohibition came in 1919, the cave once again became part of the local history and lore. DeSoto Caverns was one of the area's rougher speakeasies, with moonshine and square dancing being two of the top attractions. The third was fighting and the cavern became known as The Bloody Bucket. Visitors to the cave still can see remnants of that part of the cave's history as well.

And then there are the things that caves are most famous for - stalagmites and stalactites, formations created by the dripping of mineral-rich waters in the cavern. Viewing them is a lot like looking at clouds. It doesn't take much imagination to see angels, animals and Old Man North Wind among the crevices and layers of onyx inside the cave.

Perhaps one of the most dramatic moments during the tour comes while guests are seated in the "Great Onyx Cathedral," a grand chamber 12 stories high and larger than a football field. The guide asks, "Do you want to see how dark a cave is?" and switches off all the lights. That's when visitors learn what it means to be in a place so dark you can't see your hand in front of your face.

There are several other things do to during a visit to DeSoto Caverns. On the grounds are a scaled-down version of a ship that may be similar to the one DeSoto sailed on, a gold-panning display, a "primitive weapons" exhibition and a people-sized maze for those who would like to see what DeSoto may have felt like when he and his men found themselves looking for the right path in unfamiliar territory.

DeSoto Caverns is open, October through March, Monday through Saturday from 9 a.m. to 5 p.m. and Sunday from 12:30 to 5 p.m. From April to September, closing time is 5:30 p.m. Admission is $7.50 for adults and $4.50 for children 4-11. Children under 4 are admitted free.

On your way to the caverns, be sure and see the DeSoto Wall Mural. As you go along Alabama Highway 76 from Childersburg toward DeSoto Caverns, you'll see this painting on your right. Done in 1984 by Birmingham artist Carlton Sims, the 120 foot x 6 foot painting shows DeSoto being greeted by the Indian chief when he arrived at the village near what now is DeSoto Caverns. Just north of Childersburg, in the community of Kymulga, is the Kymulga Covered Bridge and Kymulga Grist Mill.

The 105-foot covered bridge was built in the 1860s and spans Talladega Creek.

Beside the bridge is the grist mill, built in 1864 by slave labor and restored in 1988. The 3-1/2 story water-powered mill operates three large turbines and drives millstones weighing almost 3,000 pounds. Corn still is ground at the mill and viewing the grinding operation is part of the guided tour offered there.

The mill and covered bridge sit in a 78-acre park that contains the largest cluster of white oak trees east of the Mississippi and the national champion sugarberry tree.

The Grist Mill is open on weekends only in February, March, October and November and every day from April to September. It is closed during December and January. Hours are Monday through Saturday from 9 a.m. to 5 p.m. and 12:30 to 5 p.m. on Sunday. Admission is $2.

The city of Talladega, northeast of Childersburg, has become something of a monument to transportation. In the area surrounding the city, visitors will find a covered bridge for those who want to remember the days of the horse and buggy, winding country roads for those who like to drive slow and the world's fastest speedway for those who like to watch cars go by at a record-breaking pace.

The covered bridge is in Waldo, a small community about six miles southeast of Talladega. One of the oldest covered bridges in Alabama, it is mentioned in a survey that dates from the 1850s. Spanning Talladega Creek at Riddle's Mill, the bridge may have been used by Wilson's Raiders during the Civil War. The 115-foot bridge is located on the east side of Alabama 77.

The area around the bridge now is a pioneer park with buildings that include Riddle's Grist Mill, built in the 1850s, and a log cabin.

The slower driving paths are parts of the Talladega Scenic Drive. The drive offers a 23 mile spring or fall color tour through the heart of the Talladega National Forest. The most used route begins at the southwest end of Cheaha State park and ends at U.S. 78 near Heflin in Cleburne County. Along the way are a number of scenic vistas, including the one at Sherman Cliff.

A more primitive route is the Skyway Motorway that begins at Chandler Springs on the eastern edge of Talladega and winds 11 miles through rugged but lovely mountains.

Zoomin' in Talladega

The faster driving takes place on the Talladega Superspeedway. The track, scene of NASCAR Winston Cup events and a number of other major races throughout the year, is said to be the most competitive motorsports facility in the world. A number of world speed records have been set here

Alabama Bureau of Tourism and Travel

Motorsports Hall of Fame, Talladega

and, in 1985, the fastest 500-mile automobile race ever run to that time unfolded on the Talladega track.

The Superspeedway stays busy year-round. Stock and sports cars race around the track, where the banks are 33 degrees in the turns, during the competitions. Tire, automobile and motorcycle manufacturers test their products on the track on the days when the cars aren't running.

Bus tours of the track are given daily except during races or product testing. Cost of the tour is $1 for visitors 13 and over. The tour is free to younger visitors.

Adjacent to the 2.66-mile track is the International Motorsports Hall of Fame and Museum, which houses a $6 million collection of record-breaking and special automobiles. Everything from Go-Karts to Rocket Cars that date from 1902 to the present are on display.

Among the "don't miss" exhibits are Sir Malcolm Campbell's "Bluebird," the car that set a world land speed record at Daytona Beach in 1935 and the car that Ron Bouchard drove across the finish line in the 1981 Talladega 500. In that race, he edged Darrell Waltrip out by less than two feet, making it the closest finish in stock car history. Other cars on display include those raced by Richard Petty, Fireball Roberts, Bobby Allison, Marty Robbins, Buddy Baker, Neil Bonnett, Bill Elliott, Waltrip, Roger McClusky, Dale Earnhardt, Davy Allison, Don Garlits and Bobby Isaac.

While most of the cars in the museum are gleaming examples of the car makers art, one looks like it might have been designed by Salvador Dali. During the Winston 500 in 1983, Phil Parsons' car tangled with the one driven by Waltrip. An 11-car pile-up resulted and Parsons' automobile went somersaulting through the air. Remarkably, all the drivers escaped serious injuries and the green-and-white Number 66 went to the garage on a truck bed.

Now the mangled car is on display in the museum, looking just as it did after the crash - with all parts of the automobile damaged except a fire extinguisher strapped in the middle of the car.

The museum, which fills three buildings, is open daily from 9 a.m. to 5 p.m. Admission is $5 for adults and $4 for students 7 to 17. Children under seven are admitted free.

In the city of Talladega itself, you'll learn that this is more than a city built around a race track. It's a city rich in history, with many structures dating from the early 1800s.

In the heart of town is Talladega Square and the Talladega County Courthouse, the oldest courthouse in continuous use in the state. Built in 1836, it features composite capital columns copied from the Greek and Egyptian styles.

Talladega's "Silk Stocking District" sits a block south of the square and is filled with antebellum and turn-of-the-century homes. It reflects the wealth of the city's Victorian days in its structures and tree-lined streets.

The Jemison-Carnegie Heritage Hall, not far from the courthouse, tells the history of East Central Alabama, including the Spanish exploration, Creek Indian occupancy, Civil War and Reconstruction. The museum is open Tuesday through Saturday from 1 to 4 p.m. and Sunday from 2 to 5 p.m. It is closed from December 25 to January 1. Admission is free.

Talladega College, founded by two former slaves shortly after the Civil War, sits on one border of the Silk Stocking District. On campus is Swayne

---

Hall, which began life as a high school and was the college's first building. Swayne, which became a symbol for freedom among ex-slaves, is listed on the National Register.

Another Talladega campus has become a symbol for independence among those with physical handicaps. The Alabama Institute for Deaf and Blind, founded in 1858, is one of the nation's oldest schools for the handicapped. The Institute consists of five schools - the Alabama School for the Deaf, the Alabama School for the Blind, the Helen Keller School of Alabama for the deaf-blind and multi-handicapped, the E.H. Gentry Technical Facility (a post-secondary school for the handicapped) and the Alabama Industries for the Blind.

Some of Talladega's best preserved historic buildings are on campus at AIDB. Manning Hall, the school's antebellum administration building, was constructed in 1850 by slave labor. Jemison House, built in 1898, and William F. Grace Hall, built in 1898, have been restored and now serve as residence halls for AIDB students.

The Alabama Industries for the Blind is one of the most diverse manufacturing complexes in the United States. Employees there produce items ordered through government contracts (such as some supplies for the "Desert Shield" operation in Saudi Arabia), industrial brushes, linens and paper products. While you can't buy everything that's made there since some of it is produced for specific contractors, there is a shop at the Industries complex where you can buy some items - such as linens. The store is open from 8 a.m. to 4:30 p.m. Monday through Friday.

Tours of the campus are available by appointment.

Between Talladega and Pell City, on the Talladega County side of Logan Martin Lake, is Bryant Vineyards. Five acres of muscadines and five acres of French hybrid grapes provide the basic ingredient for wines produced here. Tours (and tastings) of the vineyards and winery are available without charge from 10 a.m. to sunset Monday through Saturday.

CHEAHA – ALABAMA'S ROOF

On the northeastern border of Talladega County is Cheaha State Park and Cheaha Mountain, the highest spot in the state. This area was mentioned in records of Hernando DeSoto's 1540 expedition during which he introduced the Indians here to hogs and horses.

Hiking trails fill the forest surrounding the mountain and atop it a state park offers places to fish, places to boat and places to just enjoy the view. Overnight facilities at the park include campgrounds, chalets, a resort lodge and a group lodge. There also are a number of rustic stone cabins built by the Civilian Conservation Corps. The park is open year-round, but you'll need to get your reservations early for the peak times - in the summer and in the fall when the leaves begin to change.

Camping fees at the park are $9 to $11 per night for improved campsites and $3 to $7 per night for primitive campsites.

Within the park is the Cheaha Wilderness, nearly 7,500 acres covering the southernmost extension of the Appalachian Mountain Range. More than 1,000 of these acres rise above 2,000 feet, so the hiking and backpacking trails provide panoramic views of East Central Alabama. One trail shelter is available in the Wilderness.

Two recreation areas, Coleman Lake and Pine Glen, lie along the Pinhoti Trail not far from Heflin in Cleburne County. While much of the trail has fairly rugged terrain, sections south of Coleman Lake present a little less challenging walk. Even there, though, there are some steep grades.

The Coleman Lake Area offers swimming, fishing and boating (electric motors only). There are about 60 campsites there with improved and primitive camping available. Picnic tables and barbecue grills dot the area as well. To reach this recreational area, open May through October, take U.S. 78 east from Heflin for six miles, turn left on Forest Service Road 553 for 8-1/4 miles and then turn right on Forest Service Road 500-4. The lake is about 1-1/2 miles down this road.

Pine Glen Recreation Area is a secluded campground and picnic area. A mountain stream running through the area makes it a scenic place to spend a few hours or to stay overnight. About 30 sites for improved camping are available and there are picnic tables and barbecue grills. There also are facilities for swimming and fishing. To reach the area, take U.S. 78 west from Heflin for 2-1/2 miles then turn right on Forest Service Road 500. Pine Glen, which is open year-round, is about eight miles down this road.

Also along the Pinhoti in Cleburne County is the Shoal Creek Church, a one-story log structure. Built in the late 1800s, the church is one of six hand-hewn, hand-split log churches left in the state. Not far from the church is Cole Cemetery, burial site of many of Alabama's settlers.

Fishing Around Cherokee County

You may wonder - if you're not a fisherman - why any place would want to be known as "The Crappie Capital of the World." If you are a fisherman, however, that claim may be enough to make you want to visit the spot. Weiss Lake, in Cherokee County, is the place where anglers consistently reel in crappie weighing in at more than two pounds. The lake - off U.S. 9 - has 30,200 acres of fishing and 447 miles of shoreline.

Although crappie is the fish most people identify with Weiss Lake (Prime fishing times are February through May and September through early December), its weedbeds and stump flats also provide a haven for blue gill (early May and early June) and bass (almost all year). Weiss Lake is open year-round and there is no admission charge.

Cherokee Rock Village Park near Centre in Cherokee County sits atop Lookout Mountain and gives a 30-mile panoramic view of Weiss Lake and parts of two states, Alabama and Georgia. Dusk is one of the best times to visit this spot as the sun sets, coloring the surrounding countryside, and the lights of the surrounding cities come alive.

The "village" is made up of enormous boulders - some as large as 200 feet tall. The park has one natural arch and offers hikers and rock climbers miles

---

Northeast Alabama   **43**

of crevices, caves and trails.

In Centre is the Cherokee County Historical Museum, a new heritage museum with displays that include local newspapers, wagons, housewares, telephones, appliances, washtubs and daguerreotype photographs from 1831. In addition, there are Civil War, World War I and World War II artifacts. The museum is open Monday through Saturday from 10 a.m. to 4 p.m. Admission is $1 for adults and $.50 for children.

A few miles north of Centre, on the banks of Weiss Lake is the city of Cedar Bluff. Here, you'll find the Cornwall Furnace Park. The furnace was built in 1862 by the Noble Brothers of Rome, Georgia. The cold blast furnace was the first in the county to be powered by water and became an important part of the ironworks system used by the Confederate Forces during the Civil War.

The 5-1/2 acre park, open year-round, also contains a nature trail.

BENTON, ER, CALHOUN COUNTY

Calhoun County, southwest of Cherokee County, started out as Benton County, established in 1832 and named for Senator Thomas H. Benton of Missouri. By 1858, however, Benton's pro-North sentiments had caused him to fall out of favor with the citizens of the county and they renamed it, this time honoring Senator John C. Calhoun of South Carolina. Even though they were militant enough to change the name of their county, the citizens did still have a lot of Southern hospitality and much of that charm is preserved throughout the county today.

The oldest city in the county is Oxford, established in 1852. When the county was begun 20 years earlier, this area was called "Lick Skillet." It is said that the settlement got its name from a traveler passing through. The story goes that when he asked if there was somewhere for him to get something to eat, he was directed to a shoemaker who cared for those journeying in the area. When he was asked later if he had found anything to eat at the shoemaker's, he is said to have replied, "Yes, but I had to lick the skillet."

There might not have been much to eat in the area, but the early settlers of Calhoun County found plenty of ore that could be easily mined. With the area's ample forests providing charcoal to supply heat, a local smelting business was begun.

One of the first furnaces built was the Cane Creek Furnace near Ohatchee. This furnace manufactured part of the iron used to build the Confederate ironclad Virginia (known as Merrimack to those of the Northern persuasion).

The abundance of iron ore probably is what attracted Samuel Noble to the area. Noble's coming led to the birth of what now is Calhoun County's largest city, Anniston. The city was settled in 1872, founded by Noble, an Englishman who headed the ironworks in Rome, Georgia, before the Civil War, and Daniel Tyler of Connecticut.

They established textile mills and blast furnaces that were to help launch the South into the mainstream of the industrial revolution. In 1879, the owners hired architects, including the renowned Stanford White, who designed the original Madison Square Gardens, to design and build a modern company town. It was named after Mrs. Anne Scott Taylor (Annie's Town), wife of one of the local iron magnates. Anniston remained a private company town until it opened to the public in 1883.

There is much to see and do in Anniston, including a number of "must see" museums.

To first get a feel for the history of the city, though, drive through the Tyler Hill district on East Sixth Street and see the residential area of Victorian homes built during the late 1880s.

And be sure to put a stop on your itinerary at The Church of St. Michael and All Angels. The church, at the corner of 18th Street and Cobb Avenue, was built in 1888. It was Noble, one of the city's founders who gave many of the city streets the names of Episcopal bishops and who contributed this church to the city. The Romantic Romanesque structure, made entirely of Alabama stone, was built for the foundry workers of the area. The marble, stained glass windows and bell tower have earned it the reputation of "one of the most beautiful churches in America."

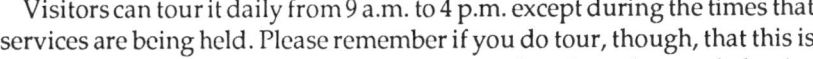

Visitors can tour it daily from 9 a.m. to 4 p.m. except during the times that services are being held. Please remember if you do tour, though, that this is a church and your behavior while inside should reflect that fact.

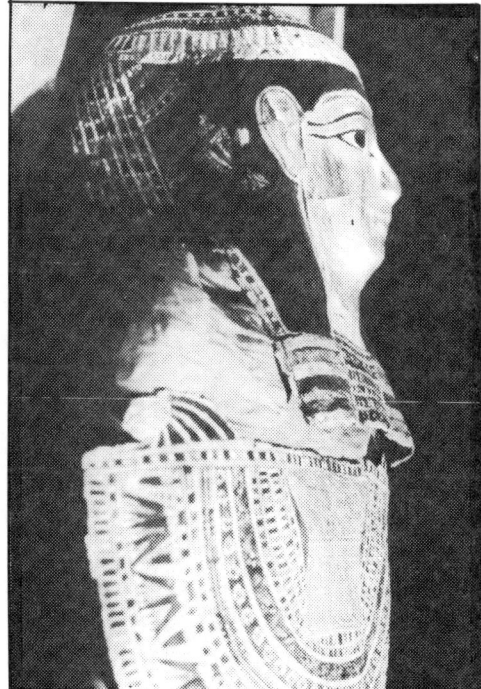

Lynn Edge
Mummy, Anniston Museum of Natural History, Anniston

ANNISTON'S ANIMAL KINGDOM

Anniston, in addition to boasting these well-kept historic structures, also is home to one of the most fascinating museums in the Southeast. The Anniston Museum of Natural History perhaps best can be described as a museum that "did it right." The collection now housed in a modern pre-cast concrete structure near the intersection of Alabama 21 and U.S. 431, began in a smaller, older building. Then it mostly consisted of an extensive collection of birds, assembled by 19th century naturalist William Werner.

And that in itself - more than 600 species of North American birds displayed in their natural habitats with authentic eggs and nests - was impressive.

But the expanded museum is breathtaking. The exhibits are displayed in various "halls," each with its own theme. Among them are Dynamic Earth, Attack and Defense, Designs for Living, East African Savannah and Man: The Versatile Adaptor.

The Dynamic Earth hall includes an authentic replica of an Alabama cave. When you enter the cool, dark and damp atmosphere, you feel as if you're in a real cave. There's not a hint that it was cleverly constructed of such everyday things as drinking straws.

Attack and Defense is a hall that's fun for kids and grown-ups alike as it teaches a basic mechanism of survival. The learning experience of the hall is seeing how animals that are predators hunt and kill their prey

Alabama Bureau of Tourism and Travel

Anniston Museum of Natural History

and how those that are prey, in response, develop protections for themselves. But the kids hardly know they are learning. How can you possibly be learning if you're getting to do such neat things as "grossing out" the girls in the group with skunk scent? The snow in the Attack and Defense Hall, by the way, won a national award for the "best artificial snow" in a museum competition.

The Regar-Werner Ornithology exhibition is housed in the Designs for Living section, which expands on the bird exhibit by showing how the design of a bird's body affects and adapts to its lifestyle.

Baobob trees, a rogue elephant, a giraffe and monkeys all fill the East African Savannah. There also is a model of a termite mound with cross section cut outs to let visitors see the workings inside.

Among the most interesting of the museum's exhibits are the mummies on display in the "Versatile Adaptor" area. In 1926, Egyptian merchants shipped the mummies from Cairo to Philadelphia expecting to display them at the Sesquicentennial Exhibition. Instead, they ended up in a customs house where they stayed until were sold to H. Severn Regar in November, 1926.

Regar donated his museum collection, including the mummies, to the city of Anniston in 1929 and it was put on display in the city's Regar Museum.

The condition of the mummies was deteriorating, however, and in 1978, they were sent to Applebaum and Himmelstein in Brooklyn, New York, for restoration. When they were returned to Anniston, they became a part of the Museum of Natural History.

Not a lot is known about the mummies. They are Egyptian and the hieroglyphics indicate they were embalmed in the third century before Christ. Their wrappings indicate that they were lower middle class or working class Egyptians.

When the museum sent the mummies for restoration, they scheduled one additional stop for them. Museum officials hoped that a visit to the Stringfellow Memorial Hospital for x-rays would help reveal some of the mummies' secrets. And they did learn a few things - the smaller mummy, based on the pelvis size revealed through the x-rays, is a woman who may have been in her mid or late 30s when she died. The pelvis of the larger mummy was crushed, so museum officials were not able to determine the sex of that person.

The wonder of Egyptian mummification processes fascinates adult visitors to the museum. The mummies' colorful decorations - including "tennis shoes" - mesmerize the youngsters.

And a few years ago, museum visitors were able to get to know "their" mummies even better through an art program that is part of the Natural History Museum's exhibition plan. For each hall, the museum commissions a piece of art work - a multi-faceted sculpture for the Dynamic Earth exhibit, a colorful portrayal of conflict for Attack and Defense, the dioramas done by Werner for the Designs for Living display. For the "Versatile Adaptor" Hall, the work is a bronze head of the female mummy sculpted by Betty Pat Gatliff. A forensic sculptor from Oklahoma, she does facial recreations for criminal investigations all over the United States. (Among her other work is a recreation of John Kennedy on the day of his assassination used by the Warren Commission during its investigation.)

Working from x-rays, Ms. Gatliff has created the face of the woman beneath the colorful mummy case. The work has a quiet dignity and beauty even without the added dimension of putting flesh onto what visitors before had seen only as x-rays.

Ms. Gatliff's work is hauntingly beautiful and it - or any of the art works - is worth the cost of admission to the museum. The museum also has an art gallery, where changing exhibits are on display.

Also adding to the museum experience are soundtracks designed to add to, not intrude on, the various exhibits. While all of them work well, none is more effective than the heartbeat that accompanies the "Attack and Defense" displays.

The Anniston Museum of Natural History is a "must see." The museum is on the grounds of Lagarde Park. In the park, you'll find picnic areas and the Eugenia G. Brannon Nature Trail. The trail, almost a mile long, winds its way through four acres of urban wilderness. Pick up a guide to the trail while you're inside the museum so you won't miss any of the trees, plants and animals waiting for you along the way.

Museum hours are 9 a.m. to 5 p.m., Tuesday through Friday; 10 a.m.-5 p.m., Saturday and 1 to 5 p.m., Sunday. Admission is $2 for adults; $1 for children 6 to 17. Admission is free to everyone on Thursdays after noon.

MARCHING THROUGH FORT MCCLELLAN

Not far from the Museum of Natural History is Fort McClellan, "The Military Showplace of the South." Opened in 1917, the 46,000 acre facility is the United State's Army Chemical and Military Police Training Center for men and women in all branches of the service. The fort also is the site of three museums - The Military Police Corps Regimental Museum, the U.S. Army Chemical Corps Museum and the Women's Army Corps Museum.

The Military Police Museum shows the history of the military police during major conflicts. The collection includes a large exhibit of firearms, including 1806 Harper's Ferry flintlock pistols, and period uniforms. There are military vehicles and Civil War photographs and artifacts, among them a field desk and chair. Along with the historical equipment, documents, displays and diagrams, visitors also will find combat art from World War I, World War II, the Korean Conflict and Vietnam. To get to the Military Police Museum (Building 3182), enter the Summerall Gate at Fort McClellan.

The Chemical Museum was established in 1921 at Edgewood Arsenal, Maryland, and moved to Fort McClellan in 1972. Closed the following year, the museum re-opened in 1982. The history of the Chemical Corps itself only predates the museum by four years. The Chemical Warfare Service was organized in 1917 to specialize in what was then a new field - chemical weapons. The name of the corps was changed to U.S. Army Chemical

Alabama Bureau of Tourism and Travel

***Statue of Pallas Athene,
Fort McClellan, Anniston***

Corps at the end of World War II.

The museum holds more than 4,000 artifacts, which take visitors through the history of chemical warfare from Biblical days to the Nuclear Age.

The Biblical weapon, a firebrand, was used to stir up fires or to throw at the enemy. The Greeks improved on this somewhat with the Fire Projector. Introduced in about 673 B.C., the projector pumped a mixture of tar, pitch and sulfur onto enemy ships. The mixture ignited when it was splashed with water.

Naturally, the museum contains large display of gas masks - including a German model with wiper blades. There also are mortars, flame throwers (another improvement on the firebrand) and gas canisters on display.

Most of the museum collection deals with wars before Korea and Vietnam, simply because of a lack of room. There are thousands of artifacts in storage, waiting for a planned expansion of the museum.

To get to the Chemical Corps Museum (Building 2299), enter the Baltzell Gate at Fort McClellan.

Fort McClellan was one of the earliest bases for members of the Women's Army Corps during World War II. It seems appropriate then that this fort would house their museum.

One of the first exhibits visitors see at the WAC Museum is a salute to Molly Corbin, who fought alongside her husband during the Revolutionary War. After this quick introduction to women in combat, the museum traces the history of the Women's Army Corps from 1942, when it was officially begun, to 1978, when it was discontinued as a separate part of the Army.

The fact that the museum has an extensive display showing the evolution of the WAC uniform over the years is not so much a concession to fashion as it is the acknowledgment that when the WACs first came into being, their uniforms weren't always readily available and often WACs found themselves wearing coats designed for men as they marched through the snow.

Other exhibits look at WAC life overseas, WAC awards and Purple Hearts awarded to WACs. On many of the flags, medals and pins of the WACs, you'll see a woman wearing a helmet. This is Pallas Athene, the Greek goddess of war and peace. A lifesize statue of the goddess is the central piece in the Pallas Athene Gardens just outside the museum.

To get to the WAC Museum (Building 1077), enter Fort McClellan at the Galloway Gate.

All three museums are open from 8 a.m. to 4 p.m. Monday through Friday with no admission charge.

ELSEWHERE IN CALHOUN COUNTY

The oldest modified Italianate style depot in Alabama is in Oxford, a municipality about three miles south of Anniston. As many as 25 trains stopped daily at this depot in 1887, when trains were the main mode of transportation. This is the second structure to stand here. The first was a casualty of the Civil War, razed in 1865. This building, one block off Main Street on Spring Street, was constructed in 1884.

Shoppers can find a haven in Oxford at the Old Mill Antique Mall and Village. Set in a century-old cotton mill, the 68,000-square foot Antique Mall houses booths and display cases of more than 150 dealers. The "Turn of the Century" Tea Room at the mall offers shoppers a place to take a break and enjoy afternoon tea. When you've had your fill of shopping for antiques, wander into the "village," which consists of eight houses - once home to mill workers - filled with goods that range from quilts to candy.

The Mall and Village are open Monday through Saturday from 10 a.m. to 5 p.m. and Sunday from 1 to 5 p.m. Admission is free.

After a day of shopping, visitors can take a break at Oxford Lake and Civic Center. There's a paved track around the lake, where swans make their home. Crossing the spillway of the lake is Coldwater Creek Covered Bridge. The 60-foot, one span bridge, built prior to 1850, recently was moved to this location and restored. The lake complex also has picnic areas, tennis courts, a driving range, a swimming pool, a baseball complex and indoor basketball courts.

Hobson City, near Anniston, is the state's first black municipality, which was formed in 1899 by some 125 black men and women. The "City of Challenged Opportunity" had been a part of Oxford until boundaries were drawn to exclude black settlements.

Before you leave Calhoun County, there are at least two more museums you'll want to see. The first, Dr. J.C. Francis' Museum and Apothecary is in Jacksonville. The building itself is worth the trip. Built in Greek Revival style, it is considered to be one of the finest examples of mid-19th century professional offices in the state. Inside, visitors go back to the "biting the bullet" days in medicine. A doctor's office and pharmacy of the 1850s has been recreated and filled with authentic medical and pharmaceutical tools of that era.

The museum, on Gayle Street west of the town square, is open to the public by appointment. There is no admission charge.

While you're in Jacksonville, drive by the First Presbyterian Church on the corner of Clinton and Church Streets. Built in 1858, it is the oldest existing church in the area. During the Civil War, the church was a Confederate hospital.

The other Calhoun County museum you need to visit is housed in the Cross Plains Train Depot in Piedmont. Construction began on the Selma, Rome and Dalton Railroad depot before the Civil War. The building, completed in 1869, now houses exhibits that span a period from the late 1830s to the early 1940s.

The depot, on Ladiga Street, is open from 2 to 4 p.m. Sunday. It is closed Thanksgiving and Christmas weeks. There is no admission charge.

In Piedmont, you may want to spend a few minutes at the Piedmont Challenger Memorial Park and Monument. The granite monuments at the site honor the seven astronauts of the 1986 Challenger crew. Building the monument, located on a site near the school in Piedmont, was an outgrowth of the interest of Piedmont's school children in the Challenger disaster and their desire to salute the astronauts who died aboard that craft.

The park is on West Memorial Drive near the intersection of Alabama Highways 21 and 9.

Etowah County

The city of Gadsden is perched on the banks of the Coosa River in the foothills of Lookout Mountain at a spot where the river makes a horseshoe-shaped bend as it twists its way southward.

James Gadsden, who negotiated the purchases of Arizona and New Mexico in 1853, was never a resident of this Alabama town that bears his name. But he was a friend of the founders - Gabriel Hughes, Joseph Hughes, John Moragne and J.C. Turrentine.

Practically since the city's beginning in 1840, Gadsden has been in the forefront of history-making events.

Union troops made their way through Gadsden in 1863 as they traveled to Rome, Georgia, where there was an important Confederate munitions base. The troops didn't just pass through the city, however, they looted and destroyed much of it.

Out of this visit from the Union Army came two unlikely heroes - 15-year-old Emma Sansom and 43-year-old John Wisdom.

Emma Sansom was at her home near Black Creek on May 2, 1863, helping to care for her brother Rufus, a Confederate soldier who was on leave because he had been wounded.

Suddenly, Union troops were everywhere. This detachment of men on their way to Rome was followed closely by General Nathan Bedford Forrest who led his men in pursuit of the Union Army. When the Union Army reached Black Creek, they crossed it on the only wooden bridge that was usable at the time and burned the bridge behind them, sure they had made a clean getaway.

General Forrest's men arrived only a few minutes later to find the bridge in flames and the river swollen by heavy spring rains. Emma Sansom volunteered to lead the Confederate troops to a shallow spot where the family's cattle often crossed the river, a place where the troops might still be able to ford the water. General Forrest's men followed the girl and found the place where they could cross the river.

Today, the young girl's courage is honored by a monument to her memory. It is at the corner of Broad Street and First Street in front of Gadsden City Hall.

On that same night, John Wisdom had a different, but no less dangerous mission, a calling that would earn him the name, "The Paul Revere of the South."

On the morning of May 2, 1863, Wisdom left his home in his horse and buggy to attend to some personal business. While he was gone, Union raiders entered the city of Gadsden and burned Wisdom's ferry boat. When Wisdom returned that afternoon, friends yelled across the river to him that the Union troops were on their way to Rome.

Wisdom turned his buggy toward the east and set out to warn the people of Rome about the Union Army's advance. Wisdom, borrowing new horses along the way, covered the 67 miles in 8-1/2 hours. When the first of the Union troops arrived in Rome, hoping to take the city by surprise, they were shocked themselves to find an armed and ready band of volunteers waiting for them.

Wisdom's Trail is marked, beginning at Broad Street Bridge to Hoke Street, then into Hokes Bluff and on to Cherokee County. There are markers honoring Wisdom at the Gadsden Community Center and also at the Hokes Bluff City Hall.

Wisdom, who died in 1909, is buried at Hokes Bluff Baptist Church Cemetery, about eight miles east of Gadsden off U.S. 278.

One structure that survived the visit of the Union Army to Gadsden is the Coates-Thornton Mansion. The home of Gideon Coates, one of earliest settlers to come into what is now Etowah County, the house is reminiscent of plantation homes in South Alabama. To reach the Coates Mansion, which is open to the public by appointment only, take U.S. 278 East from Gadsden. Turn north onto Appalachian Road. About four miles down that road, you'll come to the Coosa River. The Coates Mansion is the first house on the right after you cross the river.

Gadsden also has at least two cemeteries worth seeking out for a look at the history they hold. Forrest Cemetery, on Forrest Avenue, dates back to 1872 and the chapel there was built in the 1930s. Many Gadsdenites say they consider the chapel to be one of the most beautiful buildings in the city.

Garner Cemetery, in north Gadsden, is the burial site of a number of the city's early settlers. At least one Revolutionary War veteran is buried there as well. The cemetery recently has been cleaned and restored.

A more modern attraction in Gadsden is the Gadsden Museum of Fine Arts on Meighan Boulevard. Housed there is a permanent collection of painting, sculpture and prints. The antique china and crystal collection especially is notable. There also are monthly changing exhibits featuring the works of regional and local artists. The museum is open Monday through Friday from 2 to 4 p.m. Admission is free.

The Gadsden suburb of Attalla is where the world's first hydroelectric plant was put together and tested. William B. Lay, convinced that hydroelectric power could be harnessed and put to work, built a test facility on Big Wills Creek in Attalla. Lay used this plant, built in 1902, to perfect his concept. His dream of developing the resources of the Coosa-Alabama river system were realized in the organization of Alabama Power Company in 1906. The plant, just off U.S. 278, is in ruins now, although you still can see the remains of the dam. The bridge above the site of the dam seems to be a miniature of the Golden Gate Bridge. It was, in fact, designed by the same man who was the chief engineer for San Francisco's Bay Bridge.

Also in Attalla, just north of U.S. 278 on U.S. 11, is the burial site of

Commodore Ebenezer Farrand. A marker pinpoints the final resting place of this prominent Naval figure of the Confederacy.

In another Gadsden suburb - Hokes Bluff - you can get a taste of what life was like before interstates and superstructures spanned the bodies of water people had to cross. The Hokes Bluff Ferry still is in operation, taking people across the Coosa at a spot just off U.S. 278. The ferry runs regularly from "daylight to dark" and during that time, there is no charge for the use of the ferry. "People can cross in an emergency at night," says one Gadsden resident, "but you have to raise the ferry boat man and there is a charge."

NOCCALULA FALLS

Probably the thing that draws the most visitors to Gadsden is Noccalula Falls. The falls, once a meeting place for various Indian tribes in the area, were formed as water from Black Creek cut away at a rock overhang. Now the water spills almost 100 feet from the top of the falls to the gorge below.

The falls got their name from an Indian legend. A chief and his lovely young daughter Noccalula were said to have lived near the falls. The daughter had many suitors, but the father favored only one. When he

Alabama Mountain Lakes Tourist Association

Noccalula Falls Park, Gadsden

learned that Noccalula had fallen in love with someone else, the father forbade her to see the man she had chosen and arranged a marriage with the brave he had selected.

Despondent, the young maiden threw herself over the falls onto the rocks below. Her father, the story says, was so remorseful that he gave the falls the name of his daughter.

Neither Noccalula nor her father would recognize the falls that bear her name today. They are surrounded by a park and pioneer homestead, visited by about 500,000 people each year.

The homestead depicts the way of life for people living in the Appalachian foothills a few generations ago. Most of the structures in the homestead have been found in other locations and carefully moved to Gadsden. Among the buildings are a country store, grist mill, pioneer home, cookhouse, smoke house, "privy," blacksmith shop, chicken house, tool shed, corn crib, loom house, school house, barn, spring house and hog pen.

Also in the park is the Wilson Building, an old cotton warehouse that dates from the late 1800s. A botanical garden, nature trails and picnic areas add to the appeal of the park.

Noccalula Falls Park also has a train ride and a carpet golf course.

In the park, you'll also find the Gilliland-Reese Covered Bridge, moved piece by piece and faithfully reconstructed on this site. The bridge, built in 1899 by Jesse Gilliland, originally spanned Big Wills Creek. Because the building of the bridge improved transportation so much, volunteers turned out to work on the structure and most of the materials were donated by local merchants.

A "kissing bridge" in the true sense of the word, Gilliland-Reese has been the site of at least one wedding. In the bridge's early days, a young couple was returning from Gadsden - where they had gone to get their marriage license - when they met the preacher on the bridge. Deciding they couldn't find a better spot for their wedding, they asked the preacher to stop and marry them right then and there.

Noccalula Falls Park also is the site of Gadsden's War Memorial. "When I was a boy, I remember my uncles talking about Confederate veterans," says Joe Barnes, one of the people responsible for the memorial. "And I thought then how nice it would be to have something to remember those veterans by." After Barnes grew up and served in World War II and in Korea, he continued his interest in the War Memorial.

When he retired, he finally was able to begin the drive for such a monument. It didn't take long for him to find a lot of people who were interested in his dream. Today, the memorial honors veterans of all wars, he says, and specifically lists the names of more than 450 men from Etowah County who died in World War I, World War II, Korea and Vietnam. There also is the name of one veteran who was killed in Lebanon.

"We would like to have listed those from the Civil War and other earlier wars, but the records were just too sketchy," Barnes explains. " We dedicated the memorial in 1988. We've already had to add the man from Lebanon. I hope we don't have to add any others."

Noccalula Falls Park is open daily from 9 a.m. to 10 p.m. Admission is $1.50 for adults and children. The train ride is $1 for adults, $.50 for children. Carpet golf is $1.50 each for adults and children.

Camping is available at the park. There are 150 improved camp sites and 50 primitive camp sites. Camping costs are $12 for two campers and $1 each for additional campers after that.

The Lookout Mountain Parkway, which bills itself as "America's most scenic 100 miles," begins at Noccalula Falls. It winds its way northward through three states - Alabama, Georgia and Tennessee - passing through or near some of the area's best known attractions. A drive along any part of it offers overlooks with views of valleys and forests as well as glimpses of wildlife and waterfalls.

BLOUNT COUNTY'S COVERED BRIDGES

Blount County, Etowah County's neighbor to the west, probably is best known for its covered bridges. It has more than any other county in Alabama and among them are the two longest covered spans in the South - Swann-Joy and Nectar Covered Bridges. Horton Mill Bridge there probably is the highest covered bridge above water in the United States.

The Swann-Joy Bridge spans the Locust Fork of the Black Warrior River off Alabama 79 near Cleveland. Swann-Joy is a three-span bridge, 324 feet long that sits among stark, towering cliffs and, when rain swells the river, crosses rushing white water.

Not far from the Swann-Joy Bridge is Nectar Bridge, one mile east of Nectar just off Alabama 160. It is the longest covered bridge in the South and the seventh longest of its type in the United States. Built in 1932 of native wooden beams and timbers, the bridge spans 385 feet and has only two supports. The 14-foot wide, 10-foot high structure stands 38 feet above the Black Warrior River.

Horton Mill Bridge, off Alabama 75 five miles north of Oneonta, was built between 1934 and 1935. A two-span structure, Horton Mill is 220 feet long and 14 feet wide. It bridges the Black Warrior River, which rushes by 70 feet below the bridge. Nature trails and a roadside park border one entrance to the bridge.

Blount County's fourth covered bridge is Old Easley Road Covered Bridge, which spans Dub Branch off Alabama 160 near Oneonta. It was built in 1927 and 1928 and is the county's oldest surviving covered bridge. It also is the shortest at only 96 feet.

Although Blount County is known for its covered bridges, that's not the only things to see there. Palisades Park in Oneonta has been chosen by the National Association of County Parks and Recreation as the best park of its kind in the nation. During the summer, the park is open from 9 a.m. to 9 p.m. daily. Hiking trails, indoor and outdoor recreation centers and bicycle trails make it a favorite place for residents and visitors.

Blount County Memorial Museum in Oneonta is filled with permanent displays of arrowheads, covered bridge art and cartography. There also is a Thomas Alva Edison exhibit. Touring exhibits often make their way to this museum as well. It is open Monday through Wednesday, Friday and Sunday from 2 to 4 p.m. and Thursday and Saturday from 10 a.m. to noon. There is no admission charge.

The centerpiece of one Blount County attraction - Rickwood Caverns State Park - is a "Miracle Mile" of underground caverns filed with narrow passages, underground lakes and huge rooms waiting to be discovered. The wonders inside the cavern include a 260-million year old limestone formation, fossils and blind cave fish. In addition to the caverns themselves, the park also has a playground, picnic areas and two hiking trails. The first - Loop Nature Trail - winds through a pine forest. Fossil Mountain Trail, the second, makes its way through rock formations.

The park is open year-round. The Caverns are open on the weekend only from March through May and September through October. They are open daily from June through Labor Day and closed from November through February. Hours are 10 a.m. to 6 p.m. Cave tour is $5.50 for adults, $2.50 for children 6 to 11. Children 5 and under are admitted free. Admission to the park is $.50 per person. Trains rides, available on the weekends, are $.75 per person. Swimming (during the summer) is $1.75 per person.

Camp sites are available at the park all year long. Fees for improved camping are $7 to $9. Fees for primitive campsites are $3 to $7.

Marshall County's Shops and Sites

Any time you visit Marshall County, just north of Blount County, you're sure to find at least one of the two types of animal that migrate to the area regularly. If you're in Boaz, you'll see the Human Shopper - lots of them - filling baskets and cars with outlet buys. If you're in Guntersville, you may get a look at a Bald Eagle.

Boaz, Alabama, is the largest outlet center in the South. The more than 130 stores there sell everything from tennis shoes to teddy bears, from luggage to lipstick. But it wasn't always that way.

In 1981, half of the downtown retail stores were empty. Then something happened to turn the tide - H.D. Lee relocated its blue jean factory from the downtown area to Boaz's industrial park. Lee's parent company, Vanity Fair, transformed the vacant plant into an outlet store for its merchandise.

Other manufacturers followed and the Boaz Outlet Center was born. Since then, more outlet centers have been created and Boaz has become a city where you can shop 'til you drop. A tram provides free transportation to shoppers as they make their way through the huge parking lot at the Outlet Center. You get out of your car, hop on the tram and get off at the store of your choice. When your arms are full of bargains, just hop the tram back to your car, transfer the goodies to the trunk and start all over again.

Most of the stores in the Outlet Center are open from 9 a.m. to 9 p.m. Monday through Saturday and from 12:30 to 5:30 Sunday. A few of them close at 5 p.m. and/or are not open on Sundays.

The Bald Eagles are found at Guntersville State Park, six miles northeast of Guntersville in the Tennessee Valley. The park's almost 6,000 acres offer plenty of room for all sorts of animals, but the Bald Eagle is becoming a special favorite.

The eagles migrate to Lake Guntersville in the winter, but efforts are being made to establish a nesting population of eagles as well. Central to the success of the program are the Eagle Awareness sessions held by the park in January. Those who attend these programs get up at daylight to watch the eagles, then spend the rest of the day in seminars and field trips to learn more about the birds.

As engrossing as the eagles are, they don't provide the only reason to visit Lake Guntersville State Park, one of the best parks the state has to offer. Its  heavily wooded ridges, meadows and bluffs overlook the 69,100-acre Lake Guntersville, the state's largest reservoir.

The lodge at the park is perched on a 500-foot bluff and offers a sweeping view of the lake. The lodge even has its own art gallery, which features painting by local artists.

Twenty miles of hiking trails give visitors a chance to see parts of the forest up close. A golf course, bike trails and a marina add to the recreational opportunities at the park.

For those who would like to put their feet up and stay overnight after all that hiking, biking and other exercise, there are chalets, cabins, campsites and a lodge. Rooms at the lodge are in the $45 to $90 per night range. Cabin rental ranges from about $85 to $95. Improved campsites are about $10 per night and the rate for primitive campsites ranges from $3 to $7 per night. Fees for the golf course range from $6 to $12 and cart rental ranges from $2 to $16.

To see the structure that makes the large lake possible, you need to visit Guntersville Lock and Dam. On U.S. 431 seven miles northwest of Guntersville, the dam is three-fourths of a mile long and 94 feet high. It is open year-round and free tours are available.

If you find all the camping spots at Lake Guntersville State Park filled, don't despair. There are a couple of other places you might try. County Park Number II, off Alabama 69, has facilities for camping, hiking, boating, swimming and picnicking. Ossa-Win-Tha Resort has cottages and sites for travel trailers and mobile homes. On the banks of Lake Guntersville, the resort is open from early March to early November. The cottages are decorated in different styles - African, Persian, Early American, Modern, Seaside, Colonial, Oriental, Pennsylvania Dutch, Inca Indian and Swiss.

Rates for cottage rental range from $30 to $60 per night. Trailer, truck and camper rates are about $10 for two people, extra for other persons over 12.

Traveling between Boaz and Guntersville on U.S. 431, you'll pass through Albertville. But don't just breeze past the town. Stop at the Albertville Depot. The restored structure will take you back to the days when steam engines chugged through the countryside. Two scale model railroads fill the depot's freight area and a Red Caboose Museum houses artifacts from the area's past. The depot is open from May through late September from noon to 4 p.m. on Monday and Friday.

FORT PAYNE'S TRAIN AND MUSIC LEGENDS

There's another depot museum not far away. The Fort Payne Depot in DeKalb County northeast of Marshall County, houses the Landmarks of DeKalb County Museum. The depot, built in 1891, is an outstanding example of Richardsonian Romanesque architecture. Inside, visitors find a varied collection of Indian handiwork and artifacts. A permanent display at the museum includes farm and home items from the Fort Payne of the 1800s and early 1900s. Since the museum is set in a depot, it's natural that the exhibits also include railroad memorabilia, photographs and art.

Museum hours are 10 a.m. to 4 p.m. Monday, Wednesday and Friday and 2 to 4 p.m. Sunday.

Of course, the thing that Fort Payne probably is best known for is ALABAMA - the singing group. Three of the four members of ALABAMA come from Fort Payne and the group itself was sort of "birthed and bred" in this city. It's no surprise then that The Alabama Fan Club and Museum is here. Personal items, awards and giant photos of the group fill the museum and a 20-minute audio gives fans a close look at ALABAMA.

The museum is open from 8 a.m. to 5 p.m. Monday through Saturday and from 1 to 6 p.m. Sunday. Admission is $5 for adults, $3 for students and senior citizens and $2 for children.

While in Fort Payne, be sure to see the Fort Payne Opera House, the oldest theater in Alabama still in use. Built in 1889 during the industrial boom, the facility cost $80,000 to construct. When the Opera House opened, people proclaimed it to be the "most convenient and handsome opera house in the state."

NATURAL BEAUTY IN NORTHEST ALABAMA

While the fame of a group such as ALABAMA can leave a city a little star-struck, the real star of this area is nature. You can't get away from the breathtaking scenery, the woods and the waterfalls.

Little River Canyon is just one of the natural wonders waiting for visitors. The canyon is the deepest gorge east of the Rocky Mountains and contains the only river in the United States that forms and flows on top of a mountain. A 20-mile paved scenic drive follows the west rim of the canyon along its total length. When you stop at the various overlooks on the drive, you'll realize that canyon really is deep - its average depth, in fact, is 500 feet. At one spot, Crow's Point, the canyon is 800 feet deep.

At one end of the river is Little River Falls. You'll find it near the junction of Alabama 35 and Little River Canyon Rim Road. It's especially spectacular right after the spring rains.

At the other end of the river, near DeSoto State Park, is DeSoto Falls. This spectacular waterfall plunges more than 100 feet from a mile-long lake into

Little River Canyon below. The view from the overlook is awe-inspiring as the water tumbles through the rocks at the top of the mountain and crashes over the edge.

DeSoto State Park has cabins and chalets as well as campsites and a lodge. And for the youngsters, there's a playground. For the maybe not-so-youngsters, there is a horseshoe pitching area and a volleyball court. For everyone, there are tennis courts and a swimming pool. Don't worry, by the way, if you get to the park and the call of the volleyball court, the horseshoe pit or the softball fields overcomes you. If you didn't bring your glove and bat along, equipment can be rented at the country store in the park.

Twenty miles of hiking trails in the park wind through deep forests and past waterfalls and canyon walls.

DeSoto Park was developed in the mid 1930s by members of the Civilian Conservation Corps. The original facilities were constructed by the CCC using native stone and logs. All the original furniture in the rustic cabins

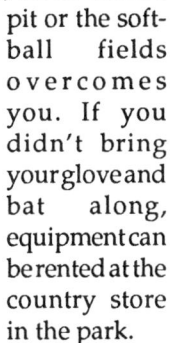

Chamber
of
Commerce
Est. 1947

Fort Payne AL

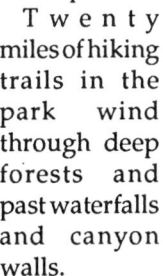

Come see what we've got in Fort Payne

---

was handmade by men of the CCC.

The park is open year round, from sunrise to sunset. Cabin rentals range from about $44 to $66. Motel room rates are from about $37 to $49. Improved campsite rentals range from $9 to $11 per night and primitive campsite rental costs are $3 to $7 per night. Admission to the picnic area is $.50.

At the north entrance to the park is the Sallie Howard Memorial Chapel, built by Colonel Milford Wriarson Howard. Colonel Howard had many claims to fame. When he was admitted to the Alabama Bar in 1881 at age 19, he became the youngest man ever admitted. He served as one of Alabama's representatives in Congress in the late 1800s. He was a script writer for a California movie company. And he was a man of determination.

His first wife, Sallie, died while they were living in California and the chapel at the California cemetery where he buried her caught his eye. It became his dream to recreate that chapel on Lookout Mountain in Alabama in his wife's memory. With the help of CCC members and residents of the mountain, Colonel Howard was able to build the church and dedicate it on June 27, 1937.

From the front, the chapel looks pretty much like a plain stone chapel, but a walk to the side reveals that the back wall of the building is a rock that crops out of Lookout Mountain. When Colonel Milford died only a few months after the dedication of the chapel, his second wife had his remains cremated and placed inside this huge rock.

The chapel is open 24 hours a day and there is no admission charge. Services are held each Sunday morning at 10 a.m.

Howard's Chapel is another place in Alabama where you're likely to find yourself becoming a guest at a wedding. A small piece of paper hanging inside the chapel simply asks brides who would like to be married there to sign their names and wedding dates and leave a phone number so the pastor of the church can get in touch with them.

SNOW SKIING IN ALABAMA – REALLY

If you say you're going skiing in Alabama, people either assume you're going water skiing or you've lost your mind. Not so. You can snow ski in Alabama at Cloudmont Ski and Golf Resort. The resort, which sits at an elevation of 2,000 feet atop Lookout Mountain, covers 1,000 acres of forest trails and waterfalls. And as soon as the overnight temperatures drop to 28 degrees or lower, eight snowmaking machines chug into service, creating a covering of white for the beginner and intermediate slopes at the resort. The snow season usually runs from mid-December to early March.

Don't worry if you've never been on skis before, the instructors at Cloudmont will have you sailing down the slopes in no time.

The ski resort is open daily from 9 a.m. to 4 p.m. and nightly from 6 to 10 p.m. during the ski season. On Friday and Saturday, evening sessions end at midnight.

Skiing costs are $25 per session (This includes equipment rental, lift and beginner lessons.) on the weekends. On the weekdays and at night, the rate is $17 to $20 per session. Lift charges, if you use the lift only, range from $12 to $14.

And what if you've never really wanted to ski or you can't make it to Cloudmont during the ski season? If you're a golfer, you've got nothing to worry about. You can play at Cloudmont from April through December. And don't think you'll be missing out on all that mountain scenery just because you aren't on the slopes. The first tee on the golf course is atop a 30 foot rock. You'll get a good view of the surrounding area from there.

Greens fees are $4 to $6. Cart rental is from $8 to $12.

If you're staying overnight, chalet rentals are $55 for four people, $5 for each extra person. The chalets are available year-round.

Just above Fort Payne and DeSoto Park is the mountain-top town of Mentone. Its quaint streets are filled with shops, restaurants and craft stores, most of them housed in historic buildings. The unusual finds - such as the "gourdies" (dolls made from gourds) - make the shopping fun and just wandering around the city is a treat in itself. Much of Mentone closes down for the winter, however, so check before you make a special trip.

A little farther up the mountain - almost into Georgia, as a matter of fact - are Sequoyah Caverns. Located 16 miles north of U.S. 11 near Fort Payne, the caverns are named for Sequoyah, the Indian who developed the Cherokee alphabet in the "Will's Town" settlement near Fort Payne.

Inside the caverns, visitors will find thousands of rock formations, dramatically lit "looking glass lakes" and rainbow falls. On the grounds are deer, buffalo and pools filled with rainbow trout. The caverns are open 8:30 a.m. to 5 p.m. from early March to Memorial Day and from Labor Day. Hours from Memorial Day to Labor Day are 8:30 a.m. to 6 p.m. Cave tours are $6 for adults and $4 for children from 6 to 12.

Inch a few miles closer to Georgia (So close that you take the Rising Fawn, Georgia, exit off I-59) and you will find Fox Mountain Trout Farm. Trout are raised here for the fisherman's pleasure. The fishing season is from early March to early November, 9 a.m. to 7 p.m. Fees are $2.50 per pound of trout caught and include fishing poles and bait as well as bagging and icing of your catch.

Buck Pocket State Park

DeKalb County does have one other state park - Buck's Pocket State Park. This is the traditional place for Alabama politicians to go and "lick their wounds" when they've been defeated in an election. You don't have to be the loser in a recent political campaign to go there, even though you might run into a few during your visit. The 2,000-acre park set in a natural "pocket" of the Appalachian mountain chain is a good place for anyone who wants to get away from the daily grind for a while to hike along the scenic trails or to try his luck at fishing. The rugged mountains and canyons are filled with wildflowers, making this a favorite spot for visitors during the spring flowering season and the fall color change.

The park is open year round from 8 a.m. to 10 p.m. Fees for improved campsites here range from $7.50 to $9 per night. Primitive campsite rentals range from $3 to $7 per night.

If you're interested in doing a little bargaining while you're visiting DeKalb County, stop by Collinsville. Every Saturday, the town hosts Collinsville Trade Day and thousands of people drop by. A tradition in Collinsville since 1950, Trade Day brings vendors of everything from antiques to livestock together so customers can buy, sell and swap. The trading goes on from sun-up to sunset and the only charge (other than for the goodies and food you buy, of course) is $.50 for parking.

Dogtown, also in DeKalb County, is the place folks go to find great buys on furniture.

Welcome To Scottsboro

Those who come to Alabama in the mood for some shopping should be sure and be in Scottsboro on "First Monday." Held in the Jackson County Courthouse Square appropriately enough on the first Monday of each month, the event dates back to the early days of this area. The trading day is said to have begun in the 1800s, when the county Circuit Court began holding its sessions on the first Monday of each month. A sort of mix of antique show, craft fair and rummage sale, First Monday is an experience not to be missed as buyers and sellers barter for goods. First Monday goes from sunrise to sunset and admission is free.

Something else you might want to buy while you're in the Scottsboro area are apples grown on Crow Mountain. To get to Crow Mountain Orchards, take Alabama 79 North through the town of Skyline. Just beyond that city, you'll see a sign that says, "Crow Mountain Orchards." Turn right at sign, go 3-1/2 miles to another sign and turn left there. The orchards are about 3-1/2 miles down that road.

In Scottsboro, too, be sure and see the Scottsboro-Jackson Heritage Center, where early life in Northern Alabama is shown through exhibits, classes and demonstrations. Set in an 1880s Greek Revival home, the museum is open from 9 a.m. to 4 p.m. Tuesday through Friday. Admission is $1 for adults and $.50 for children.

In this same complex, you'll find "Sage Town," a pioneer log cabin village. Among the structures are a blacksmith shop and a one-room school house. Jackson County's 1868 courthouse is on the grounds as well.

Also near Scottsboro is the Goose Pond Recreational Complex, a 360-acre park set on a peninsula that juts into the Tennessee River. The facilities at this municipally-owned park include an 18-hole championship golf course, a marina, a pool and hiking trails. There also are cottage, cabins and campsites available.

Fees at Goose Pond, which is open year-round, include $1 for parking and greens fees ranging from $7 to $14. Camping fees begin at $10 per night.

About 35 miles north of Scottsboro is the Stevenson Railroad Depot Museum. This depot sat at an important junction - near where Alabama, Tennessee and Georgia meet - so it was a crucial spot in the Confederacy's lifeline during the Civil War. Built in the 1850s, the little depot was heavily guarded as the war raged all around it. During the Union occupation of Stevenson, the structure was protected by two extensively fortified redoubts and several blockhouses. Today, it houses a collection of military and agricultural memorabilia as well as local artifacts.

The museum, on Main Street in Stevenson, is open Monday through Friday from 9 a.m. to 5 p.m. January through March. From April to December, it is open Monday through Saturday from 9 a.m. to 5 p.m. and Sunday from 1 to 4 p.m. Admission is free.

A LITTLE CAVE HISTORY

In the northeast corner of Alabama, closer to Tennessee than anything else, is some of the state's earliest history - a cave shelter called Russell Cave National Monument.

Stone Age man made his home here about 9,000 years ago. The site was discovered in 1953 and has been excavated meticulously by a team of archaeologists to yield a wealth of information about early human settlement in this region.

The cave, a limestone chamber 210 feet long and 107 feet wide, is part of a much larger cavern stretching about one mile into the side of a gray limestone hill.

Inside are charcoal remains of ancient campfires, bones of humans buried there and other evidence found more than 20 feet beneath the cave floor. These indicate that nomadic Indians began living in Russell Cave as early as 7,000 B.C. They probably returned to the cave each autumn, when the summer's supply of wild plant foods dwindled and cold weather set in. From the refuge of the cave, they would venture out to collect firewood, gather nuts and seeds, fish in a nearby stream and hunt animals for meat and hides.

Their tools were simple - awls, fish hooks and sewing needles made from bone, stone knives and short spears tipped with stone points.

The Indians' way of life changed little for more than 6,000 years. Then, in about 1,000 B.C., the cave's inhabitants began using dramatically different tools, a change that indicates a new lifestyle. Their spear points grew more refined, suggesting that the bow and arrow had been adopted as the weapon for hunting. Pottery appeared for the first time, as did jewelry of bone and shell.

Gradually, the Indians learned to farm and began to establish larger, more permanent villages. By 500 A.D., Russell Cave, the oldest regularly used site of human habitation in the Southeastern U.S., no longer was needed as a seasonal shelter for the community.

The cave and the 310 acres of surrounding countryside were given to the United States by the National Geographic Society on January 4, 1961. Today, the site is managed by the National Park Service and is maintained in its natural state.

Visitors to Russell Cave take a self-guided tour of the cavern then go to

---

Northeast Alabama

visitor center, where there are exhibits of tools and artifacts from the excavation. Nature trails wind their way up the mountain covering Russell Cave and meet on top at a point where the view of the surrounding area is spectacular. Along the way up the trail are markers identifying the indigenous plant life and telling how early man might have used it.

Russell Cave National Monument is eight miles west of Bridgeport off U.S. 72, via County 91 then County 75. The cave is open daily except New Year's Day, Thanksgiving and Christmas from 8 a.m. to 5 p.m. It is free.

WHERE TO STAY

There are a number of chain hotels and motels throughout this part of the state. In addition, there are privately owned facilities. Among them are:

In Anniston: American Inn, The Carriage House Inn, The Heart of Anniston Inn, Lenlock Inn, Liberty Inn, McClellan Inn, Mid-Town Inn, Nelford Inn, Royal Inn and Vann Thomas Motel.

In Ashland: Country Inn Motel.

Alabama Bureau of Tourism and Travel

Russell Cave, Bridgeport

In Cedar Bluff: Lakeshore Motel.

In Centre: Pruett Fish Camp and Cabins, Centre Motel.

In Childersburg: Lynn Motel, River Terrace Motel.

In DeKalb County: Shady Grove Ranch (a Dude and Guest Ranch with two group lodges and two guest rooms) and Adams Outdoors (The rustic cabins here surround a common kitchen/bathhouse building and hiking trails lead in all directions through the surrounding countryside. Adams Outdoors is closed for much of the winter.).

In Gadsden: Gadsden Motor Inn, Friendly Village Inn, Gadsden Airport Motel.

In Guntersville: Mac's Landing Lodge, Overlook Mountain Lodge.

In Jacksonville: Gamecock Motel.

In Lincoln: McCaig Motel.

In Mentone: Nippersink Lodge (Set in a home built in 1935, the lodge has nine rooms with baths, living room, dining room, kitchen and screened porch overlooking the river.).

In Oneonta: Windwood Inn of Oneonta.

In Oxford: The Executive Inn and Travelers Inn.

In Roanoke: Harry's All-American Inn.

In Scottsboro: The Liberty Inn.

In Sylacauga: The Towne Inn.

In Talladega: Colony House Motel.

In Wedowee: Old English Inn.

Bed and Breakfast Inns in this region of the state include:

The Victoria in Anniston. An elegant 1888 home forms the core of this inn.

The Noble-McCaa-Butler House in Anniston. This bed and breakfast is set in an 1886 Victorian home. It has six guest rooms, including one three-room suite. There are some shared baths.

Mentone Inn Bed and Breakfast in Mentone. Located atop Lookout Mountain, this inn offers lots of porches for sitting on to enjoy the view. Menton Inn is open from early April through November.

Governor's House Bed and Breakfast in Lincoln. Set in a 150-year-old house, this bed and breakfast sits on a ridge overlooking pastures and lakes.

Shinbone Valley Country Inn in Clay County. This inn sits at the base of Cheaha Mountain. The inn is open for lunch on the weekends.

Stamps Inn in Arab.

Campgrounds in the area besides those in state parks and recreation areas include:

In Cedar Bluff: Riverside, Big Oak Campground, J.R.'s Marina Campground, Last Resort Campground, Little River Canyon Mouth Park, Riverside Campground, Three Rivers Resort Campground and Driftwood Family Campground.

In Centre: Bay Springs Campground, Bay Springs Motel Campground,

Bay Springs Restaurant Campground, John's Grocery Campground, Peek's Grocery and Tackle Campground, Pruett's Sunset House Restaurant Campground and Cowan Creek Grocery Campground.

In Grant: Honeycomb Campground.

In Guntersville: Street Bluff Fishing Camp, Riverview Campground and Beech Creek Fishing Camp.

In Ider: Thunder Canyon Campground and RV Park (Table tennis, volleyball, horseshoes and a children's fishing pond are among the extras here.).

In Leesburg: CedarPoint Campground and Pine Cone Marina Campground.

In Ohatchee: Willow Point Marina and Campground (Facilities include spots for swimming, covered picnic tables and setups for volleyball, badminton and horseshoes.).

In Valley Head: Sequoyah Caverns KOA Kampground.

WHERE TO EAT

In Anniston: Victoria, Annistonian, Betty's Bar-B-Que, China Luck, The Courtyard, The English Tea Room, Los Mexicanoes, Mata's Greek Pizza and Grinders, Mikado Japanese Steak House, Old Smokehouse Bar-B-Q, Peking's, Top O' The River and Village Inn.

In Ashland: Lee's Country Kitchen and Magnolia Inn.

In Boaz: Mrs. Tupper's, The Lunch Box and The Original Mill Street Deli.
In Cedar Bluff: Lighthouse Restaurant.
In Centre: Muffins Cafe and the Cotton Patch.
In Childersburg: Taylor's and Mister J's Family Steakhouse.
In DeKalb County: Terri's Time Saver Deli.
In Gadsden: The Choice, Manny's, The Fisherman, Hunan Chinese Restaurant, Good for You! Express, Hungry Hut, J.C. Garcia's, Oasis On The Drive, Penny Profit Bar-B-Q, Pruett's Bar-B-Q, The Q's, Silver Dragon, Tiffany's Cafe, Banquet Table Buffet, Bar-B-Q Bob's and Bullship Restaurant.

In Guntersville: The Glover (located in a restored Guntersville landmark hotel), Northtown Cooker, Reid's, Val-Monte and Local Option.

In Lincoln: BJ's Family Restaurant, Dot's Drive In, Dot's Hickory Pit and Frank's.

In Mentone: The Log Cabin Deli, Mentone Springs Hotel Restaurant (open Thursday through Sunday only) and Cragsmere Manna (It's located in an historic house and open only on the weekends, but those who have caught it open and eaten there recommend it.).
In Oneonta: The Landmark, Little Joe's and Round the Clock.
In Riverside: The Ark and Hal's Hungry Bear Restaurant.
In Roanoke: Galley Steak and Seafood and City Cafe.
In Scottsboro: Liberty Restaurant.
In Sylacauga: Bob's Steak House, J. Oliver's and Szechuan Village.
In Talladega: Seafood Galley.
In Wedowee: Charlie's Catfish and The Hub (appropriately named since Wedowee is the center of Randolph County).

ANNUAL EVENTS

Among the annual events that draw visitors to this area are:

Eagle Awareness Weekends, Guntersville, January

Black Heritage Festival, Anniston, February.
Boat Show, Oxford, February.
A Taste of Cherokee, Centre, February
Arts and Crafts Exhibition, Anniston, March.

April in Talladega, Talladega, April.
Charlie Miller Domino Tournament, Talladega, April.
Indian Dance and Country Crafts Festival, DeSoto Caverns, Childersburg, April.
Art-On-The-Lake, Guntersville, April.
Poke Salat Festival, April, Arab.

Indian Day, Bridgeport, April.
Festival Of The New Spring Moon - Youth Pow Wow, Gadsden, April.
Sequoyah Open Road Run, Valley Head, April.
Sap Rising Celebration, Gadsden, April.
Championship Pro Rodeo, Oneonta, April.
Easter Festivities, Boaz, April/May.

Pontiac Oakland Car Show, Talladega, May.
Sunshine Saturday, Talladega and Sylacauga, May.
Winston 500, Talladega, May.

Alabama Bassmaster Invitational, Guntersville, May.
Art on the Rocks, Gadsden, May.
Hobby Show, Oxford, May.
Rhododendron Festival, Mentone, May
North Alabama Catfish Festival, Scottsboro, May.
Rhododendron Art Show, Scottsboro, May.

Air Show, Sylacauga, June.
Chalaka Arts and Crafts Show, Sylacauga, June.
Gem and Mineral Show, DeSoto Caverns, Childersburg, June.
Miss Motorsports Hall of Fame Pageant, Talladega, June.
Super Sports Weekend, Sylacauga, June.
June Jam, Fort Payne.
Gerhart Chamber Music Festival, Guntersville, June.
Fitness and Nutrition Show, Oxford, June.
Cheaha Mountain Spring Arts and Crafts Show, Cheaha State Park,
Delta, June.
Blount County Industry and Farm Tour, Oneonta, June.
Riverfest, Gadsden, June/July

DieHard 500, Talladega, Talladega, July.
International Motorsports Hall of Fame Induction, Talladega,
July.
Freedom Festival, Albertville, July.
Star Spangled Celebration, Guntersville, July.
Gold City Homecoming, Glencoe, July.
Mentone Crafts Festival, July.
Blueberry Festival, Lineville, July.
Alabama Bicycle Classic, Fort Payne, July.
Antique Automobile Club Invitational Meet, Gadsden, July.
Salvation Army Doll Auction, Oxford, July.
ARCA 500K, Talladega, July.
Mountain Lakes Triathlon, Guntersville, July.

Crazy Daze, Sylacauga, August.

Auto and Truck Show, Sylacauga, August.
Boys and Girls Clubs' Rodeo, Gadsden, August.
Summerfest, Guntersville, August.
Four Hundred Fifty-Mile Yard Sale, Gadsden, August.
Anniston Museum Day, Anniston, August.
Cherokee Pow Wow and Green Corn Festival, Gadsden, August.
St. William's Catholic Church's Seafood Festival, September.
Fall Harvest Festival, Childersburg, September.
Fayetteville County Fair, Sylacauga, September.
September Fest, DeSoto Caverns, Childersburg, September.
Waldo Sorghum Sopping Days, September.
Seafood Festival, Guntersville, September.
Motorcycle Show, Oxford, September.
Sequoyah Caverns Arts and Crafts Festival, Valley Head, September.
Renaissance Arts Festival, Boaz, September.

Farm-City Week, Sylacauga and Talladega, October.
Falls Fest, Gadsden, October.
Harvest Festival, Boaz, October.
Oxfordfest, Oxford, October.
Blount County Fair, Oneonta, October.
Fall Cheaha Mountain Arts and Crafts, Delta, October.
Renaissance Feastival, Guntersville, October.
Blount County Covered Bridge Festival, Oneonta, October.
Alabama Wildfowl and Wildlife Festival, Guntersville, October.
Fall Festival, Centre, October.
Mentone Fall Colorfest, October

Renaissance Feastival, Albertville, November.
Alcazar Car Show, Lineville, November.
Megabuck B.A.S.S. Tournament, Guntersville, November.
Fall Arts and Crafts Show, Oxford, November.
Christmas Parade, Albertville, November.
Christmas Parade, Centre, November.
Miniature Train Exhibit, Sylacauga, November.
Winter Market, Anniston Museum of Natural History, Anniston,
November/December.
Christmas Festival of Lights, DeSoto Caverns, Childersburg,
November/December/January

Christmas Parades in Talladega, Sylacauga, Guntersville and Blount
County, December.
Parade of Lights, Guntersville, December.
Holiday Arts and Crafts Show, Oneonta, December.
Christmas at the Cabins, Sylacauga, December.

Northwest Alabama's Treasures

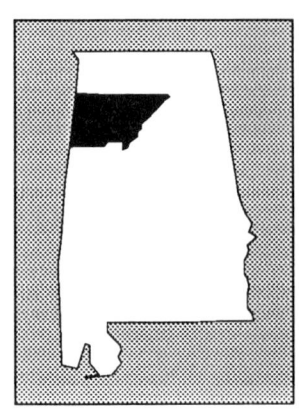

 A sandstone bridge formed more than 200 million years ago, a "Free State" formed during the Civil War and an entire world in miniature created by one man's hands all are found in a slice of North central Alabama reaching from the Mississippi border almost to the Appalachian foothills.

Natural Bridge, the 60-foot high sandstone bridge, is near Natural Bridge, the city which sits just at the Winston/Marion County border. The bridge was created through the natural erosion caused by a tributary stream that ran through the area hundreds of millions of years ago. The two 148-foot long spans of sandstone form the the longest natural bridge east of the Rockies. All around the bridge are natural gardens, filled with mountain laurel and giant magnolias. A hiking trail that winds through the area of rocky bluffs leading to the bridge and nearby Brushy Lake is short, but strenuous. Still, the scenery is worth the effort. Camping and picnicking are available along the lake shore.

Natural Bridge is open daily from 8 a.m. to sunset. Admission is $2 for adults, $1 for children six to 16.

Winston's "Secession"

The town of Natural Bridge is in Winston County, Alabama's own Liechtenstein. Don't be surprised if you hear the county referred to as "The Free State of Winston," a name it gained during the Civil War.

Most of the early settlers of Hancock County (In 1858, it became Winston County to honor Alabama Governor John A. Winston), were fiercely independent folks. Isolated by the hills and less affluent than the planters to the south, they generally had less political influence in state government.

As a war between the North and the South became inevitable, these people found themselves caught in the middle of the controversy. While they didn't want their fellow Southerners to lose the conflict, they could not brings themselves to fight against what they still considered to be their nation. Charles Christopher Sheats, a school teacher, was elected by the people of Winston County to represent them at the Secession Convention in

Montgomery in 1861. Sheats was one of only 24 convention delegates who refused to sign the Ordinance of Secession. Alabama left the Union in January, 1861.

Early in 1862, the anti-secession movement in Winston County decided the time had come for these people to be heard. Six riders went out in all directions, telling of a meeting to be held at Looney's Tavern, just north of the present day town of Addison. On July 4, 1862, more than 2,500 representatives of Winston and surrounding counties met at the tavern for a "neutrality meeting," at which Sheats was the main speaker. The people voted overwhelmingly to adopt a resolution stating that if a "state can lawfully and legally secede or withdraw from the Union, being only a part of the Union, by the same process of reasoning, a county could cease to be part of the state." The resolution asked that both the North and the South leave the people of Winston County "alone, unmolested, that we may work out our political and financial destiny here in the hills and mountains of Northwest Alabama." Unfortunately, the politics of this war didn't allow for neutrality.

When the Confederacy

Northwest Alabama

This region of six counties lies in the East Gulf Coastal Plain of Alabama, the state's largest land area. Within this region is some of Alabama's most primitive history as well as some of her most advanced waterways. Reaching from the Mississippi border to the center of the state, this area is home to more than 230,000 people. Cullman, Fayette and Jasper are the largest cities in the region.

needed manpower, the Conscription Act, which did not recognize the neutrality of the "Free State of Winston," was passed. The men who were hiding in the mountains, led by Sheats and Bill Looney, began to assist the Union Army in scouting and recruiting. More than 700 men from Winston County joined the Union Army while only 112 served the Confederacy and the people of Winston County led hundreds of volunteers through Confederate battle lines to serve with the Union Army.

Because of his violent opposition to war, Sheats was jailed and spent much of the war imprisoned. But the Unionists of Winston County made a significant contribution to the victory of the Union even with their leader behind bars. They sheltered Confederate deserters, fought as guerrillas, furnished intelligence to the Union and served as guides.

Each year, the story of how the Free State of Winston was formed is told in the new drama "Incident at Looney's Tavern." The play is presented in a new 1,500-seat amphitheater complex near Double Springs. The complex

Scene from "Incident at Looney's Tavern," Double Springs

also has restaurant and picnic facilities. The amphitheater is about 29 miles west of I-65 on U.S. 278. The production is presented on Thursdays, Fridays and Saturdays from mid-June to Labor Day. There are Saturday shows only after Labor Day. The show closes in late September. Pre-show entertainment begins at 7:15 p.m. and the play begins at 8:15 p.m. Ticket prices are $11 for adults and $6 for children for box seats and $9 for adults and $5 for children for mezzanine seats. There is a senior citizens discount.

BANKHEAD FOREST

The majority of Bankhead National Forest, Alabama's largest national forest, lies within Winston County. The nearly 200,000 acres of timberland, rivers and natural wonders hold the remains of Indians who lived here long before Columbus discovered America. Waterfalls, bluffs, canyons, springs and lakes provide a backdrop for such scenery as the state's largest tree, a 500-year-old, 150-foot poplar.

In the Bankhead Forest are four recreation areas - Brushy Lake, Corinth,

Houston and Clear Creek.

Brushy Lake Recreation Area, north of Double Springs, provides a remote environment. The 400 acres there encompass a 33-acre manmade lake, created by a concrete arch-design dam constructed by the Civilian Conservation Corps in the early 1930s. Camping areas have sites for improved camping, picnic tables and barbecue grills. The lake provides fishing and boating and there are hiking and biking trails and a ballfield. Pets are permitted. The camping area is open year-round and fees for camping are less than $5.

Four miles east of Double Springs is the Corinth Recreation Area. A less secluded camping ground is on the shore of 21,000-acre Lake Lewis Smith. The recreation area contains two camping loops, where each campsite is equipped with a picnic table, grill, lantern pole and camping pad. In the day-use area, there is a sand swimming beach and spots for fishing, boating, hiking and cycling. The camping area is open 24 hours a day from early May to late September. The day-use area is open from 7 a.m. to 10 p.m. from early April to late October. Camping fees are $5 for singles and $10 for doubles. Swimming fee is $2 per vehicle. Pets are permitted.

The Houston Recreation Area is 12 miles east of Double Springs off U.S. 278. Adjacent to Lewis Smith Lake, the area has three camping loops. Campsites here have the same equipment as those in the Corinth Area. The Houston Area provides another quiet, secluded place in the Forest to pitch a tent, picnic in the shade of century-old trees or to try your hand at fishing. There is a sand swimming beach, as well as natural trails and areas for cycling, boating and canoeing. The camping area is open 24 hours a day from mid-May to late September. The day use area is open from 7 a.m. to 10 p.m. during the same months. Camping and swimming fees are the same as in the Corinth Area. Pets are permitted.

The newest recreation area in the Bankhead Forest is the Clear Creek Recreation Area, located about 14 miles north of Jasper. The more than 400 acres spread out next to Lake Lewis Smith and are filled with waterfalls and bluffs. This new facility, opened in 1988, offers picnic sites, a playground, a white sand beach and swimming. Four camping loops, with a total of 104 camping sites, here feature single and two-family units in a lakeside forest setting. Each camping unit is equipped with electrical and water hookups and a camper's boat ramp.

The day-use area has individual picnic sites next to the lake, a white sand beach, a swimming area and three large group picnic shelters. Parallel to the shoreline of the lake is a mile of asphalt bicycle trail that crosses two large hollows on specially-designed contoured bridges. The bicycle trail connects the day-use area with the camping area.

There is a 2.5-mile trail that hikers may use for exercise or nature study. It crosses the scenic rock bluffs that are well-known in the Bankhead Forest. When it rains, the water flows over the rock bluffs creating magnificent waterfalls.

The camping area is open 24 hours a day all year. The day-use area is open from 7 a.m. to 10 p.m. from early March to late October. Fees for camping are $9 and $10 for singles, $14 and $17 for doubles. Group camping fee is $20. The day use fee is $2 per vehicle. Rental for the picnic shelters (make reservations in advance) is $25 to $35. Pets are permitted. Also within the Bankhead Forest is Sipsey Wilderness, 26,000 acres of wild land that has been described as "a real paradise for hikers and canoe enthusiasts." Gorges, canyons and virgin timberlands are filled with exotic plants and rare birds and mammals.

THE SIPSEY WILDERNESS

To get an idea of where the Sipsey Wilderness is, look at an Alabama map showing Winston and Lawrence Counties. Draw a line from just below Moulton in Lawrence County to Haleyville in Winston County. Most of the wilderness lies above this line and within the Bankhead Forest. The line also is approximately the location of the Tennessee Divide, at the end of the Appalachian foothills. Water that falls above this line flows into the Tennessee River, water that falls below it flows into the Sipsey and eventually into the Black Warrior.

The wilderness contains about 120 acres of "virgin timber." If, like many people, you aren't sure exactly what that is, the U.S. Forest Service defines it as "a large stand of timber that never has been commercially harvested." The wilderness area also has second-growth timber, the timber that comes up, either naturally or through planting, after an initial harvest.

While you're in the Sipsey Wilderness, you can fish in the Sipsey Branch of the Black Warrior River or swim in a number of creeks that feed the river.

The Sipsey Wilderness has a total of 22 miles of hiking trails, designed for various skill levels of hikers. For example, the 2.7-mile Borden Creek Trail, which can be handled in an afternoon, is for the casual hiker. This trail offers the opportunity to visit areas with high bluffs and rock outcroppings.

A six-mile trek, which brings you along the 1.2-mile Bee Branch Trail, requires a little more stamina and knowhow. This trail runs along the Bee Branch, which feeds into the Sipsey River. While on this trail, you can see some virgin timber that includes oak, poplar, hemlock and hickory trees. There also is a 500-yard descent that goes down into the Bee Branch Canyon. On the hike along Bee Branch from Forest Road 208 to the junction of Bee Branch with the Sipsey River, you'll encounter a rock-trimmed box canyon with sheer vertical walls rising 100 feet or more.

The Sipsey Wilderness has no developed camping sites. Camping is permitted, however. The Forest Service hopes to encourage "no-trace camping," meaning campers should remove all evidence of their campsite and carry refuse out of the wilderness area. Campfires are permitted, but the use of small backpacking stoves is encouraged.

The Sipsey Wild and Scenic River, the only Alabama river included in America's Wild and Scenic Rivers System, is created, for the most part, in the Sipsey Wilderness. Border, Flannagan, Haygood, Braziel, Hubbard, Tedford,

Alabama Bureau of Tourism and Travel

Sipsey Wilderness

Thompson and Montgomery Creeks - all in the Wilderness area - come together through Bee Branch to form the river about 1/2 mile north of the Sipsey Picnic Grounds on the southern edge of the wilderness.

Sipsey Picnic Grounds were constructed by the CCC. At Kenlock Springs, there is a CCC camp where there's a natural water slide, carved from the rock by the flow of water across it. Today, visitors to the area enjoy a trip down a rock slide that Mother Nature thought up long before there were water theme parks.

Canoe trips down the Sipsey Wild and Scenic River have become a favorite activity for many people - both experienced canoeists and those who are new to the sport. Visitors from as far away as Canada have come to the area for a trip down the Sipsey. The best time for a canoe trip is the spring (February or March to early June) or the fall - at the times when Alabama has gotten recent rains.

The dry weather of 1990 has many of the Sipsey's tributaries running low on water, and the same thing happens during the seasons when the state gets less rain. Because of the way the Tennessee Divide influences the levels in the Sipsey, runoff water leaves the area quickly during a dry season, making the river less navigable.

Probably the best way to see the Bankhead Forest and the Wilderness is first to stop at the Ranger Station in Double Springs on Alabama 195, just south of the Wilderness. The station is open from 7 a.m. to 5 p.m., Monday through Friday, and is stocked with trail maps of the various areas in the Forest. The people there also can give you directions to different parts of the wilderness.

If you go on the weekend, stop by the Handy Pack at the intersection of

Northwest Alabama   75

Wilderness Parkway, U.S. Highway 278 and Alabama Highway 195. You can't miss the store, it's directly under a huge American flag. When you get there ask for Neal Shipman. Not only does his Handy Pack have all the maps and information that the Ranger Station has, but Shipman is something of a local expert on the area.

He and other members of his family have helped develop a number of trails in the Bankhead Forest, among them a motorcycle trail for offroaders that opened recently. He also can point you toward the horseback riding trail in the northeast corner of the forest. Shipman can give you directions for a number of different hikes through the Wilderness area, one of which is an eight-mile hike that is one way only. Hikers are dropped off at the starting point and picked up at the end of the hike.

Another is a trip through the area for senior citizens and others who may have some difficulties in getting around. That route covers 20 miles of wilderness, but the trip is made in vehicles and directs visitors into the Forest for a while and then back out again to explore a new part. It takes them to such locations as the natural water slide, Brushy Lake and a natural bridge that's "not THE natural bridge."

Also part of this "tour" is a stop at a jail in Houston that was built during the Civil War. Like many jails of that time, nails have been driven through the logs to keep prisoners from sawing their way to freedom.

TUMBLING DOWN TO SMITH LAKE

Once the Sipsey River makes its way to the Sipsey Picnic Grounds, it tumbles down to Wilburn Ford, a ford used to cross the river during the Civil War. It is there that Lewis Smith Lake forms.

One of the nicest ways to see Smith Lake is to take a cruise on the "Free State Lady," a paddlewheeler that churns along the waters of the "old Sipsey." There are two different trips on the lake offered from mid-April to late October by Smith Lake Tours. The first leaves from U.S. Highway 278 Dock (about a mile from Looney's Tavern and 30 miles west of Cullman). Tour One consists of afternoon "Regular" and evening Dinner Cruises on Thursdays, Fridays and Saturdays.

Tour Two leaves from Duncan Bridge Marina Dock, about 12 miles north of Jasper. On Wednesdays, you can take a Regular afternoon or an evening Dinner Cruise from this location. On Sundays, there is an afternoon Lunch Cruise, an afternoon Regular Cruise and an Evening Dinner Cruise. All cruises last 90 minutes to 2 hours and are hosted by a guide who not only tells you where you are, but entertains and tells folk stories as well.

Tour rates are $7.50 for adults, $5 for children three to 12 and free for children under 3. There is an extra charge for lunch or dinner.

Leaving the Bankhead Forest, travel west on U.S. 278. On Cullman County 11, just north of 278 is the Clarkson (Legg) Covered Bridge, the state's largest covered truss bridge. The 277-foot long, 90-foot high bridge, completed in 1904, is at the site of the Civil War conflict the Battle of Hog Mountain. The bridge is set in a park that has hiking trails, a working grist mill, log cabins and a picnic area. Clarkson Covered Bridge is open from 7 a.m. to sunset daily.

COMING INTO CULLMAN

Back on U.S. 278, you can continue west about nine miles into Cullman. From the day it was born, this city was meant to be a little bit of Germany. The city was founded in 1873 by Col. John G. Cullman, a German immigrant who wanted to build a self-sustaining colony of German refugees and immigrants.

He bought a little more than 5,000 square miles of land from the L&N Railroad and settled five German families there. Cullman sent a brochure to German immigrants describing the place he had found in Alabama.

"After traveling around the country and arriving in North Alabama, the impression was made upon my mind that if this country was filled up with good farmers it would be the garden spot of America," Cullman wrote. "I found here all that I had been looking for, all that I regarded as necessary to make good homes: there was here combined these things to an extent not equaled by any other place that I had seen."

By 1880, there were 6,300 people - many of them German - living in Cullman's little city. Today the population is more than double that number and the city still is home to a number of people who trace their roots back to Germany. All of the city's residents are able to enjoy a piece of Col. Cullman's legacy. He laid out the town that bears his name and the people there still enjoy its 100-foot wide streets.

Much of the history of Cullman County is contained in an eight-room house - the Cullman County Museum. The museum is housed in a replica of Col. John Cullman's home. (The original was destroyed by fire in 1912.)

A tour of the museum begins in the Archaeological Room, where there are displays of Indian artifacts as well as a seven-foot tall carving of an Indian warrior created from the wood of a Sweet Gum tree. The Primitive Room shows visitors the kinds of tools used at the turn of the century to make a living on the hilly land of Cullman County. Rafters and walls in the room are taken from area barns.

The Clothing Store lets visitors "window shop" among outfits from the 1850s. Main Street shows how downtown Cullman might have looked more than 100 years ago. Along the brick street are a Hobby Shop, Dry Goods Store, Drug Store and Doctor's Office, General Store, Jewelry Shop, Book Store, Photographer's Studio, Trophy Store, Department Store and Gun Shop. Between the stores are a wishing well, a school bell and a replica of a beer wagon that's piled high with scrapbooks of Cullman life.

Just off Main Street is a child's room complete with china dolls, wicker baby carriage, wooden blocks and miniature doll house. The South Room of the museum shows the era of fainting couches, grand pianos and love seats.

The final room on the tour is Col. Cullman's Room, a recreation of the

Colonel's bedroom with his own rocking chair, bed and sofa.

The museum is open Monday, Tuesday, Wednesday and Friday from 9 a.m. to noon and from 1 to 4 p.m., Thursday from 9 a.m. to noon and Sunday from 1:30 to 4:30 p.m. Admission charge $1 for adults and $.50 for children 12 and under.

Beside the museum is a large bronze statue of Col. Cullman, walking cane in hand and sporting a heavy beard.

Near the museum is Weiss Cottage, Cullman's oldest home. The South still was recovering from the Civil War when Dr. Aldo Weiss pulled into Cullman in the 1870s to set up practice. He purchased land from the L&N Railroad and in 1875, completed his home there. The structure served as Dr. Weiss' living quarters, an office for his practice and (downstairs) a shelter for his goats. The cottage has been restored and is shown by appointment only.

The Sacred Heart of Jesus Church in Cullman certainly is worth a stop. The Romanesque-style building is constructed of native Cullman stone. The cornerstone was laid in 1913 and the building dedicated three years later.

Alabama Mountain Lakes Tourist Association

Weiss Cottage, Cullman

The church's twin spires reach more than 100 feet in the air and the front doors are nearly 11 feet high. The stained glass windows in the church were manufactured by the von Gerichten family in Germany.

Seven miles north of Cullman on U.S. 31 is Hurricane Creek Park, where an observation platform gives visitors a wonderful view of the nearby gorge. A tour of the park includes a walk across a swinging bridge and looks at rock formations, a cave and waterfalls. Admission charges are $2 for adults and $1.50 for children from three to 18. The park is open year-round (except when there is ice on the trails) from "sunrise to sunset," according to the supervisor there.

Sportsman Lake Park is within a few blocks of downtown Cullman, just off U.S. 31 north. This family park offers picnicking, camping, carpet golf, a mini zoo and fishing in a lake stocked with bream, bass and catfish. The park is open daily from 7 a.m. to 7 p.m. from April through September.

Southwest of Cullman on the banks of Smith Lake is Smith Lake Park. This 22,000-acre lake is impounded by Smith Dam and has 500 miles of shoreline. Recreation facilities here include camping hookups, miniature golf, a swimming pool, a water slide and a boat launch. The park is open from May through September from 8 a.m. to 8 p.m. on Monday through Thursday and from 8 a.m. to 10 p.m. Friday through Sunday. Admission to the park is $1.50, children five and under are admitted free. There is a $15 per month charge for RV hookups and a $2 charge for the water slide.

It's a Small World at Ave Maria Grotto

Cullman, with its German heritage, would have an international flavor even without one of the attractions it's most noted for, but Ave Maria Grotto is much more than "just another place to see while you're in Cullman." The world in miniature created on the rolling hillsides at St. Bernard Abbey is a lesson in architecture, art, world landmarks and determination.

Ave Maria Grotto (literally translated, "Hail Mary Cave") with its more than 150 recreations of shrines, buildings and churches is the work of Brother Joseph Zoettl. Born Michael Zoettl in Landshut, Bavaria, "Brother Joe" knew early in life that he wanted to become a priest. In 1892, at the age of 13, he left his homeland never to return. His destination was Alabama and St. Bernard Abbey, the state's only Benedictine monastery. Brother Joe was one of the first students at the newly established school.

While studying for the priesthood, he was injured in an accident at the Abbey. While helping to hoist the bell into the tower of St. Bernard's first building, he hurt his back and was left crippled for life.

In those days, a priest had to be in perfect health and Brother Joe no longer qualified for what he considered to be his calling. Instead of becoming a priest, he became a monk and stayed to work at St. Bernard. In 1910, shortly after his accident, Brother Joe was put in charge of the power plant at the Abbey, shoveling coal into the furnace. And, when his work was done for the day, he would create his now-famous works of art.

Using just a few hand tools and odds and ends he discovered on the grounds, he shaped his first work, "The Main Grotto," and placed it in a rock quarry created when the monks removed huge slabs of stone to build the school's administration building. When another monk saw the small buildings and shrines Brother Joe shaped from the things other people left behind, he thought they were good enough to sell to people who visited the monastery.

The income from the sales helped finance Brother Joe's work, as he made his way through the rock quarry, landscaping it and making it ready for his miniature creations.

As more and more people saw his work, Brother Joe began to receive donations from visitors - not just cash, but beads, broken jewelry and empty cold cream jars - anything he could use to build another of his miniatures.

Over the next 48 years, Brother Joe continued to build and display his world in miniature. Visitors wonder at the exactness of the reproductions, even more so when they learn that Brother Joe saw only a few of the structures he recreated - St. Martin's Catholic Church in his hometown, the Statue of Liberty and the buildings at St. Bernard. Many of the others -

Alabama Bureau of Tourism and Travel

Ave Maria Grotto, Cullman

among them St. Peter's Basilica and the Alamo - he did from pictures that people sent him. Those that it was impossible for Brother Joseph to see - Noah's Ark and Jesus' birthplace in Bethlehem, for example - he fashioned from his imagination.

Brother Joe also built memorials to those students from St. Bernard who died during World War II and in Korea. In 1958, with his health failing, he added the final two pieces to his Grotto. One, an American flag made of glass, was placed beside his replica of the World's Peace Church in Hiroshima, Japan. The other, a miniature of the basilica at Lourdes, he created to honor its 100th anniversary.

Three years later, Brother Joe died. He is buried in the Abbey Cemetery, just a short walk from the Grotto. The path to his gravesite is marked with the stations of the cross.

Ave Maria Grotto is open from 8 a.m. to sunset daily. Admission is $3.50 for adults, $2 for children 6 to 12 and $2 for senior citizens.

WALKER COUNTY: TALLULAH AND OLD YORK

South of Cullman County is Walker County, a place that has given Alabama a number of her better-known native sons. The Bankheads - politicians William, John and John II - are from this part of the state. The family home in Jasper saw distinguished politicians visit and provided a place for Tallulah, William's granddaughter, to begin her acting career. In the attic, she would "play lady," taking wedding dresses and evening gowns from where they were stored in trunks. Draped in the fine gowns of silk and satin, Tallulah and her sister would act out endless stories during the childhood days they spent in Jasper. Although the home is not open for public tours, you can drive by and see it. And as long as you're in Jasper, you might as well drive by and see the family home of George "Goober" Lindsey, another Jasper resident who's gone on to fame in the big city.

William Bankhead's funeral was held at First United Methodist Church in Jasper, a two-story marble structure built in 1921. Among those attending the funeral was Franklin Delano Roosevelt.

Walker County also offers you a wonderful place to get away from it all and slow down the pace of your life a bit. Harold Corry, owner and builder of Old York U.S.A. Heritage Park near Oakman, says to get there you "travel down Alabama Highway 69 South less than a mile from Oakman, then turn right and go back 100 years in history."

Corry has officially adopted a theme for the park, built around his great-grandfather's home - "Life in the Slow Lane."

Corry's great-grandfather bought the home in 1852. The post office was in his house from 1848 until 1867. The end of the Civil War brought the end of the post office as well. When a post office was re-established, it was located in various homes throughout the community.

The heritage park Corry created is on 15 acres that has belonged to his family for more than 100 years and gets it name from one of the community's former names - York. It was changed because there already was a York in Alabama.

On Corry's great-grandfather's land in the 1880s was a house, a grist mill and a cotton gin. As the community around his property began to grow, a boomtown of sorts sprang up.

Corry's great-grandfather helped lay out the town, where there soon was a saloon, livery stable, barber shop, general store, bank and church.

The park that Corry has built is a reconstruction of one street from the town that sprang up in 1880s. Once again, there are dancing girls in the saloon, "gun fights" in the streets and choirs in the church. Corry's park also has a bandstand, which provides the setting for many of the events held there.

There are annual festivals, where local residents give demonstrations of what life was like in the 1880s - they make syrup, church butter and plow with mules. "About three times a day, a gun fight breaks out outside the saloon," Corry says. "Of course, it's all acting, but we have some letters written during the 1880s that show it's not too far-fetched to think that this might really have happened."

Each year, a festival also re-enacts the swearing-in ceremonies for Company K of the 50th Regiment, Alabama Volunteers, on February 16, 1862. The men were sworn in on the front lawn of Corry's great-grandfather's home. During the re-enactment, descendants of those men take their parts. As they ride off to battle, a narrator recounts what happened to each of them during - and, for those who survived, after - the war.

Because Corry's family has lived on the property continuously since 1852, he calls the Corry family log home at the park, "The House Made of Memories."

Each December, there's a Christmas party and lighting ceremony at the park. More than 22 different church groups carol during the festivities as the lights come on all around and atop the 13 different structures in the park. Admission to the Christmas party is free. The park's lights shine throughout the Christmas season.

For the time being, Old York, U.S.A., is a "special events park," says Corry, and open only for these annual events or for school or church tours. When the park is open, admission is $3.

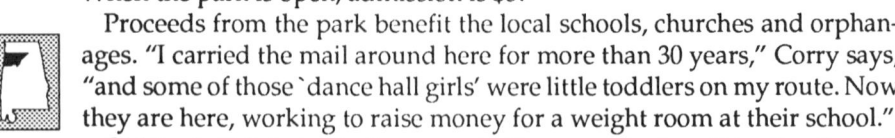

Proceeds from the park benefit the local schools, churches and orphanages. "I carried the mail around here for more than 30 years," Corry says, "and some of those `dance hall girls' were little toddlers on my route. Now they are here, working to raise money for a weight room at their school."

Old York, U.S.A., isn't a theme park, Corry emphasizes. It is a family park for people "who want to enjoy history."

FAYETTE COUNTY: MORE THAN FROGS AND RUBES

When you're through with life in the slower lane, maybe you'd like to get into something really competitive. If you've ever thought you might like to enter your frog in frog jumping contest that's an official preliminary for the "biggie" in Calaveras County, California, you need to be in Fayette in September. Fayette, the county seat of Fayette County in northwest Alabama, once was the town of Frog Level. That's why they have an annual Frog Level Festival on Labor Day weekend. And owning the winning contestant in the Frog Jumping Contest there will qualify you and your frog to compete in the national competition in California.

Even if you don't own a frog, put Fayette on your list of places to stop. The art museum in the Civic Center filled with works by local artists. Especially interesting is the work of Jimmy Lee Suddeth, a Fayette resident, who uses a number of natural materials such as clay in his paintings. The Civil Center is on the Old Fayette Elementary School, built in 1930. It is open Monday, Tuesday, Thursday and Friday from 9 a.m. until noon and from 1 to 4 p.m. Admission to the art museum is free.

Guthrie Smith Park, also in Fayette, is a 100-acre facility with a lake, tennis courts, picnic areas, baseball fields and an area for band concerts. It makes a nice stopover for a rest - or some recreation - on your way.

Just as each state has her native born actors, painters, writers, statesmen and other famous offspring, each state must have her infamous "children" as well. For Alabama, the best known of those probably is Rube Burrow. Born in Lamar County in 1854, Burrow, gained a reputation for his strength, athletic ability and sharpshooting before he was 18 years old. At that age, he is said to have found the country around his hometown boring. To cure that boredom, he struck out for Texas. He helped on an uncle's farm there, but

quickly became bored with that as well.

Before long, Rube was joined in Texas by his brother Jim and together, they went into the cattle rustling business. On the morning of December 1, 1886, Rube and Jim - along with two companions - decided to rob the train at Bellevue, Texas. Not only did they net $300 from the heist, they also relieved a squad of U.S. soldiers of their guns. Rube used those weapons throughout most of the rest of his career. Their next train robbery about a month later brought in more than $2,000.

The brothers returned to Alabama after their third train robbery and were welcomed home by the people of Lamar County who thought they had come by their wealth due to their success as Texas farmers.

They left again and went to Arkansas and Mississippi to pursue their real careers again. Jim was captured and jailed - some accounts say in Montgomery and others say in Arkansas - and Rube made several unsuccessful attempts to free his brother.

Even though he wasn't the sort of native son a county would erect a statue to honor, Rube Burrow didn't fall out of favor with the people of Lamar County until he shot and killed the local postmaster in an argument over the delivery of a false mustache Rube had ordered through the mail.

That's when a posse was organized. The governor of Alabama even sent troops to help in the search, but Rube eluded capture and made his way into Florida. But a team of detectives, probably hired by the railroads, was looking for Burrow as well. They tracked him through Florida and back into Alabama, finally arresting him near Myrtlewood in Marengo County.

Determined not to let Rube slip through their fingers again, they took special precautions to be sure he didn't escape. Burrow did manage to trick his guards and get away - but it was his last escape. He didn't leave town, but instead went to get his gun and money from one of his captors. Burrow was shot and killed, probably by Jefferson Davis "Dixie" Carter.

After his death, the railroad officials - who weren't terribly sorry to see him go - gave Rube one last free ride. Of course, they stopped along the way to his final resting place so that people could view the remains. Rube finally was buried in his native Lamar County at the end of the trip. You can visit Burrow's grave in Fellowship Cemetery near Vernon.

And if you go to Vernon to see where the notorious outlaw is buried, you might as well see a couple of other things there. Faulkner's Antique Mall in town is home to 30 or 40 exhibitors with all sorts of antiques and collectibles.

If you're sportsminded, the public fishing lake there is loaded with bream.

WHERE TO STAY

There are a number of chain hotels and motels in the larger cities in this part of the state. In addition, there are independently owned facilities. Among them are:

In Hamilton: Holiday Motel.

In Cullman: Anderson Motel.

In Vernon: Montreat Lodge.

Campsites are available in almost all the parks and recreation areas of this region. You also will find a few private campgrounds. Among them is Sleepy Hollow Campgrounds in Jasper.

WHERE TO EAT

In addition to the chain and fast food restaurants in this area, there are some well known locally owned eateries and some not so well known, but recommended by the people who live in the various towns. Among them are:

In Hamilton: Hamilton Bar-B-Que and Danilli's Pizza.

In Double Springs: Looney's Tavern Restaurant (The restaurant is open even during the theater's off season.).

In Cullman: All Steak (The orange rolls, according to one source, draw customers from all around.).

In Holly Pond: Holly Pond Cafe. (You can't get this close to the birthplace of Gov. Guy Hunt and not stop in on Holly Pond Cafe. The restaurant opens at 6 a.m. every day. It's open until 9 p.m. during the week and until 10 p.m. on weekends. Holly Pond is 13 miles east of Cullman on U.S. 278.).

In Bremen: Bug Tussle (Located about 18 miles southwest of Cullman on Alabama 69, this restaurant is known for its steaks. People from all around make pilgrimages just to eat here. The steak house is open from 11 a.m. to 8:30 p.m. Sunday through Thursday and from 11 a.m. to 9:30 p.m. on Friday and Saturday.).

In Jasper: Uncle Mort's (This restaurant is known for its country breakfasts, served any time during the day.).

In Vernon: Kountry Kitchen.

ANNUAL EVENTS

Among the annual events in this part of the state are:

"Bloomin' Festival Arts and Crafts Fair and Ave Maria Grotto
"Free Day," Cullman, April. Kudzu Festival, Hamilton, May.
Mayday For Maywood, Hamilton, May.
Historic District Homes Tour, Cullman, May.
Spring Festival, Old York, U.S.A., Oakman, May."

Incident at Looney's Tavern," Double Springs, June-September.

Oakman Reunion, Oakman, June. Classic Street Machines Car Show, Cullman, July.
Anderson's Bass Classic Tournament, Cullman, July.
Fayette Arts and Crafts Festival, Fayette, August.Mule Day, Winfield, September.
Fayette County Fair, Fayette, September.
Frog Level Festival, Fayette, September.
Cullman Lions Club Fair Parade, Cullman, September.
Cullman County Band Exhibition, Cullman, September.
Cullman County Fair, Cullman, September.
Old Time Festival, Old York, U.S.A., Oakman, September.
Mule and Wagon Days, Old York, U.S.A., Oakman, September.
Hamilton C.J. Fall Festival, Hamilton, October.
Cullman Oktoberfest, Cullman, October.

Bluegrass Super Jam, Cullman, November.

Christmas in the Slow Lane, Old York, U.S.A., Oakman, December.

Tuscaloosa & Alabama's Black Belt

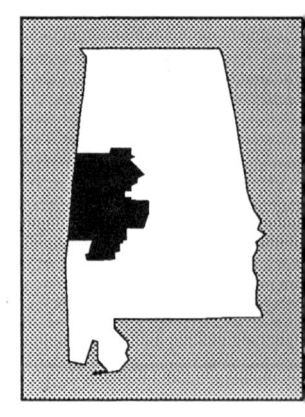

To geologists, Alabama's Black Belt, cutting a path from the Mississippi border just below Columbus across to Montgomery, is a layer of decayed limestone filled with fertile black soil. To antebellum farmers, it was the perfect place to grow cotton - and plantations. The rich soil made the area attractive for growing things. The presence of several of the state's major waterways made it simple to get goods to and from market and added to the affluence of this part of pre-Civil War Alabama.

Some of the state's most lavish homes were in this area when the Civil War and the boll weevil brought an end to that way of life.

Fortunately, many of the homes and early businesses in this area have been preserved and mixed with the new look in the Black Belt.

START IN PICKENSVILLE

To get a better understanding of what the rivers meant - and still mean - to the counties that cluster around them, visit the Tom Bevill Resource Management and Visitor Center in Pickensville. At first, you might not recognize the center for what it is - it has the look of an antebellum home, built in a much earlier time to give its owners a magnificent view of the Tombigbee River.

The look is no accident. The builders took the best parts of a number of antebellum homes and put them together in this structure. The landscaping and the interior color schemes and furnishings are patterned after those popular in the late 1700s to the mid-1800s. Much of the wood in the floors of the visitors center came from an 1830s plantation house in Perry County. The cupola is fashioned after one on Kirkwood mansion in Eutaw. The porch design copies that of Waverly mansion in West Point, Mississippi. The columns are like those on Rosemont mansion in Greene County.

SEE THE WATERWAY

Inside the center, there are displays, models and artifacts telling the story of the Tombigbee River and the series of locks and canals that now link it to the Tennessee to form the Tennessee-Tombigbee Waterway. The history of the people who lived around the river also is traced in the exhibits and audio-visual displays. One of the nicest features of the center is the cupola, from which you get a bird's eye view of the river, lock and dam behind the center.

And the center offers a chance to get on the water, even if it is in a very limited sense. The U.S. Snagboat "Montgomery" is moored permanently beside the center and is open - from pilot house to engine room - to visitors. The 180-foot "Montgomery," one of the last steam-powered sternwheelers to ply the waters of the South, served the Mobile District from 1927 to 1982. The vessel was used to remove submerged stumps and fallen trees from the channels of seven major rivers.

The center, a half mile south of the junction of Alabama 14 and 86, is open seven days a week year-round, except for some Federal holidays. Hours usually are 8 a.m. to 4 p.m. Monday through Friday. Hours on Saturday and Sunday vary according to the season. Admission is free.

THE FACE IN THE WINDOW

About 10 miles northeast of Pickensville, you can go ghost hunting at the Pickens County Courthouse in Carrollton. The ghostly spectre you're looking for here is called "the face in the window."

The image, which is said to be indelibly stamped on the lower

---

Tuscaloosa and The Black Belt

Alabama's Black Belt, where the state's cotton industry was born, crosses this region of seven counties. In this part of the state, which reaches eastward from the Mississippi border, many of the cities are built on the banks of the Black Warrior and Tombigbee Rivers. More than 250,000 people live in this area, where the population centers include Tuscaloosa, Northport, Demopolis, Eutaw, Greensboro and Marion.

---

right pane of the garret window, is supposed to be that of Henry Wells, a black man who had been convicted of several charges including robbery. Wells was imprisoned in the courthouse in the 1800s and the heat of the sultry, humid afternoon mixed with too much corn whiskey to produce a lynch mob, ready to kill him for the crimes he was supposed to have committed.

The authorities, hoping to stave off the mob, hid Wells in the garret of the courthouse but the hiding place was quickly discovered. Wells peered from the window, watching the mob coming toward him. "I'm innocent," he is said to have shouted down, "If you kill me, I am going to haunt you for the rest of your lives."

Just as the crowd was about to enter the building, a bolt of lightning struck, illuminating Wells as he stood at the window. No one is sure how Wells died. Some say he was killed by the lightning, others say he was hanged. Either way, that was the last night of his life.

The next day, when some of the townspeople passed the courthouse, they looked up to see Wells' image still pressed against the garret window glass. It is said that the image remains, a reminder of people who were determined to mete out their own brand of justice.

ALICEVILLE THROUGH THE LOOKING GLASS

In nearby Aliceville, a museum outlines the history of the area with exhibits of artifacts from West Central Alabama. Buttons once were produced here using the shells of mussels gathered from the river. Examples of those buttons and some of the equipment used in making them are in the museum. Also there are pieces from another period in Aliceville's history - when the city was the site of a World War II prisoner of war camp.

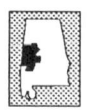

The place where the camp was located now is the Sue Stabler Park. The camp itself was torn down after the war, but pieces of the construction remain at the park. Among them is a chimney built by the German prisoners. Many of those builders wrote their names - which still are visible - in the rocks of the chimney.

The museum, in the Aliceville Civic Center, is open by appointment only until renovations on the Civic Center are complete.

Also at Aliceville is the grave of James McCrory, George Washington's bodyguard at Valley Forge. McCrory, who chose this area as his home at the end of the Revolutionary War, died in 1840 and is buried in Old Bethany Cemetery.

MA'CILLE'S MUSEUM

Pickens County also has one of the most unusual museums to be found in the state. It's sort of a cross between a taxidermist's workshop and a glassmaker's storehouse. Ma'Cille's Museum of Miscellanea has everything from a stuffed mule's head to 19th century china dollheads. Ma'Cille is short for Mama Lucille - Lucille House. Mrs. House, who is 80-plus years old, has been creating this unusual museum for more than 30 years.

Because her family didn't have a lot of money, she learned early in life to save things. Apparently, it was a hard habit to break. When Ma'Cille visited museums in Birmingham and Tuscaloosa, she started thinking about how nice it would be to have one of her own. So she started shopping the flea markets for bottles that appealed to her and began putting together the collection that would be part of her museum.

The stuffed animals - in addition to the mule head, there are stuffed squirrels, fish, a bull, a hog, a pig and a chicken with three feet - became a part of the museum when Ma'Cille's son killed a deer and wanted to have the head mounted. Mrs. House couldn't afford to pay a profession to do the work, so she bought a "do-it-yourself" book on taxidermy and, well, did it herself. Ma'Cille stuffed many of the animals in her museum, but some were done by professionals and donated to the cause.

Ma'Cille's real "pride and joy" exhibit at the museum is the doll collection. While digging for bottles once, Ma'Cille found the china doll heads. She created bodies for them, added clothes and dolls became a permanent part of the museum. The doll collection has expanded to include some that date from the early 1800s, modern dolls and foreign dolls. Ma'Cille's favorites are the "First Ladies of the White House," some of which she made. All of the First Ladies dolls wear replicas of the gowns their live counterparts wore to their husbands' Inaugural Balls.

Other people have made contributions to Ma'Cille's Museum - the county sheriff gave up a confiscated whiskey still, for example - but most of the work is Ma'Cille's.

Ma'Cille's Museum of Miscellanea is located off Highway 86 between Gordo and Carrollton. "It's on a dirt road, but there are signs to guide you," the people at Gordo City Hall assure visitors. There are no set hours since Ma'Cille lives in her museum and there is no admission charge.

GREENE COUNTY

Greene County, set against the Mississippi line about 20 miles south of Pickensville and wrapped around the Black Warrior, Tombigbee and Sipsey Rivers, is in the northern part of the Black Belt. The history of the county dates from 1819, but the "golden era" of the area was in 1840 to 1860, when more than 15,000 people lived there.

Farmers in pre-Civil War Greene County grew cotton and corn and the rivers that ran through the county made getting their goods to market easy. When cotton no longer was king in Alabama, Greene County farmers turned to timber and beef for their livelihood. In the county seat of Eutaw, the past and the future mix pleasantly.

Many historic sites, including almost 50 antebellum structures, still can be seen there. One of the most striking is Kirkwood, built in 1860. Outside, eight large Ionic columns grace the entrance and, at the door, colored glass sidelights depict the four seasons. Kirkwood is open for tours, but hours and days vary. Check with the Historical Society for current hours. Admission is $3.

A number of Eutaw's historic homes are built in the raised cottage style. Among them are the Archibald-Tuck House, constructed with the main living area on the upper level and interior chimneys, and Merifield, built in 1840 by William F. Pierce, one of Eutaw's first settlers.

The Alexander-Webb-Wilson House, was built in 1836 in Erie (the first county seat of Greene County) as a stagecoach inn. It later was moved to Eutaw.

The Greene County Courthouse visitors see today was built in the late 1800s on the foundations of the original courthouse, which burned in 1868. The First Presbyterian Church, built in 1851, still has its original whale oil lamps and chandeliers. The lighting fixtures, however, now use electricity.

Kirkwood is the only home in Eutaw open to the public, but others can be seen on a walking/driving tour. Brochures for the tour are available at the Historical Society Office on Main Street. ("If no one is there, you'll find the brochures in the mailbox," according to one member of the Historical Society.)

Near Eutaw is Greenetrack, where the greyhounds race from the first week in January through the third week in December. Races are held nightly except for Sunday and there are matinees on Wednesday and Friday at 4 p.m. and Saturday at 1:30 p.m. No one under 18 is admitted, so this is an "adults only" outing. Admission is $2 for clubhouse seating and $.50 for general admission. Parking is $.50 for self-parking and $1 for valet.

As long as you're in the area of Eutaw, it's worth a quick side trip to Forkland, about 14 miles south, off U.S. 43. The mansions here aren't open to the public, but certainly deserve a look from the outside. Thornhill is a two-story frame mansion with six massive Ionic columns and Rosemont, considered by many to be Alabama's most beautiful mansion, is a 20-room structure. Also in Forkland is the board and batten St. John's-in-the-Prairies Episcopal Church, built in 1859.

Thornhill and Rosemount are not open to the public, but can be viewed from the outside. Services are held once a month at St. John's, which was designed by John Upchurch, founder of the American Institute of Architects

The doggies run almost daily at Greenetrack, Eutaw

Shoals to Sand Dunes

and designer of the Trinity Episcopal Church at the head of Wall Street in New York.

OVER TO GAINESVILLE

Northwest of Forkland is Gainesville, a Sumter County town that once was the third largest city in the state with more than 4,000 citizens. Gainesville was incorporated in 1835 on land that originally belonged to the Choctaw Indians. When Colonel Moses Lewis acquired the land on the banks of the Tombigbee, he divided it into lots and named his new town after Colonel George Strother Gaines, an American agent to the Indians. Soon afterward, families from other parts of Alabama and from other states began moving into Gainesville, building large homes and establishing businesses.

The homes of Gainesville's settlers reflected the elaborate lifestyles of the time when the city was a thriving riverport. The centerpiece of the Lewis-Long House, a Federal-style structure built by Moses Lewis, is the elaborate hand-carved wooden staircase. The home also has two underground cisterns for storing food and water. Other homeowners used different architectural styles to express their tastes. The Magnolias, built in the mid-1800s, is in the Greek Revival style. The 1840 Lewis-Jones-Fields House combines two antebellum styles - the two-room floor plan with separate entrances and the Greek Revival style facade with inset portico.

The Lewis-Long House and the Lewis-Jones-Fields House are not open to the public. The Magnolias is open by appointment only and admission is $4 per person.

Other pieces of Gainesville's past still exist. Among them are the Kring Coffin Shop, which dates from the 1830s. The coffin shop is open by appointment and admission is free. The Confederate Cemetery is the burial place of 250 unknown soldiers who were cared for in a hospital in Gainesville during the war.

Also in the cemetery is a cannon that was made to be used during the Civil War but never saw active duty. The cannon was made in Selma and shipped down river to Mobile. Mobile had fallen by the time the cannon reached that city, so it was sent back upstream to Gainesville. By the time it reached Gainesville, the war was ending and, to prevent the Union troops from capturing the weapon, the cannon was sunk in the river. Later, the cannon was retrieved and placed in the cemetery.

The Winston Cemetery in Gainesville is the burial place of Alabama's first native born governor John Winston. Also buried in the city is Maria Fearing, a former slave who gained prominence as a missionary to the Congo.

Gainesville's Old High School was the first public school in the state to provide free transportation.

When Gainesville was in its prime, it was a social and cultural center. The American Hotel was a popular night spot for dancers from throughout the area. The town had a bank, an ice house, doctors' and lawyers' offices, two newspapers and a Town Square. Today the hand-pump well in Old Town

---

Square and the ice house are all that remain from this prosperous time in the city's history.

The people who settled Gainesville established a number of churches there. Many of the buildings that housed these congregations still stand. The Presbyterian Church, built in 1837, still has many of its original fixtures, including the pump organ and the whale oil lamps. The church, where Maria Fearing was a member, also still has the original bell, inset with 500 silver dollars to give it its unique tone.

Also in Gainesville is Clark's Chapel, which dates from the mid-1800s and was built for one of the first independent black congregations in the area.

For those interested in more modern pursuits, Gainesville Lake and Recreation Area, with more than 6,000 acres, offers boating, fishing and skiing. On the campus of Livingston State University, about 20 miles south of Gainesville is the Alamuchee-Bellamy Covered Bridge. West Alabama's only remaining covered bridge was moved to this site in 1969 and has been fully restored. It originally was built over the Surcarnoochee River near Livingston before the Civil War. It is made of handhewn heart pine timbers, joined with wooden pegs.

DEMOPOLIS' FRENCH INFLUENCE

The city of Demopolis, at the southern end of the Tennessee-Tombigbee Waterway, might never have been established if the men and ladies of France in the 1800s had thought things through before they jumped into a new project.

The name of the town - meaning "City of the People" - is about all that remains of the dreams brought to America by a group of exiles from Napoleonic France in July, 1817. The group came to establish a "Vine and Olive Colony," planning to produce grapes and olives for French-made wines and olive oil. From Congress, they received land grants for four townships. The thing they didn't think about ahead of time was that the soil and climate weren't suited for raising the crops they had planned. They also didn't realize that ladies of the French court and officers of Napoleon's army weren't necessarily suited for the wilderness, either.

By the mid-1820s, the colonists had scattered. Others came to cultivate the soil and this time, they found a crop that would grow. Cotton plantations flourished in antebellum Demopolis and, after the war, left behind a heritage of architecture that remains today.

Adhuc hic hesterna - "Still Here are The Things of Yesterday." So says an elaborately lettered sign posted on the grounds at Gaineswood in Demopolis. The restored antebellum mansion has been described by architects and historians as everything from "an Alabama plantation palace" to "the most magnificent of all" antebellum Alabama mansions. But there's more to this Southern belle's story than just beauty.

Her story begins with Nathan Bryan Whitfield, a major general in the North Carolina militia who moved with his family to Demopolis in 1835. Whitfield, who had visited and admired Demopolis before the move, established a plantation south of the city and later purchased a second plantation, where he decided to build his dream home.

In those days, neighbors lived miles apart and to ease the isolation, plantation owners built elaborate, massive homes to accommodate the social life that would bring together family and friends for days-long visits. The homes, with their ornate columns, fine furnishings and landscaped gardens, breathed Southern hospitality to their guests. So it was with Gaineswood, when in 1843, it began to rise in the midst of General Whitfield's new 1,400-acre plantation. The home, 17 years in the building, reflected the personality of its owner, who was an architect, engineer, builder, decorator and inventor. General Whitfield conceived the basic design of his home, built shops on the grounds for the carpentry and plaster work that would go into the mansion and made lathes with which to fashion columns and cornices. His mansion was built in the best tradition of Greek Revival architecture with Doric, Ionic and Corinthian elements. Then, as now, the home was painted in a sandstone color with white trim.

And then, as now, none of the house's four sides match, which has led to a years-long debate as to which side of the house was supposed to be the front. The floor plan also is highly unusual, with no definite traffic flow pattern and no real feel of unity from room to room. Each room, in fact, seems almost to have been a separate project. The drawing room has elaborate columns, pilasters and friezes. Twin full-length mirrors imported from France are mounted on opposite ends of the room, creating many reflections and illusions of spaciousness. The dining room and library flank each other with a hall between and both have domes topped by windowed cupolas. In the library, a flutina is on display. This one-of-a-kind musical instrument, resembling an upright player piano, was invented by General Whitfield.

Although Gaineswood has a second floor, it is built in two unconnected sections with separate stairways leading to each. Gaineswood was completed in 1860, just before the Civil War began. General Whitfield invested heavily in Confederate bonds and when the Confederacy was defeated, he found himself with no ready capital for the upkeep of the mansion. He also was in poor health as the result of a fall he suffered while working on a canal for the city. The house was sold to his son, Dr. Bryan Whitfield, for $40,000. Though his son now owned the mansion, General Whitfield continued to live in Gaineswood until his death in 1868.

The house then went through a succession of owners. With each new one came a new realization of the impracticality of General Whitfield's dream. Because of its design, Gaineswood was impossible to heat. The roof leaked and its extraordinary arrangement, covering several separate but interconnected sections and about 5,000 square feet, made it difficult to repair. Gaineswood finally stood vacant, suffering the indignities of vandalism and neglect. A leaky skylight caused one floor to rot away and a mulberry tree grew up through the rotted boards. Goats wandered through the ballroom.

The mansion's salvation came in 1966 when the State of Alabama acquired the house and began an extensive restoration project. General Whitfield's descendants sent Gaineswood's original furnishings "home" to once again grace its halls. Today, visitors enter Gaineswood's wrought-iron gates (each weighing a ton), turn the silver doorknob and enter a structure where things of the past truly still do exist.

Gaineswood is located on Whitfield Street East and is open from 9 a.m. to 5 p.m. Monday through Saturday and from 1 to 5 p.m. Sunday. Admission is $3 for adults, $1 for students and $.50 for children 12 and under.

ANOTHER BEAUTIFUL HOME

Gaineswood isn't the only magnificent home in Demopolis. Among the others is Bluff Hall, built in 1832 as a wedding gift for the daughter of Allen Glover. The planter and merchant, utilizing slave labor, had the mansion constructed in the Federal style. The structure no longer is strictly Federal in design. At some point in its history, a Greek Revival gallery was added.

The house, on the White Bluffs of the Tombigbee River, is open Tuesday through Saturday from 10 a.m. to 5 p.m. and Sunday from 2 to 5 p.m. The last tour begins at 4:30 p.m. Admission is $2 for adults, $.50 for students and children.

YOU CAN FISH, TOO

If there are those in your family who would rather fish, camp or boat than look at mansions, Demopolis has plenty for them as well. Lake Demopolis, a 10,000-acre lake with a 397-mile shoreline, has facilities for fishing, boating, waterskiing and camping. There are boat ramps, picnic areas, a playground, ballfields and camp sites at Foscue Creek Park, two miles west of Demopolis off U.S. 80.

MARION'S BIG HISTORY

A great deal of history is tucked into the small Perry County town of Marion. The beautiful college town set in the middle of Alabama's Black Belt is the hometown of Governor Andrew Barry Moore and Coretta Scott King. Sam Houston was married in one of the city's homes and both Samford University in Birmingham and Alabama State University in Montgomery were established in Marion. The city has been home to Nicola Marschall, designer of the Confederate flag, silversmith Roswell Huntington, band leader Hal Kemp, Tennessee poet laureate John Trotwood Moore and artist Arthur Stewart.

Originally named Muckle's Ridge after an early settler who built a cabin in the area in 1817, Marion changed its name in 1822 to honor Francis Marion, a hero of the American Revolution. The city has almost 100 antebellum sites within its city limits. Among the most famous are Judson College, built in 1838, Marion Military Institute, which dates from 1842, and Marion Female Seminary, built in 1850.

Lincoln Normal School, founded in 1867 by Congregationalists, is the forerunner of Alabama State University. First Congregational Church of Marion on Clay Street is closely associated with Lincoln School. The building is the only reconstruction period Black church in Marion remaining without major modifications to its design.

Judson, one of America's oldest colleges for women, is home of the Alabama Women's Hall of Fame. At Marion Military Institute is the Alabama Military Hall of Honor. Plaques honoring Alabamians who had distinguished themselves in the U.S. Armed Forces are displayed in the Institute's Chapel. Marion, an all-male junior college, is the site of old Howard College (which now is Birmingham's Samford University).

Tied with the history of Howard College is that of "Harry the Slave." Harry, a servant of Dr. Howard Talbird, president of Howard College, died on October 15, 1854, while helping to save residents of the school from a fire. He is buried in Marion Cemetery.

Marion Female Seminary, which now belongs to the Perry County Historical Society, was built in 1856. The seminary has come to be known as the "birthplace of the Stars and Bars," the Confederate flag. "It's not the battle flag like the one that flies over the Capitol," a member of the Historical Society points out, "but the actual Confederate flag." The flag was designed by Nicola Marschall, an artist who was a teacher at the school. Marschall, who left the South not long after the end of the war, also is credited with having designed the gray Confederate uniform.

Looking at the elegant homes which serve as reminders of Marion's antebellum past, it is hard to believe that the city began in 1817 with one log cabin. Michael McElroy, who lived in that cabin left the city not too long after that, saying it was becoming too crowded as more people moved in. And that was before circuit riders, schoolteachers and plantation owners got there.

Among the homes of Marion which are open during annual pilgrimages are Magnolia Hill, where one of the largest magnolia trees in the state grows, and the Lea-Collins Home, where Sam Houston took Margaret Lea as his bride in 1840.

Antique shoppers will be convinced that there's no place like Marion once they've peeked inside the many stores tucked throughout the city. Camellia Place, one of the city's older homes, now houses an antique shop. And the Antique Mini Mall is set in an old hotel that dates back to 1848. In its heyday, the hotel - The King House - was noted for its great Southern cooking and for its fourth floor ballroom. In 1921, a fire at the hotel gutted the upper floors and destroyed the ballroom. The landmark didn't just disappear, however. It immediately was rebuilt as The Marion Hotel. Today, a number of the hotel rooms are open as antique shops.

HALE COUNTY

Hale County, set in the midst of the Black Belt, is a county that was carved out of several others after the Civil War. When the Legislature created the county in 1867, it took parts of Greene, Marengo, Perry and Tuscaloosa

Counties and put them together to make Hale County. The county was named for Stephen F. Hale, who was killed at Gaines Mill, Virginia, while leading the Eleventh Alabama Infantry Regiment.

Even though the county didn't come into being until after the war, many of the homes and buildings in Greensboro - which became the county seat - were there when the county was born. The 1828 Gayle-Tunstall-Sledge Home, built in the Federal style, Magnolia Hall, a structure that dates from the 1850s, and the Hale County Courthouse, built in 1867, all are reminders of the area's history.

Perhaps the most magnificent structure in Greensboro, though, is Magnolia Grove. The home, which sits on a 15-acre estate at the head of Main Street, was built about 1840. It is the birthplace of Admiral Richmond Pearson Hobson, who was responsible for sinking the "Merrimac" to blockade the Spanish fleet in Santiago Harbor during the Spanish-American War.

The Greek Revival mansion was built by Colonel Isaac Croom and his wife, Sarah. The design of the home is elegantly simple - wide central halls on both floors are flanked by two large rooms on either side. Downstairs, the hall ends with an unsupported winding staircase on the right. The wall of the house curves to match the shape of the stairway. The room on the right at the front of the house was the formal dining room when the house was built. Today, it is a museum of mementos of the Hobson and Croom families. Hours at Magnolia Grove, the only historic home in Greensboro open for public tours, are from 10 a.m. to 4 p.m. Tuesday through Saturday and from 1 to 4 p.m. on Sunday. Admission is $3 for adults, $2 for students and $.50 for children under 12.

A TRIP TO THE MOUNDS

Long before Christopher Columbus came to the New World, there was a sophisticated society of people living in parts of Northwestern Alabama. These Indians, referred to as Mound Builders by archaeologists, constructed huge, flat-topped pyramids that served as the foundations for their temples and other important buildings.

These Mississippian Indians were highly skilled and had a complex class structure made up of priests, nobles, warriors, craftsmen and workers. As skillfully as their workers built the massive mounds, their artists created works in stone, pottery, bone and copper.

On a bluff overlooking the Black Warrior River situated between Greensboro to the south and Tuscaloosa to the north, Moundville annually draws thousands of visitors curious about these ancient residents.

Even though many skeletal remains of the Mound people have been found in the area, the mounds were not burial mounds. They were, one scientist says, substructures for buildings. But it was common practice of these Indians to bury their dead beneath the houses, so there are burials in the mounds.

While excavations and studies have taught scientists much about the

Mound Dwellers, they still remain something of a mystery. Through the work of archaeologists and students at Alabama colleges, it has been learned that the Mississippians were of average size and many had artificially flattened the backs of their heads. Not all members of the tribe lived in the mound village. Many lived in huts in outlying areas and tended the crops.

In addition to raising crops, the Mound Dwellers picked wild plants for food and developed small lakes that they stocked with fish.

And they built mounds - one basket load of dirt at a time. The largest one, which stands some 60 feet high, is believed to have been the site of a sacred temple, the center of the tribe's religious life. Probably once a year, people from the surrounding villages gathered in the mound community for a festival, honoring the gods.

The mounds and how the Indians knew the methods for building them are a mystery, but perhaps the greatest mystery surrounding the Mississippians is what happened to them after the late 1400s. By the year 1541, when DeSoto came through this part of the state, the Mound Dwellers probably were gone.

There are theories about what happened to the Indians. Even though no evidence supports the belief, some say that the mound builders succumbed to a disease. Another theory is that as other tribes moved near, the land became a battleground. A third possibility discussed is that the earth, stricken by drought or pestilence, no longer yielded enough crops.

In the park museum are exhibits showing the lifestyles of the Indians who lived in the area as well as artifacts that have been uncovered in scientific digs.

Those visiting Moundville may hike down one of the park's nature trails which wind their way throughout the acreage. The trails are covered with towering trees which filter out the sunlight and create a perfect home for wildflowers, ferns and mushrooms. Some of the Indians' smaller mounds are sprinkled throughout the woods.

Picnic areas overlook the river near a model of an Indian village. Here parents sit and enjoy the view as they watch children dash to the village and pretend they are the Indians they've just learned about.

The mound area and museum are open seven days a week from 9 a.m. to 5 p.m. Admission is $2 for adults and $1 for children.

Tent and trailer camping sites are available at Mound State Park. The campgrounds are closed from mid-December through mid-February.

ROLLING INTO T-TOWN

The University of Alabama is in Tuscaloosa, a city which served as Alabama's capital from 1826 to 1846. The University itself was founded in 1831 and a few of the buildings on campus survived the onslaught of Union soldiers who burned much of the campus. All of that is pretty simple to understand. This next part may be a little difficult for those who don't live in Alabama. While the University of Alabama is in Tuscaloosa and cross-state rival Auburn University is in Auburn, the University of Alabama plays some of its home football games in Tuscaloosa and some in Birmingham. Until recently, Auburn played one home game every other year in Birmingham, but now plays them all in Auburn. You don't really need to know all of that unless you travel to Tuscaloosa during football season. If you do, you may have to get reservations for your accommodations well in advance.

Even if you aren't a football fan, a trip to Tuscaloosa is well worth your time. And if you are a football fan who has made lots of trips to Tuscaloosa but never seen any of the sights beyond the stadium parking lot, you've missed much of what the city has to offer its visitors.

The city and the University of Alabama campus are filled with things to see and huge slices of history sit there just waiting to be discovered.

Denny Chimes at The University of Alabama, Tuscaloosa

Antebellum structures on the campus truly are "one of a kind" sights to see. They are the only buildings in the area that survived the passage of Union troops through Tuscaloosa. One of those is the 1827 Gorgas House, built as a dining hall for the University. In 1879, it became the residence of Josiah and Amelia Gayle Gorgas. Gorgas was a brigadier general in the Confederate Army and the seventh president of the University. Amelia was the daughter of an Alabama governor. It was their son General William C. Gorgas, however, who became the home's most famous resident. He gained international fame for his work in helping to eradicate yellow fever epidemics in the early 1900s and thus opening the way for the construction of the Panama Canal. Today the Gorgas House is a museum with historical exhibits and memorabilia from the Gorgas family.

The house is open Monday through Friday from 9 a.m. to 5 p.m. and on Saturday from 11 a.m. to 4:30 p.m. Admission is free.

The Old Observatory, built in 1844, is the only pre-Civil War classroom building still standing. The Little Round House once was used by students on guard duty. It was fired on, but not destroyed by Union troops.

Smith Hall, a Greek Revival style structure built in 1909, houses the Alabama State Museum of Natural History. The museum exhibits portions of Alabama's geological formations and fossils in recreated natural habitats. Smith, which also is the home of the University's Geology and Geography departments, is open from 8 a.m. to 4:45 p.m. Monday through Friday, from 10 a.m. to 4 p.m. Saturday and from 2 to 5 p.m. Sunday. Admission is free.

You can't cross the campus without enjoying Denny Chimes, the 115-foot tall carillon which sounds the quarter-hour throughout the day. In the afternoons, concerts are played on the chimes.

BEAR BRYANT'S MUSEUM

William Gray Little probably didn't know what he was starting when he organized the first football club at the University of Alabama in 1892. But what he launched was a team that inspires fan loyalty and devotion unmatched by almost any other college. The history of that football team is traced in the Paul W. Bryant Museum on the Alabama campus.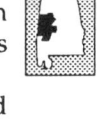

Part of that history, of course, are the coaches - especially Bryant - and their careers are chronicled as well as those of the players. A visit to the museum begins with a showing of "The Bryant Legacy," a short film narrated by sports commentator Keith Jackson. Included in the film is some half-time locker room footage, showing the coaching that fans didn't get to see on the field.

Employees at the museum say they've been told by visitors that seeing Bryant's trademark hound's-tooth hat sculpted in Irish crystal is worth the price of admission. The hat, created by Miraslav Havel of Waterford Crystal, is encased in a lighted, burglar-proof case equipped with a security alarm. The hat Bryant wore was hand-carried from Tuscaloosa to Waterford, Ireland, by a Waterford official and used as a model for Havel's replica.

The museum has its share of static exhibits - jerseys, photographs, game balls, trophies and the 1926 Rose Bowl Championship banner. But a lot of things in this museum move. Video screens set attractively into architectural elements of the museum roll vintage film clips as well as highlights from Alabama's most recent games.

Also in the museum is a research library open to sport scholars. The library has scrapbooks, programs, films, photographs and other sports publications. The emphasis, of course, is on Alabama football and the Southeastern Conference, but items in the library cover all college sports.

The museum is open Tuesday through Saturday from 10 a.m. to 4 p.m. and Sunday from 2 to 5 p.m. (Check on museum hours if you are planning a visit to Tuscaloosa during school holidays.) Admission is $2 for adults and $1 for students and children under 12. Admission is free to members of

---

Tuscaloosa and the Black Belt

Alabama Alumni Association.

Tours of the entire campus are given Monday through Friday at 10 a.m. and 2 p.m. The tours, on the "Bama Bound" bus, leave from the Rose Administration Building.

ELSEWHERE IN TUSCALOOSA

A number of Tuscaloosa's historic buildings sit within a nine square block area not far from the University campus.

The Mildred Warner House is a museum for lovers of historic structures, and for lovers of fine art, and for lovers of antiques. It's sort of hard not to find something to like here. The house itself began in 1822 as a two-room cabin with open hearth fireplaces. A large four-story Georgian-style brick portion was added in the 1830s. Jack Warner bought the house in 1977 and completely restored it, naming the finished product in honor of his mother. It is furnished with antiques dating from 1700 to 1865 and houses a comprehensive collection of American art with paintings by more than 40 artists. The home is open Saturday from 10 a.m. to 6 p.m. and Sunday from 1 to 6 p.m. No admission is charged.

The Dearing-Swaim Home, built in 1835, is said to be among the best examples of Greek Temple style architecture (with columns around three sides) remaining in Alabama. The house was so well built that it never has needed restoration and its original sheet metal roof lasted 125 years. The roof was duplicated exactly when it finally was replaced. The house was spared in 1864 because the lady of the house scrambled the last turkey eggs she had and fed the troops who were sent to burn the structure. The home, a privately owned landmark, sometimes is open for tours but a drive-by look at the exterior should be included in any trip to Tuscaloosa.

Set in the midst of all the historic buildings is something new - C.H.O.M. (Children's Hands-on Museum), a "must-see" if you're traveling with children. Inside the museum, they can visit an Indian village, make a loan at a bank designed just for them, try on historic clothing in Grandmother's Attic, make a TV news show or watch the stars in a planetarium show. The museum is open Tuesday through Friday from 9 a.m. to 5 p.m. and Sunday from 1 to 5 p.m. Admission is $3 per person. Children under four years old are admitted free.

Alfred Battle wasn't kidding around when he built what now is called the Battle-Friedman House on Greensboro Avenue; he meant for it to last. The interior walls are 18 inches thick. Constructed in the 1830s and acquired by the Friedman family in 1875, the house today is filled with fine antiques. Outside, there are period gardens that spread across a half block of land. The Battle-Friedman House is open Tuesday through Saturday from 10 a.m. to 4 p.m. and from 1 to 4 p.m. Sunday. Admission is $3 for adults, $2.50 for senior citizens and $.50 for children.

Also on Greensboro Avenue are the First Baptist Church, the oldest church in Tuscaloosa County, and First United Methodist Church, with a bell that was cast by the Paul Revere Company in the 19th century.

---

houses a collection of religious objects that date as far back as the 15th century. A panel depicting the Annunciation was created in South Germany in the 1400s and the church's baptismal font is 16th century Italian. The pulpit is Gothic, carved in oak and crafted by a 15th century Frenchman. The stained glass windows in the chapel next to the church were created in various parts of Europe and date from the 16th century. Furniture there includes 18th century French Provincial pieces and many of the fixtures are 18th century brass.

In 1907, Willie Turner, a member of the First African Baptist Church, made bricks on a site behind the McLester Hotel and the men of the church cut the trees to make cypress logs for the construction of the church structure that now stands on Ninth Street. This church, where Civil Rights groups were headquartered during the 1960s, owns one of the oldest church bells in the city. Purchased in 1885, the bell is now used for weddings and other events.

ANOTHER STATE CAPITAL

Tuscaloosa once was Alabama's capital and the buildings in the Historic Capitol Park complex on University Boulevard West are from that period in the city's history. Among the structures here is the McGuire-Strickland House, the oldest wooden house standing in Tuscaloosa. This home has  hand-hewn timbers, wooden pegs and square nails. It still sports its original shutters, window panes, pine flooring and mantels. Built in 1820, it was occupied by the Strickland family for about 100 years. It now is the County Preservation Society Headquarters. It is open from 8 a.m. to 4 p.m. Monday through Friday and there is no admission charge.

The Old Tavern, also in the park area, was built in 1827 and was the home of Alabama Governor John Gayle. It also has served as an inn and stagecoach stop. The Old Tavern is open Tuesday through Saturday from 10 a.m. to 4 p.m. and from 1 to 4 p.m. Sunday. Admission is $3 for adults, $2.50 for senior citizens and $.50 for children. On Bryant Drive (off University Boulevard several miles east of the campus) is the Murphy-Collins House. Built in the early 1920s by Will Murphy, the first black mortician in Tuscaloosa, the structure now houses black heritage memorabilia. The Murphy-Collins House is open by appointment only. Admission is $3 for adults, $2.50 for senior citizens and $.50 for children.

The University of Alabama isn't the only college in Tuscaloosa. Stillman College, established by the Presbyterian Church in 1876 to train black ministers, today is a four-year co-educational liberal arts college.

The architecture on campus includes the city's only example of Corinthian columns.

ART AND PAPER

While Gulf States Paper Corporation sounds more like somewhere you'd go to stock up on school supplies than something you'd make a trip to Tuscaloosa to see, it will surprise you. Four Oriental-style buildings on the grounds of the corporation's national headquarters house an outstanding

---

grounds of the corporation's national headquarters house an outstanding art collection. The art includes primitive artifacts from Africa and the South Pacific, Oriental art and works by Frederick Remington, Charles Bird King, Bierstadt and Wyeth. Among the most popular paintings with visitors to the galleries are the wild bird portraits of Basil Ede, considered to be the foremost painter of birds of all time.

Outside the buildings is a Japanese Garden, a grassy, green area of quiet set around a pond filled with ducks.

Regular tours of the facility are offered on the hour Monday through Friday from 5 to 7 p.m., Saturday from 10 a.m. to 7 p.m. and Sunday from 1 to 7 p.m. There is no charge for the tour.

KENTUCK IS NORTHPORT HIGHLIGHT

Across the Black Warrior River from Tuscaloosa is the city of Northport, which originally was called "Kentuck." The city, was the site of an early ford used by travelers making their way across the Alabama Territory. Soon a community sprang up at the river crossing and, probably because there was a port on the north side, before long became Northport.

Each year, the city recalls the time when it was Kentuck with a weekend of music, art, crafts and folklore. The festival began in 1971 as a tiny street fair and now takes over almost the entire city as artists and craftsmen display their wares and demonstrate their skills.

While Festival weekend gets a lot of attention, it is only the showcase of the art and crafts community that has grown up in Northport. In fact, "The Traveler's Guide to American Crafts" recently called the city, with its Kentuck complex, "Alabama's craft center" and "home to a growing number of good-quality studios and galleries."

Near the festival area, on the site of Northport's original blacksmith shop, is the Kentuck Art Center. It houses space for six top national craftsmen and their studios. "Working in clay, wood, canvas, glass and metal," says Kathy Bailey of the Kentuck Museum, "these artists are an integral part of Northport's presenting contemporary art in an historical setting." Studio hours at the art center vary, but they usually are Tuesday through Saturday from 10 a.m. to 4 p.m.

The Northport Civic Center, just minutes away, houses the Museum. This facility offers a year-round schedule of changing exhibitions of contemporary art, traditional craft and folk art. The museum is open Monday through Friday from 9 a.m. to 5 p.m. and Saturday from 11:30 a.m. to 4:30 p.m.

Four buildings from the 1800s make up the piece of Alabama history called the North River Historical District. The Old Center Church, built of hand-hewn logs held together with pegs, served at various times as a school, civic center and place of worship. Gravestones in the adjacent cemetery date from 1824. Umbria Schoolhouse is a restored one-room building that served as central Alabama's earliest schoolhouse. The Gainesville Bank was moved from that city and restored in 1970. The high-ceilinged building has a vault that is enclosed with hand-molded brick. The Dogtrot Cabin is typical of that style of architecture. This one, though, has a full length porch across the front protecting windows of German hand-blown glass. The North River District is open by appointment.

The Northport First United Methodist Church was built in 1913 by Arthur Laycock, who came to America from England in 1882 and settled in Northport. The church's bell was rung April 3, 1865, to sound the alarm as General John Croxton's army approached Northport and Tuscaloosa. Only a short time later, Croxton's troops were burning the University of Alabama.

LAKE LURLEEN

Lake Lurleen State Park, 12 miles northwest of Tuscaloosa, offers something for the entire family. The serious fisherman (or woman) can pursue his hobby while the rest of the group enjoys swimming, boating and hiking. There are picnic facilities and a playground area at the 1,625-acre park as well as sites for primitive and improved camping. Fees are charged for use of some of the park facilities. Pets are allowed if kept on leashes.

A few miles northeast of Tuscaloosa, just off Interstate 59, is Bama Scenic Rock Gardens. Nature trails here are set among natural rock formations dotted with native wildflowers and ferns. The gardens are open from 8 a.m. to 5 p.m. seven days a week and admission is $2.50 for adults and $1 for children under 12. Overnight camping facilities are available at the gardens. The fee for camping there is based on the kind of trailer or RV you're using. Admission to the gardens is included in the camping fee.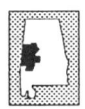

WHERE TO STAY

Since Tuscaloosa is a college town and because a number of the cities in this area have annual events that draw large crowds, there are several chain motels and hotels in this part of the state. In addition, there are independent facilities. Among them are:

In Tuscaloosa: Bel-Aire Motel, Dill's Motor Court, Moon Winx, Ole English Inn, Stagecoach Inn and Thunderbird Inn.

In Demopolis: Riverview Inn and Windwood Inn.

There is a bed and breakfast inn, Blue Shadows Guest House, in Greensboro. The inn is open all year except Thanksgiving week. Nature trails and a lake on the grounds make this an ideal getaway spot.

Several public parks and facilities offer camping in this area. Camping also is available near Aliceville at Cochrane Campground, operated by the U.S. Army Corps of Engineers. There are 50 campsites in the improved camping area and 10 for the primitive camper. User fee for an individual campsite is $8. In addition, there are several private campgrounds. Among them are:

In Tuscaloosa: Lake Tuscaloosa.

In Demopolis: Forkland Park, Deer Lick Run, Runaway Branch.

WHERE TO EAT

In addition to chain restaurants and fast food establishments in the area, there are a number of privately owned eateries. Among them are:

In Tuscaloosa: The Landing (Fresh snapper is the specialty here.), The Waysider (known for its great breakfasts), Dreamland Cafe, (Everyone has heard of the barbecued ribs at Dreamland - stories about them even have appeared in newspapers "up north."), Storyville and Trey Yuen. (The chef here has more than 30 years experience in cooking authentic Chinese cuisine.).

In Northport: City Cafe (a city landmark where folks gather daily), Cypress Inn (overlooks the Black Warrior River) and Moe's Original Bar-B-Que and Steaks.

In Aliceville: The Plantation House (located in a home that dates from 1903).

In Demopolis: Riverview Landing, Ellis V, The Pig, Red Barn, Camphouse and Mr. G's.

In Marion: Calico Kitchen, Billy's Place.

In Eutaw: The Cotton Patch.

In Moundville: Miss Melissa's.

ANNUAL EVENTS

Annual events in this part of the state include:

Historic Spring Pilgrimage and Antique Show, Marion, April.
The Road To Calvary, Moundville, April.

Spring Arts And Crafts Festival, Moundville, May.
Fireworks on the River, Demopolis, July.

Folk Roots Festival, Eutaw, August.
West Alabama State Fair, Tuscaloosa, September.

Art in the Park, Demopolis, October.
Moundville Native American Festival, Moundville, October.
Alabama Catfish Festival, Greensboro, October.
Kentuck Festival, Northport, October.
City Fest and University Homecoming, Tuscaloosa, October.

Christmas on the River, Demopolis, December.
Candlelight Tour of Gaineswood, Demopolis, December.
Christmas in the Canebrake, Demopolis, December.

Birmingham: Heart of The Heart of Dixie

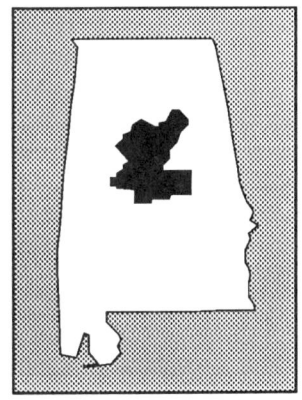

To feel the heartbeat of Alabama, place your fingers on the pulse point that is Birmingham, the state's most populous city. Geographically near the center of Alabama, Birmingham seems to set the pace for the entire state. Once contained in just a valley amid Alabama's rolling hills, the city has sprawled in all directions, creating a major metropolitan area of more than 900,000 people.

Birmingham offers a delightful mix of downhome comfort with uptown sophistication.

It would take months to explore all of Birmingham's hidden treasures. To truly experience the metropolitan area would take years. Probably the best way to even taste a sample of what this part of the state has to offer is to bite off small chunks and try to see it a little at a time.

STARTING IN BIRMINGHAM'S CENTER

Begin your exploration of Birmingham in the heart of the city. Linn Park, one of Birmingham's oldest city parks, sits at the north end of 20th Street downtown surrounded by municipal buildings. It recently has undergone a $2.5 million renovation and with its new fountain, trees and walkways, the park always is a pleasant place for a break in the middle of a hectic day. It also often is the site of concerts and other special events.

On the west side of the park is City Hall, on the east side, the County Courthouse. Next to the courthouse is the Linn-Henley Research Library. For almost 50 years, it was "The Library." Now it is part of a complex that stretches across two blocks and spans one downtown street. The newer part of the complex, an award-winning strong geometric design, echoes without imitating the older building which sits across 21st Street North from it. This "new" (even though it has been around for a about five years now, it's still the new library building to most Birminghamians) library houses the "basics" that any library offers in addition to an art gallery and a collection of prints and art objects that can be checked out the same way the books can. And while the new facility adds a dramatic look to a library's basic functions, the "old" library building is truly a work of art as well.

105

This neo-classical structure, made of Indiana limestone, was opened in early 1927. It took two more years to complete the ground-floor interior, done in marble, brass and oak. Even without its crowning glory - murals of figures from world literature painted by New York artist Ezra Winter - the library looked just the way a library should by the beginning of 1929. The murals were completed that year. Time and changes in the decor of the library took their toll on the magnificent interior design, however. And the library's collection of works outgrew the facility.

While the new library building was being completed, the old building was being renovated and restored. The murals were cleaned and brought back to their original beauty. Today the older building houses the Tutwiler Collection of Southern History and Literature, the Rucker Agee Map Collection, the Department of Archives and Manuscripts and other research collections. Library hours are Monday and Tuesday 9 a.m. to 8 p.m., Wednesday through Saturday, 9 a.m. to 6 p.m., and Sunday, 2 to 6 p.m.

The Heart of Dixie: The Birmingham Area

Jefferson County, the state's most populous county, and the counties that cluster around it make up this region of six counties. Birmingham, of course, is the largest city in the region. But nearby cities like Hoover are seeing dramatic population increases while the City of Birmingham's population tapers off.

As the Birmingham metropolitan area increases, the cities nearby grow with it. Other population centers in this area are Leeds, Bessemer, Clanton and Pell City. The geographical center of the state lies within this region, where almost 900,000 people live.

THE MUSEUM OF ART

Just north of Linn Park is the Birmingham Museum of Art, the largest municipally-supported art museum in the Southeast. The permanent collection has examples representing art history from ancient Egypt to the present. Especially notable is the Beeson Collection of Wedgwood porcelain, with more than 1,400 objects. This collection is considered the largest outside of Great Britain. Other particularly fine collections are those of Asian and African art.

The museum is open Tuesday, Wednesday, Friday and Saturday from 10 a.m. to 5 p.m.; Thursday from 10 a.m. to 9 p.m. and Sunday from 1 to 5 p.m. There is no admission charge.

Despite the fact that you have to journey under a rumbling interstate highway, it's a pleasant stroll on the Garden Walk from the back of the art museum to the Birmingham-Jefferson Civic Center. In addition to providing a home base for The Birmingham Children's Theatre and the Alabama Symphony Orchestra, the Civic Center complex offers a spot for touring company performances, circus rings, trade shows and basketball games.

The Civic Center presently is undergoing a $140 million expansion that will increase the present hotel to 700 rooms and create a Medical Trade Mart. Other facilities will be expanded as well.

Also in the Civic Center is the Alabama Sports Hall of Fame Museum. Here, the state's athletic history - including the football from Coach Paul "Bear" Bryant's 315th win, major league baseball uniforms from the 1920s and 1930s and video clips from memorable moments in sports - is on display. The museum is open Monday through Friday from 8 a.m. to 5 p.m., Saturday from 10 a.m. to 5 p.m., and Sunday from 1 to 5 p.m. Admission is $1.50 for adults, $.75 for children under 19 or $4 per family.

Oak Hill Cemetery, just north of 11th Avenue North and 19th Street near the Civic Center, is the city's oldest cemetery. Many of Birmingham's early leaders are buried here along with Confederate and Union soldiers, ex-slaves and paupers. Among the more interesting mausolea and tombstones is that of Charles Linn, for whom Linn Park is named. The city's first banker, Linn selected the site for his mausoleum long before his death in 1882. Linn chose the plot on high ground so that "on Judgment Day, I can walk out to view the greatest industrial city in the South."

MORE DOWNTOWN LANDMARKS

Heading away from the Civic Center and back toward downtown, you'll find a wonderful blend of old and new buildings. The new ones tower over the city streets and house retail businesses and offices. Many of the older ones have been restored to their former beauty and now are office buildings, restaurants and even living quarters.

The Steiner Building on the corner of 21st Street and First Avenue North, was built in 1890 and restored in 1980. It originally was a bank and now houses the offices of an investment banking firm and an architect's office.

The iron front exterior of the Zinszer Building at 2117 Second Avenue North doesn't give away the secret inside - a breathtaking three-story atrium. When it was built in 1889, the building was home to Birmingham's first and largest "easy payment" furniture house. Restored in 1985, it now is a law office.

When the Empire Building rose on the corner of First Avenue North and 20th Street in 1909, it became the third "skyscraper" at that intersection. Citizens called this spot, then the heart of the Birmingham business district, "The Heaviest Corner on Earth." The building, restored in 1982, now houses a bank. Especially lovely is the elevator lobby, where the original Italian marbles and fixtures have been uncovered and repaired.

The restoration work on the Alabama Power Building at 600 18th Street North is impressive in itself. The history of the building and the lore of

"Electra" make it a "must see." When the building was constructed in 1925, it was more than a corporate headquarters - it was a monument to Alabama's natural resources. All the structural steel, limestone, marble, brick, colored tile, cast-iron pipe, cement, lime and pine lumber used in the building originated within 60 miles of Birmingham. The Gothic-Modernistic style building has three limestone figures over the main entrance. The three women are said to represent Power, Heat and Light.

There's another woman atop the building. Unlike her counterparts below, Electra chose not to be clothed for her appearance over Birmingham's city streets. Golden Electra holds aloft sheaves of lightning, symbolizing Alabama's electrical progress. Birminghamians like to say that Electra is the girlfriend of Vulcan, the massive statue that stands on Red Mountain and overlooks the city (and Electra). A replica of the Statue of Liberty that once stood atop the Liberty National Life Insurance Company between the two was said to be the chaperon keeping the two lovers at a respectable distance. (Not an easy task when you consider that Electra was wearing nothing and that Vulcan has a bare bottom).

The other mystery of Electra - who posed for the statue - may never be solved. Various Birmingham belles have claimed to be Electra's alter ego and others say that Electra is a combination of the best features of several of Birmingham's most attractive young ladies. And, indeed, a number of women have claimed portions of Electra's anatomy as their own. Bring your binoculars, have a look at Electra and make your own decisions.

The Iron Age Building at 212 20th Street North was constructed in 1888 to become a newspaper press office and is one of the city's two remaining cast-iron-fronted buildings. The restoration, done in 1990, has removed aluminum store fronts that covered the cornices and columns of cast iron and has re-established the original look of the building.

Other restorations in the area include the Birmingham Realty Building, 2114 First Avenue North; The Woodward Building, 20th Street and First Avenue North; the Russell-Olshine Building, 313 20th Street North; the Denechaud Building, 2107 Second Avenue North; the Saks Building, 1900 First Avenue North; the O'Neill, Gilreath, Eubank and Drennen Buildings, 2017-2025 Third Avenue North; the Walker Building, 324 21st Street North; the Harris Building, 115 21st Street North; Avondale Land Company Building, 2122-2124 First Avenue North; the Penny-Liberman Building, 2210 Second Avenue North; Mercantile Supply/Alabama Title Building, 2233 Second Avenue North and the McAdory Building, 2013 First Avenue North.

AROUND FIRST AVENUE...

Along First Avenue North and in the area surrounding it are a number of warehouses that have been restored and converted to multi-use facilities. In most cases, the buildings now house businesses on the lower floor and living space on the upper floors. These lofts are home to a collection of young and old, artist and businessman and reflect the varied tastes of their owners. Some of them have been decorated in such a way that you'd never know you were in an old warehouse. Other owners have chosen to "work with what's here" and one residence still has the warehouse walls - with painted advertisements - intact and in view.

Perhaps the best way to see the restoration work being done in the downtown area is to attend the annual "A Day in Old Birmingham" festival. During this event, many of the restored buildings - including the loft apartments - are open to the public and costumed guides tell the story of the city's beginnings.

<h3 style="text-align:center">HISTORICAL CHURCHES</h3>

Essential to the history of Birmingham are the churches of the city. Many of the structures still used for worship services today are as old or older than the city itself. Landmark churches in the downtown area include First United Methodist Church, built in 1891, on the corner of 19th Street and Sixth Avenue North; First Presbyterian, built in 1888, at 21st Street and Fourth Avenue North and St. Paul's Cathedral, built in 1893, at 22nd and Third Avenue North.

Cathedral Church of the Advent on the corner of 20th Street and Sixth Avenue North was built in 1893 and offers not only a look at a lovely structure, but a quiet place to stop in the middle of the city. Advent Gardens, with outdoor seating scattered throughout a flower and shrub garden, is open from 8:30 a.m.-4:30 p.m. and there is no admission charge.

The part of Birmingham's history that the entire nation watched being written was penned in part

Belle Features

Sixteenth Street Baptist Church, Birmingham

Birmingham: The Heart of Dixie   109

at another downtown church. On the northwest corner of Sixth Avenue North and Sixteenth Street stands Sixteenth Street Baptist Church. It was there that a Sunday morning bombing killed four children and turned the city's and the nation's attention to racial unrest in the South. Open daily to the public, the church, which dates to 1873, was a rallying point for Civil Rights leaders of the 1960s.

Inside the church is a stained glass window, given as a memorial to the slain children by the nation of Wales. Tours of the church can be arranged by calling the church office.

Kelly Ingram Park, with a statue of Martin Luther King Jr., is northwest of the Sixteenth Street Baptist Church. The park, over the years, has served as an assembly spot for marches, rallies and prayer services.

Also in this area is the Alabama Penny Savings Bank. Located at 310 Eighteenth Street North, it was the state's first black-owned bank and the nation's second largest black-owned financial institution.

Plans are in the works for a Civil Rights Mu-

Belle Features

Martin Luther King Jr. Statue, Kelly Ingram Park, Birmingham

seum in this area in the near future.

Rising beside the First Avenue North viaduct near where Birmingham's north and south sides meet, are the hulking smokestacks of Sloss Furnaces, a monument to the iron and steel industry that built Birmingham. James Withers Sloss, the son of an Irish farmer, built the furnaces in 1882. Not long after they were completed, iron began to flow from Sloss' furnaces, built at the crossing of a number of railroads. The casting sheds and ovens of Sloss continued to belch molten metal until 1971, when production stopped there. It seemed the furnaces were doomed to destruction, but a group of supporters, determined to salvage this reminder of the glory days of Birmingham's iron industry, came up with a plan to make Sloss vital again.

A museum/visitor's center now fills one of the brick buildings at Sloss and a tour winds its way among the furnaces and pipes. The main casting shed serves as an amphitheater for concerts and community events. The furnaces, said to be haunted, also provide the setting for a "Kid's Day" safe Halloween celebration - complete with trick or treating and ghost stories each year.

Sloss Furnaces, a National Historic Landmark, is open Tuesday through Friday from 10 a.m. to 4 p.m.; Saturday from 10 a.m. to 4 p.m., and Sunday, from noon to 4 p.m.

Guided tours may be arranged on weekdays. On weekends, tours are available, without reservations, at 1, 2 and 3 p.m. There is no admission charge. The furnaces are on the southern side of the First Avenue Viaduct. The entrance is on 32nd Street North.

Also bridging north and south Birmingham is Morris Avenue. The cobblestone streets still exist in this part of the city, which has tried for several comebacks and still refuses to die. Many of the old warehouses along Morris Avenue now are home to stylish offices. The street also is home to a restaurant, a private club and "The Peanut Depot," where everyone goes to get fresh roasted hot peanuts.

BIRMINGHAM'S COLLEGES

Just over the north/south dividing line in Birmingham is one of the city's many colleges. There are those wags in Birmingham who would tell you that the University of Alabama at Birmingham reminds them a little of "The Blob" of movie fame. Oozing, spreading, growing, the school complex really does personify the word "sprawl." Virtually a city in itself, UAB encompasses 70 city blocks and is Birmingham's largest employer, with more than 12,000 faculty and staff.

Anchored by University Hospital and its related facilities - internationally known for the health care they provide - UAB also includes classrooms, the Hulsey Fine Arts Center, the Mervyn Sterne Library, the UAB Visual Arts Center and the UAB Arena, home of Blazers basketball.

On campus is the Alabama Museum of Health Sciences, where Birmingham's medical growth and the development of the health sciences in Alabama are documented. On display are materials such as medical instruments, photographs and equipment related to medical history. At 1700 University Boulevard in the Lister Hill Library, the museum is open

Birmingham: The Heart of Dixie

Monday through Friday from 8 a.m. to 5 p.m. There is no admission charge.

Also in the Hill Library is the Reynolds Historical Library, which houses ivory anatomical mannequins, Benjamin Franklin's original writings, rare medical and scientific books and three of George and Martha Washington's letters to their dentist. The hours are the same as those for the Museum of Health Sciences and there is no admission charge.

HISTORIC FIVE POINTS

When you've passed UAB, you've arrived at Five Points South, one of Birmingham's most eclectic neighborhoods. Parks, theaters, restaurants, bars, shops and historic structures fill this circular intersection at the south end of 20th Street. Day and night, yuppies, families, teens, artists, students, joggers, couples and Birmingham's older set make their way to Five Points South. It's a great place to people watch.

Incorporated as the Town of Highland in 1887, Five Points South offers a varied collection of architecture as well as people. The Spanish baroque Highlands United Methodist Church, commands a view of the entire circle. In front of it is a fountain that soon (perhaps as soon as early 1991) will sport a sculpture by Birmingham artist Frank Fleming, known for his mythical creations and wry looks at life.

Across one street is the Art Deco Munger Building, across another are the Ware and Medical Arts Buildings, also done in the Art Deco Style and now combined to created Pickwick Place, a sort of shopping plaza.

Also across one of the streets that radiates from Five Points South is the statue of Brother Bryan. Rev. James Alexander Bryan came to Birmingham in 1889 to minister to the city's poor. He began his work at Third Presbyterian Church as a 26-year-old minister. He continued as pastor there until his death in 1941.

Rev. Bryan quickly became known in Birmingham as "Brother Bryan" and although his pastorate was Third Presbyterian, his workplace was the entire city. As concerned for the physical well being of Birmingham's poor as for their spiritual condition, Bryan ran a soup kitchen and a clothing distribution center during the Depression. He started college scholarship funds and established a club where women could make and sell quilts.

Bryan's work was underwritten by every part of the Birmingham community. Bakeries donated leftover bread to his soup kitchen, businesses and individual supplied monetary support without Bryan even having to ask for it.

The work of Brother Bryan knew no social, economic or racial boundaries. Anyone who was in need - physical or spiritual - could find an advocate in Bryan. The minister was known for his deep belief in the power of prayer and was just as likely to be found praying in a pool hall as in a church building.

It is fitting, then, that Birmingham's memorial to this man of prayer depicts him on his knees with his face upturned in supplication. The statue of Brother Bryan, done by Birmingham sculptor Georges Bridges, was unveiled in the Five Points South neighborhood in 1934. It was moved to Vulcan Park in 1966 and returned to Five Points South in 1982. It sits today as a serene reminder of what one determined man can do if he believes in his calling.

TWO GREAT MUSEUMS

Just off Highland Avenue, one of the streets that radiates from Five Points South, are two of the city's most interesting museums.

The Discovery Place, at 1320 22nd Street South, was the state's first museum for children. But, in truth, adults find as much fun as the children do. The hands-on activities include everything from generating electricity by riding a bicycle to giving the news and weather at the museum's simulated television station.

The Up Space, which used to be an attic storage room before the museum was forced to grow in that direction, offers a number of "Discovery boxes" for children and grown-ups to explore together as well as a library and natural history and science related books.

The museum looks to be a single level facility from the outside, but clever use of the existing space has created a multi-level, fun place to learn inside.

The Discovery Place is open from 9 a.m. to 3 p.m. Tuesday through Friday and 1 to 4 p.m. on Saturday and Sunday. During the summer, Saturday hours are expanded to 10 a.m. to 4 p.m. Admission is $2 for adults and $1.50 for children.

Special programs and seminars are scheduled for Saturdays and Sundays and a quick call to The Discovery Place will outline the upcoming events. The Discovery Place is closed during the month of September for repairs, renovations and creation of new exhibits.

Next to The Discovery Place is a museum that tells so much of Birmingham's natural history, it takes a whole mountain to hold it all - the Red Mountain Museum. It took the highway department to locate all that history for Birmingham. When the city was looking for a better way than going over Red Mountain to link downtown with "over the mountain," someone came up with the idea of going through the mountain. And the Red Mountain Cut began.

A massive chunk of the mountain was removed to create the highway (which, for the uninitiated, has a variety of names - U.S. 280 East, the Red Mountain Expressway, the Elton B. Stephens Expressway) and the terraced cut revealed layer upon layer of geological history. The walkway along the 220-foot long, 1/3-mile high cut, has interpretive information to help visitors understand the 150-million year development of the earth's layers shown preserved in the rock.

Inside the museum building are exhibits focusing on science, geology and paleontology. They show artifacts from Alabama's history, a presentation about the age of the dinosaurs, a look at what makes up the sun and such hands-on activities as computer games that teach natural history. A large central exhibit room houses a 14-foot-long mosasaur skeleton that was found in Greene County.

On the grounds outside are picnic tables, trees and grassy spots.

The star of the grounds, though, is Seymour, the dinosaur. He's not scientifically correct, but he's got a great personality. The figure, which started life as an advertisement for a Sinclair gasoline station, patiently permits children to clamor over him and slide down his tail. Perhaps because he is so patient, he has been the object of a number of graduation night high school pranks. Stolen and found, replaced again and again, Seymour almost met his demise in what everyone in Birmingham hopes was the last such episode. To prevent his removal, his feet had been firmly planted in the ground at the museum, so the vandals removed his head. A weeks-long search finally located the head and a plan was devised to reattach it while children - and adults - of Birmingham flooded Seymour with get well cards. The plan worked, Seymour is restored and once again oversees the grounds at Red Mountain Museum.

The museum and grounds are open Tuesday through Saturday from 10 a.m. to 4:30 p.m. and Sunday from 1 to 4:30 p.m. There's no required admission, but the museum asks for donations of $1 per visitor.

THE ZOO AND BOTANICAL GARDENS

Before he went to live at Red Mountain Museum, Seymour lived at The Birmingham Zoo, just over the mountain from the museum. There, he was atop the reptile house, which didn't make him any more scientifically correct and did make him less accessible to children. Even without Seymour, the zoo is worth a visit. It is the Southeast's largest zoo and the 70 acres are filled with about 250 species of animals. For a while, the zoo was less than a place of pride. The facilities for the animals were outdated almost to the point of being inhumane. But a recent renovation and building program has corrected much of that, placing many of the animals in settings that resemble their natural habitats.

The animals are grouped not so much by species as by lifestyle. One of the newer buildings, for example, is for Social Animals. Colorful panels between the exhibits show how the animals interact and also relate their interaction to man's interaction with other men.

The Predator House shows how one species of animal may rely on another for food and how that food is captured. Again using the large colored panels, the relationship of predator and prey is explained.

The zoo has the almost-mandatory zoo train that makes a circuit of the exhibits. A new restaurant - set in a railroad dining car - is near the train station. The zoo has begun a number of new programs, including a "Breakfast with the Zookeeper," designed to familiarize the humans with the animals. There is a zoo auditorium that's used for many of these programs as well as films and, recently, a live theater production of a play about the South American rainforest. Picnic areas at the zoo always are available to zoo visitors. From time to time, they are the site of "Concerts in the Park" by the Alabama Symphony Orchestra.

*A friend you'll see
at the Birmingham Zoo*

A marked path throughout the zoo indicates an exercise trail used by walkers who like to have more than the walls of a gym to look at while getting in their aerobic activity.

The zoo is one of the few places that is open rain or shine every day of the year including holidays. Hours are 9:30 a.m. to 5 p.m. Admission is $3 for adults, $1.50 for children ages 2 to 17 and adults over 65. Children under 2 are admitted free. The train ride is an additional $1 per person.

Across the street from the zoo are Birmingham's Botanical Gardens. More than 25 individual garden areas fill the almost 70 acre facility. Probably best known is the Japanese Gardens, a 7-1/2-acre garden that visitors enter through a Torii or "Gateway to Heaven." The central feature of the garden is a teahouse, originally built for the 1964 New York World's Fair and given to Birmingham by the people of Japan. The Bonsai collection in this part of the Botanical Gardens is world famous. On any given day - but especially during the spring and summer - that you visit the Japanese Gardens, you may find yourself a guest at someone's wedding. This garden is one of the most popular spots in the city for outdoor ceremonies.

Though the Japanese Gardens may be the best known part of the Botanical Gardens, it isn't the only part. The Native Plant Garden, filled with flowers and trees native to the state, is the next largest section. Other gardens to explore here include the Rose Garden, Wildflower Garden, Fern Glade, Camellia Garden and Vegetable Garden. In addition to the thousands of plants in the garden, more than 200 species of birds make their home here.

Birmingham: The Heart of Dixie

The greenhouse and conservatory, the largest of its kind in the Southeast, have tropical and exotic plants from around the world.

Outside the conservatory is the "flower clock," a giant clock that marks the time in flowers. This spot is a favorite of younger visitors to the gardens.

One area of the Botanical Gardens, the "Touch and See Nature Trail," is designed for visually impaired visitors. Plaques written in Braille tell about the flowers and trees in the area and guide visitors as they touch and experience the plants growing there.

At the entrance to the gardens is the Garden Center, a relatively new building designed to be used for community, educational and social events. Rather than intruding on the gardens, the Center - which has a great many windows opening onto the gardens - seems to sit naturally among the rose bushes and other plants that surround it. In the Garden Center you'll find a reception area, gift shop, restaurant and meeting rooms. There also is an Orientation Room, where visitors learn more about the Botanical Gardens.

The Garden Center also houses the Horace Hammond Memorial Library, with its large collection of horticultural literature.

Outside the Garden Center is a sculpture by Jesus Bautista Moroles. The piece is a gentle fountain of free-standing stone trunks, some of them as much as 12 feet tall. The trunks twist and taper and reach from bases to tops that slowly release bubbling water. This work by Moroles, hailed as "one of the cultural pleasures of this place, a work of art that complements its setting and heightens the beauty of nature," is just one more reason to make time in your schedule for a trip to the Botanical Gardens.

The Botanical Gardens is open daily sunrise to sunset and there is no admission charge.

Vulcan: Towering Over Birmingham

Not far from the Botanical Gardens and the zoo is Vulcan, the world's largest cast-iron statue and the second largest statue in the United States. Only the Statue of Liberty surpasses it in sheer size.

The 56-foot tall statue, which weighs 60 tons, was designed by Italian sculptor Guiseppe Morretti and cast in Birmingham foundries. Vulcan, the Roman god of the forge, was to be Birmingham's display at the 1904 St. Louis World's Fair.

And the appearance of the gigantic work did cause quite a stir at the Fair. At the close of the exposition, Vulcan was declared to be "the greatest fair exhibit in man's history" and had been seen by nearly 20 million people. In fact, Vulcan's popularity at the Fair was second only to that of the ice cream cone, which was born at that World's Fair.

When the Fair ended, a number of cities offered to buy Vulcan, but the Commercial Club of Birmingham, which had sponsored the statue at the Fair, said Vulcan was coming home to his native city.

He got a free trip back to Birmingham on the L&N Railroad, but Vulcan quickly learned that fame was fleeting. Back at home, a lot of people said he had an ugly face and needed to have his bare bottom (which peeks from beneath his leather apron) covered. No one could decide where his permanent home should be. In truth, everyone seemed to want him in someone else's neighborhood. Finally, the L&N solved the problem of a temporary home by reclaiming its freight cars and dumping the metal giant in a field near Red Mountain.

The Alabama State Fair asked to have Vulcan as an exhibit there about 18 months after he was left alone in the field and grateful sponsors happily placed him on loan to the Fairgrounds. He stayed there for 30 years, enduring all sorts of abuse from losing a thumb to having bees take up residence in his right arm, which had been attached backwards.

In the mid-1930s, talk began again about finding a proper home for the statue and in 1936, work began on a 124-foot tower/pedestal for him atop Red Mountain. Finally in May, 1939, the statue was in place at Vulcan Park - his face turned toward the city, the other side facing the communities "over the mountain."

Even the gods show their age and Vulcan had begun to do so until the grounds and pedestal of Vulcan Park got a recent facelift. Now a landscaped park surrounds the base of the pedestal and visitors no longer have to take the stairs to get to an observation platform just below Vulcan's feet. A glass-encased elevator whisks them to the deck and its spectacular view of the city below.

The Vulcan, Birmingham

Unfortunately, you no longer get a close-up view of the huge statue from the observation platform. But viewing Vulcan from the ground, you will notice a lighted torch in his uplifted right hand. The torch burns green if there have been no traffic fatalities in Birmingham during the last 24 hours and red if there has been one. During the hostage crisis in Iran, Vulcan's torch burned yellow as a reminder of the plight of the Americans in the Embassy there.

Vulcan Park is open daily from 8 a.m. to 11 p.m. and the night views of the city are lovely. Admission is $1 for ages 7 and up. Children under 7 are admitted free.

BEAUTIFUL SAMFORD UNIVERSITY

Samford University, a Baptist liberal arts college, is on Lakeshore Drive in the Birmingham suburb of Homewood. Its Georgian style buildings set on beautifully landscaped grounds give the campus a "college" look that's picture perfect.

Speaking of pictures, be sure to have yours made with the life-size statue of Ralph Beeson, a Samford benefactor. Beeson's statue sits on a bench at the foot of the Centennial Steps leading to the Harwell Davis Library on campus. Visitors and students alike have made it a tradition in the few years the statue has been there to sit beside Beeson (or in his lap) for a photograph session.

The students have become so fond of the likeness of Beeson, sculpted by Glynn Acree, that they provide it with a Santa hat at Christmas and make sure it wears a muffler in cold weather. It is said that Beeson, who died in late 1990, enjoyed the tales of how students took care of his statue.

On campus is a magnificent carillon. If you're there when it's being played, you're in for a treat. Even if you miss the music, don't miss the murals in the Center for the Healing Arts.

The building, Georgian in style to fit with the look of the campus, was completed in 1988. Among its interesting architectural features are its copper dome and the 55-foot rotunda beneath. Light streams into the rotunda through an oculus at the top of the dome.

But the building has more to offer than spectacular architecture. Around the second floor of the rotunda are murals done by D. Jeffrey Mims. Done in the style of the Old Masters, the four murals depict scenes of healing from the Bible. Mims worked with the architect long before the building was completed, making his works seem a part of the building, rather than an "added attraction."

Lewis Arnold

Ralph Beeson sitting with his statue at Samford University, Birmingham

In the courtyard of the Healing Arts Center is a bronze statue of a healing angel. Designed by Birmingham artist Constantine Breton, it was cast in Italy by sculptor Urbano Buratti.

You can see the building, which houses the Ida V. Moffett School of Nursing, the Rotunda Club and guest rooms for campus speakers and other visitors, during regular school hours. Visitors are welcome to enjoy the architecture and artwork of the Healing Arts Center, but are asked to remember that it is a classroom building and a degree of quiet is required.

Overlooking the Samford campus, atop Shades Mountain at the intersection of U.S. 31 and Shades Crest Road, is Temple Sibyl. Once the structure graced the grounds of the home of former Birmingham mayor George Ward.

Ward, it is said, was visiting Italy when he saw the ruins of what historians say was the Temple of Vesta, the Roman goddess of fire and the hearth. Fascinated by the Roman culture, Ward adopted the plan of the Temple for his home. Ward called the home he built in 1924 "the Temple of Vesta" and in so doing, also named the Birmingham suburb of Vestavia.

Three years after he built the home, he constructed the gazebo - which served as an entrance to a bird sanctuary on the Ward estate - and called it the Temple of Sibyl.

Ward, so the story goes, believed it to be a reproduction of the temple in  Tivoli, Italy. Of late, there has been much discussion about whether the structure actually does reproduce that temple or is instead a reproduction of the temple of Vesta. The question arose when a group of students at a Birmingham high school questioned whether the original Temple of Sibyl was round. Their contention was that the Temple of Vesta in Rome was the round structure and the Temple of Sibyl in Tivoli was rectangular.

The question of whether or not Ward misnamed his temple came up long after his death and continues to be a topic for discussion among Birminghamians today. What is known is that Ward was so "into" his Roman lifestyle that he made his servants wear togas and gave them and his dogs Roman names.

When Ward died in 1940, the home with its temple and gazebo began to crumble. In 1948, it was bought and converted into a restaurant and tourist attraction. Ten years later, it was bought by a Baptist church, which used it for worship services for about 10 more years. When the church built a new sanctuary, the home was torn down, but the gazebo was spared. It was moved to its present site in 1973.

Today, the restored gazebo sits surrounded by a landscaped garden. Off-highway parking gives visitors access to Temple Sibyl, its garden and picnic areas. There is no admission charge.

MISS LIBERTY
South of Temple Sibyl, U.S. 31 intersects with I-459, Birmingham's southern bypass loop. Traveling north on 459 will take you to Liberty Park. The office park takes its name from the replica of the Statue of Liberty that stands in

the middle of a landscaped area at the entrance to where the office buildings are being developed.

For 30 years, Miss Liberty imposed her rather hefty presence between Vulcan and Electra as she sat atop the Liberty National Life Insurance Company office building on Birmingham's Southside.

She came into being in 1952, when Frank P. Samford Sr., then president of the insurance firm, decided to bring the company's corporate symbol "to life" with a copy of the Statue of Liberty. He commissioned Lee and Archer Lawrie, a father and son team, to sculpt the replica. Four years later, the job was finished.

The Lawries had created a duplicate of the statue, done to scale and exactly one-fifth the size of the original. Unfortunately, even at one-fifth the size of her big sister, Miss Liberty was too large to be cast at a U.S. foundry for a price the company was willing to pay. Liberty National officials located the foundry in France that had cast the only other known large replica of the Statue of Liberty (That one overlooks the Seine in Paris now.) and the Lawries model went to France in 1956.

Two years later, the finished Miss Liberty came to New Orleans from France and then was brought to Birmingham on railroad cars. That journey took a while because the crates containing pieces of Miss Liberty were so large the train could travel at only 25 miles per hour and only in the daytime.

Once it got to the city, the statue - 31 feet tall and weighing 10 tons - was reassembled and decked out in red, white and blue bunting for the big day when she would be placed on top of the building that would be her new home. On September 13, 1958, a crane lifted her into place.

On December 3, 1988, cranes lifted her down from that perch and she was placed temporarily in a vacant lot until she could undergo renovation and be taken to her new location, where she oversees the traffic passing by at a much quicker pace than that she watched over downtown. The view of the statue is particularly interesting at night when floodlights silhouette Miss Liberty against the night sky.

A few miles west of Liberty Park on I-459 is the exit that leads to Hoover Metropolitan Stadium - the "Hoover Met" or just "The Met" to those who go there regularly. It is here that the Birmingham Barons play baseball, beginning in April and lasting until sometime in September, the exact finishing date depending on whether or not the team has made it to the championships. In 1990, the Barons were the Division AA affiliate of the Chicago White Sox. That may or may not be true in 1991 and following years. The team's contract with the White Sox is up for re-negotiation and Barons' owners hope to move the team up to AAA status.

No matter what the Big League affiliation of the Barons or what division the team plays in, the team has proved time and again that it has a "won't die" attitude and always is good for an exciting evening at the ballpark.

The Barons came to their new home at The Met in 1988 and the new facility provides a great backdrop for the game. No matter what boasts you hear from other cities, The Met is one of the best baseball facilities in the Southeast. There are few, if any, bad seats in the house and even the cheap seats provide a good view of the spitting, chewing, scratching and solid hitting and pitching that goes on at The Met.

Even if you're in town when the Barons aren't playing, drive by and see The Met. You don't want to pass up an opportunity to visit the place where baseball legend-to-be Frank Thomas got his call "up to The Bigs."

The old home of the Barons was Rickwood Field, on the west side of Birmingham. When the Barons played there, they bragged that Rickwood was the second oldest professional ballpark in the country. And with the demise of the original Comisky Park, Rickwood has moved up in status to become the oldest park still standing.

Even though the glory of the park has faded and the Barons have left, drive by the field at 1137 Second Avenue West, just to say you've seen it.

Then begin your exploration of the western part of Birmingham.

You Choose: Roll Tide or War Eagle

In Alabama, there are some things you just don't make jokes about. The Alabama-Auburn football game is one of them. Marriages between Alabama fans and Auburn fans are considered to be mixed marriages and not given much of a chance of survival.

For many years, the sacred ground upon which this most important of all games was played was Legion Field in Birmingham. For the confused - the University of Alabama is in Tuscaloosa, Auburn University is in Auburn. There probably are more Alabama and Auburn fans in Birmingham than in either of the other two cities. So the teams, taking turns being the home team, would make the pilgrimage yearly to clash on the grass - and in recent years artificial turf - of Legion Field, where the fans would be divided half for the Tide and half for the Tigers.

The Iron Bowl ended in 1988, when it became a true "home and home" game. In 1989, for the first time, Alabama traveled to Jordan-Hare Stadium in Auburn for the game. In 1990, the game returned to Legion Field and the 1991 game also is to be played there. Then the present contract is up and the future of where the game will be played will be decided when a new contract is signed.

Even if the Iron Bowl no longer exists or if you don't come to Birmingham during college football season, Legion Field is a "drive by must see." Heisman Trophy winners have played on this field, Bear Bryant won his 315th game there, marriages have been proposed there during games and some of the greatest rivalries of all times have been fought to the finish between the hash marks.

Alabama and Auburn are not the only two schools which play football games at Legion Field. High school teams tee it up there most weekends, and the stadium also is home to other special college football games. The All-Amerian Bowl also was played at Legion Field.

A few blocks west of Legion Field on Eighth Avenue West is Birmingham-

---

Birmingham: The Heart of Dixie   **121**

Southern College, a Methodist liberal arts college. On the campus is Robert R. Meyer Planetarium, where changing programs seem to bring the stars within reach. Each year, a special Christmas show examines the story of "The Star of Bethlehem." Other shows about the stars and planets are presented throughout the year.

Reserved shows are offered at the planetarium on weekdays at 9, 10 and 11 a.m. Public shows, which don't require reservations, begin at 2 p.m. on the first and third Saturdays and Sundays each month. Visitors should arrive 30 minutes before showtime since late arrivers are not admitted. Admission is $2 for adults and $1 for students and senior citizens.

THE ARLINGTON HOME

Leaving Birmingham-Southern, take Arkadelphia Road south until it intersects with Cotton Avenue. Travel east on Cotton until you reach Arlington Antebellum Home and Gardens, the area's only remaining antebellum home. This two-story, Greek Revival mansion, completed in 1842, is authentically furnished with period pieces, some dating back 200 years.

Unlike antebellum homes that were destroyed during the Civil War, this one survived because it was used as headquarters for Union officers.

Arlington, which predates the city of Birmingham by more than 20 years, is another spot in Birmingham where you might find yourself an impromptu guest at a wedding. The gracious home is a favorite of local brides and in the spring and summer, outdoor weddings are set in the surrounding gardens.

The home is open Tuesday through Saturday from 10 a.m. to 4 p.m. and Sunday from 1 to 4 p.m. Admission is $3 for adults and $2 for children ages 6 to 18. Children under 6 are admitted free.

TUXEDO JUNCTION

Music lovers can't leave Birmingham without making a pilgrimage to "Tuxedo Junction." Leaving Arlington, go west on Eighth Avenue West until in becomes Bush Boulevard. Continue west on Bush until it intersects with Ensley Avenue. Take Ensley Avenue North to its intersection with Twentieth Street and your at "The Junction."

The junction is at the site of what once was a streetcar crossing of the Ensley-Fairfield line in the Tuxedo Park residential area. At the junction is the Nixon Building (1728 Twentieth Street), a two-story brick structure, built in 1922, which housed offices on the bottom floor and a second floor dance hall, once the social center for the city's Black community.

Much of the action in the area went on at Tuxedo Park, a nearby amusement park where Hawkins and his music became popular with the area's residents.

Hawkins' popular tune was written as a filler for the flip side of a recording of Sammy Lowe's "Gin Mill Special" which Hawkins and his band had done for RCA's Bluebird label. The tune was one the band used as a sign-off during its performances.

The title for the then-unnamed tune was suggested by the band's valet.

Words were added in the mid-40s and "Tuxedo Junction" became a Big Band staple. Benny Goodman, Glenn Miller and Gene Krupa all recorded versions of the song, which stayed on the Top Ten list for years.

Don't think that just because you've seen Birmingham's Westside, you've seen all there is to see in the city. The eastern part of Birmingham holds some treats as well.

The last undeveloped remnant of the Red Mountain Ridge, Ruffner Mountain Nature Center, covers 538 acres east of downtown Birmingham and provides a nature oasis in the middle of modern day hustle and bustle. The Visitors Center at Ruffner gives an overview of the kinds of things you'll see as you hike the wooded area and go atop rocky outcroppings along the trails.

But it is the trails that make a visit to Ruffner worthwhile. Winding throughout the Nature Center land, the more than seven miles of hiking paths offer glimpses of plants, animals, unusual geologic formations and springs. Trails vary in length from 1/2 mile to five miles and have benches for resting placed strategically along the way. The places where the trails top the mountain offer incredible views of the surrounding area.

The Nature Center, at 1214 81st Street South, is open Tuesday through Saturday from 9 a.m. to 5 p.m. and Sunday from 1 to 5 p.m. There is no admission charge.

Throughout the year, Ruffner offers special education programs and such activities as "Night Hikes." There usually is a small charge for these events, but they are well worth the expense.

SOUTHERN MUSEUM OF FLIGHT

When you leave Ruffner Mountain, head north toward the Birmingham Airport. Tucked away just east of that facility is the Southern Museum of Flight. As the planes from the airport roar overhead, visitors to the museum get a close-up look at the magic of flight.

Pieces of history from the more than eight decades of flight in the Southeast are on display here. In addition, there are mementos of the Red Baron's encounter with Canadian pilot Roy Brown during World War I, uniforms of military and commercial pilots and an extensive reference library on aviation.

There are some model airplanes of the size you might put together and store on your trophy shelf, but most of the models you'll see are life-size, either replicas or the real thing. Among the planes on display are replicas of monoplanes from the 1900s, a 1912 Curtis Pusher and one of Delta's first planes, built originally to be used as a crop duster. You'll also see a World War II Link trainer, used to teach pilots to "fly blind."

You can see the museum on a self-guided expedition or guided tours are available with reservations. Southern Museum of Flight is open Tuesday through Saturday from 9 a.m. to 5 p.m. and Sunday from 1 to 5 p.m. Admission is $2 for adults and $1 for students. There is no charge for preschoolers.

It's a little tricky to find the museum, so the Greater Birmingham Convention and Visitors Bureau suggests this route: Turn right off Airport Highway onto 37th Avenue. Turn left on 65th Street, then right on 43rd Avenue and follow the green "Southern Museum of Flight" signs and turn left onto 73rd Street North. The museum is on the right.

If you are a fan of horse racing, check on the status of the Birmingham Race Course while you're in the city. A truly magnificent facility, the course unfortunately has been plagued with financial problems since its birth a few years ago. In late 1990, the Racing Commission still was trying to make a decision as to whether or not there would be a 1991 racing season.

If the horses are running, its worth a trip to the Race Course.

Obviously, unless you plan to spend a lot of time in Birmingham, you're not going to be able to see even all the things that lie within 20 minutes of downtown.

You can get a good overview in a couple of ways, however. One is to see the city's historic districts.

They include:

• **Anderson Place**, roughly bounded by 14th and 16th Avenues South and 15th and 18th Streets. Includes large turn-of-the-century residences.

• **Cullom Street/12th Street South**, roughly bounded by 11th and 16th Avenues South and 13th and Cullom Streets. Early residences that date from 1902 to 1920.

• **Fourth Avenue**, 1500-1700 blocks of Fourth Avenue North. In the 1910s and 1920s, early Black-owned businesses concentrated here. District includes the Pythian and Masonic Temple Buildings and Carver Theater, which is being renovated as a live venue theater.

• **Glen Iris Park**, 40 acres on Birmingham's Southside. First Birmingham neighborhood designed by noted national land planner, Samuel Parson Jr. of Boston.

• **Phelan Park**, bounded by 13th Place to 16th Street South and 13th to 16th Avenue South. Includes more than 100 early 20th century residences.

• **Pratt City Carline District**, Pratt City. Sixty-one properties along historic streetcar line passing through the city's oldest mining boomtown.

• **Roebuck Terrace**, Roebuck, just west of Roebuck Golf Course. About 65 country estates and tiny bungalows.

• **Smithfield**, bounded by Eighth Avenue and Fourth Terrace North and First and Sixth Avenues West. Includes more than 400 modest cottages and large residences dating from the 1890s through the 1920s and representing the city's earliest and most substantial concentration of black, middle-class homes. Also has fine examples of the work of black architect Wallace A. Rayfield.

• **Joseph Riley Smith (College Hills)**, 300 and 400 blocks of Tenth Avenue West and 100 to 400 blocks of Ninth Court West. Sixty-four residences, including seven associated with the planter-physician-developer after whom it is named.

RED MOUNTAIN AND THE ARTS

Another way to see the best of Birmingham is to take a drive along the crest of Red Mountain. The city especially is beautiful at night from the streets that cut across the top of the mountain. You'll find one of these by taking Arlington Avenue off Highland Avenue. Arlington meets Argyle at Key Circle and you can take Argyle to Stratford, which overlooks the city. You won't be the first person to discover this spectacular view of the city, however. In fact, a family that lives in one of the houses along Stratford likes to say they would indeed be rich if they had a nickel for every young bride who tells them, "I got my engagement ring right there across from your house."

You'll find as you make your way around Birmingham that there are dozens of parks scattered throughout the city. They range from parks with swimming pools and golf courses (George Ward Park, for example) to those with picnic tables, swings and slides (Brother Bryan Park on Southside is one of these) to parks with nothing more than a grassy spot beside the road. On Altamont Road you'll find one of those grassy stops. This particular one has a cannon to climb on and a wonderful view of the city.

Arts are a big part of the Birmingham entertainment scene. There are at least a half-dozen legitimate theaters in the city, including Town and Gown Theatre, Birmingham Festival Theatre and Terrific New Theatre.

Colleges in the area - UAB, Samford and Birmingham-Southern among them - offer theatrical productions by their drama departments. In fact, these college productions are done in some of the most sophisticated theater structures in Birmingham. 'Southern's theater, for example, had the first turntable stage in the nation.

In recent years, there has been a significant growth of professional theater in Birmingham. Birmingham Children's Theatre presents plays and musicals aimed at kindergartners through young adults. Just because they are for children does not mean that the acting, plays, scenery and productions are of anything but top quality. In fact, BCT's productions travel throughout the United States.

For more than a decade, Birmingham's summers have been filled with music, thanks to Summerfest. Each year three musicals are presented. Many feature stars brought in for the shows, but all feature a young and enthusiastic ensemble of actors, often getting their first professional experience. Among those who've danced and sung in Summerfest are Broadway star Rebecca Luker and "Saturday Night Live" star Victoria Jackson. Performances are at Boutwell Auditorium, where dining is available along with the show.

Joining the professional theater scene is Birmingham Repertory Theater, which has ambitious plans for the future. It has presented such interesting plays as the Mystery of Irma Vep. At present, it is using existing theater buildings to present its productions, but plans call for a $4 million renovation of the Lyric Theatre at the corner of Third Avenue North and 19th Street

---

Birmingham: The Heart of Dixie

downtown. This magnificent structure once was Birmingham's best vaude-ville house and the acoustics and sight lines are reputed to be virtually perfect.

When it is restored to its former glory, it will join with the Alabama Theatre, a classic movie palace complete with a mighty Wurlitzer organ, and the Carver Theater in giving Birmingham a new theater district.

In the meantime, south of Birmingham in Hoover, a unique and lavish entertainment facility opened in December 1990. Called Carnegie's, it features a dinner theater presenting popular plays and musicals. But it's more than that. It's also a place where you can go see intimate, unusual plays, have a meal while you're serenaded by singing waiters, participate in a mystery play or dine and dance - all under one roof.

You might not think you'd come to Birmingham just to see a high school play, but you will when the high school is the Alabama School of Fine Arts. ASFA is the nation's only state-supported secondary school for students with special artistic talents. And the quality of the theatrical productions here reflects the talent and dedication of those students.

In addition to its Theater Arts Department, ASFA also has departments of Creative Writing, Dance, Music and Visual Arts. Student dance and music presentations, readings and art exhibits all are worth a trip to Birmingham. The same kind of drive that makes theater presentations at ASFA superior is present in the other departments and shows through in the performances.

Seeing any student presentation at ASFA may just give you the chance to say, "I saw him when he was just a high school student" about future Pulitzer Prize winners, nationally known dancers, Tony Award winning actors or reknowned painters and sculptors.

In addition to the Alabama Symphony Orchestra and the Birmingham Youth Symphony, musical presentations are given regularly by such groups as Birmingham Opera Theater, Birmingham Heritage Jazz Band, Birmingham Boys Choir, Birmingham Concert Chorale, Red Mountain Chamber Orchestra, UAB Super Jazz Band, Samford's A Capella Choir and Birmingham-Southern's Hilltop Singers.

The State of Alabama Ballet, Southern Danceworks, Ballet UAB and the Birmingham-Southern Dancers are among the dance groups that perform regular in Birmingham.

On any given day or night in Birmingham, you probably can find many fine arts performances that you'd like to attend. Choosing just one is the problem.

ART AND MORE ART

The Birmingham Museum of Art is the city's largest storehouse of paintings, sculptures and other works of art. But it's by no means the only place in Birmingham to see art. There are a number of small, private galleries scattered throughout the city. And in addition to those, you'll find art galleries in hospitals, banks and at least one grocery store (Vincent's Market in Brookwood Village).

Birmingham's night life also includes a number of clubs offering different types of entertainment - from music to comedy. The Comedy Club, on Green Springs Highway, plays host to first-rate stand-up comedians. The stage and technical facilities at The Comedy Club are state-of-the-art. Owner Bruce Ayers says no other comedy club in the country has all the extras his does. The late Waylon Flowers and his irreverent puppet Madam appeared often at The Comedy Club. Among the other celebrities who have had audiences rolling in the Comedy Club aisles are Sinbad, Marsha Warfield, Elayne Boosler, Wil Shriner and Willie Tyler and Lester.

The Comedy Club, which offers dinner along with the guffaws, has performances nightly Tuesday through Saturday. There are two shows on Friday night and three on Saturday. A recent addition to The Comedy Club's offerings is the Kids Comedy Club, once-a-month afternoon performances of children's classic plays.

Birmingham once had a staple diet of cabaret comedy in a group called "Wit's Other End." Made up of five local performers, "Wit's" had audiences in stitches every weekend for a number of years. "Wit's" specialized in music and satire - particularly on politics, religion and Southern life.

The group broke up and only appeared sporadically for a while. Then they sort of disappeared from the scene. In late 1990, however, "Wit's" was regrouping, replacing two members who had left the comedy fivesome with new local talent. The new "Wit's Other End" will make appearances in various nightspots around town now and then. When you're in Birmingham, it's worth checking a local newspaper to see if you can catch one of their acts.

Music also is a part of Birmingham's night scene. There are dozens and dozens of clubs where jazz, rock, pop, rap and country are played. Among the best known and "hottest" spots in town are Grundy's Music Room, 1924 Fourth Avenue North (for Jazz), Louie Louie and Flamingo, both on Highland Avenue (for rock). Writer's Night at Flamingo gives you a chance to hear songwriters performing their own works.

The Nick, at 2514 19th Avenue South, looks a little strange from the outside. But The Nick is legendary for its introduction of new music that quickly becomes hot.

So your nights in Birmingham will be busy and your days filled with seeing the sights. You'll probably like Birmingham so well, you'll want to take home a souvenir. You'll find lots of those.

SHOPPING AROUND

There's a funny T-shirt that reads, "Whoever said money can't buy happiness just doesn't know where to shop." In Birmingham, people say, "Whoever says there's no place to shop in Birmingham just isn't looking."

The single largest shopping complex in the city is the Riverchase Galleria which has more than 200 stores and specialty shops. The Galleria complex is anchored at one end by the Wynfrey Hotel and at the other by an office tower.

Hoover's Riverchase Galleria is one place to shop 'til you drop around Birmingham

Other malls in Birmingham include Brookwood Village, Century Plaza, Eastwood Mall and Western Hills Mall, all recently renovated and spruced up for a move into the 1990s.

On Into Bessemer

Before the Birmingham area was known for its sports or its medical facilities, it was known for its iron and steel industry. Many of the cities that grew up around Birmingham proper were born because of the area's industrial heritage. Bessemer, about 14 miles southwest of Birmingham, was founded in 1887 by Henry F. DeBardeleben and named after Sir Henry Bessemer, who also lent his name to the steel-making process he invented.

The few furnaces that gave the city of Bessemer birth quickly became many furnaces and the community grew along with the industry. By the 1930s, Bessemer ranked second only to Birmingham as a center for heavy industry, producing iron, steel, cast-iron pipe, steel railway cars, explosives, fertilizer and building materials.

Today Bessemer still is a town dominated by industry. And it is a town that remembers its past.

The Bessemer Hall of History Museum, housed in the city's 1916 Southern Railway Depot, offers exhibits showing pioneer life in Jefferson County. Photographs and articles from the early days of the Bessemer area are displayed along with artifacts from nearby Indian mounds. The museum, at Alabama Avenue and 19th street in Bessemer, is open Tuesday through Saturday from 10 a.m. to 4:30 p.m.

Even before there was a Bessemer, there were settlers in western Jones Valley. Among them were men who would play prominent roles in founding the new city. A number of their houses have been preserved and are available for visitors to tour.

To get to the McAdory, Owen and Sadler Homes from the Hall of History, go north on 19th Street until you reach U.S. 11. Take U.S. 11 West to where it intersects with Highway 150. Take 150 South to Eastern Valley Road. Take Eastern Valley Road west.

About 1.5 miles down Eastern Valley Road is the McAdory House. Built in 1840 by Thomas McAdory, this dog-trot cabin was the birthplace of Thomas' son Robert, who became Bessemer's first mayor, and his grandson, Thomas M. Owen, who founded the Alabama State Department of Archives and History. Two more miles down Eastern Valley is the Owen Home.

Thomas H. Owen built what now is the rear portion of this house in 1833 for his 17-year-old bride. As his finances grew, so did the house. About five years later, he enlarged the home into the two-story structure that stands today.

Continue down Eastern Valley for another 2.5 miles to find the Sadler Home. Part of this home was built about 1818 by John Loveless, whose widow sold the property to Isaac Sadler. Sadler added to the house, completing the present structure - a two-story home with a dog-trot - in 1830. The house is furnished with several pieces original to the family and there is a hand-operated loom on display in one of the bedrooms.

The grounds of these three houses are open daily and there is no admission charge. The homes may be toured by appointment. There is a charge for these tours. You can make arrangements for one by calling the Bessemer Convention and Visitors Bureau.

TANNEHILL HISTORICAL STATE PARK

About 5 miles west of the Sadler Home, in a small triangle where Jefferson, Bibb and Tuscaloosa Counties meet, is Tannehill Historical State Park, the site of the Tannehill Furnaces. Iron first was manufactured at Tannehill in 1830, when Tannehill Ironworks, tucked away in the backhills of Roupes Valley, began as just a small forge. The ironworks had been established to manufacture kitchen utensils, but before the history of iron-making at the site was completed the furnaces and forges would be used to create the implements of war. The first charcoal blast furnaces was added in 1850 under the supervision of noted ironmaster Moses Stroup. Before long, Tannehill was a community in itself. The area also had a blacksmith shop, a grist mill, a saw mill, a tannery and living quarters for the workers.

The ironworks themselves expanded again in 1863, when two more furnaces were added by the Confederate government. The furnaces of Tannehill became major suppliers for the Confederate Army.

Each day, more than 20 tons of pig iron were produced in the furnaces and used to make cannon balls, gun barrels and other munitions. Iron ingots were shipped from Tannehill by rail to the Selma Arsenal for conversion into naval plate for warships.

The centerpieces of the Tannehill Ironworks were Furnace No. 1 and the Double Furnaces. Standing side by side on the banks of a creek, the furnaces were joined to a nearby cliff by wooden bridges. Across those bridges came the iron ore, limestone and charcoal used to feed the furnaces.

Twenty-four hours a day, seven days a week, the firebreathing giants consumed the raw materials, heated them to more than 2,000 degrees and reduced them to molten metal. The hot, glowing liquid flowed through tap holes and into the molds that would give them their finished shape.

The Confederate Army knew how much it depended on the iron that flowed from Tannehill's furnaces. Unfortunately, the Union forces knew the value of Tannehill's products as well. In March, 1865, Union troops moved toward the Confederacy's industrial heart.

Shortly after daybreak on March 31, 1865, three companies of the Eighth Iowa Cavalry - led by Captain William A. Sutherland - swooped down upon Tannehill. The workers there, forewarned of the attack, had fled to the surrounding woods. When the Union soldiers arrived, two of the furnaces were in blast. The metal that was molten on that day more than 100 years ago still lies, solidified now, in the bottoms of the furnaces.

In a matter of moments after the troops reached Tannehill, the ironworks were in flames. Almost everything, including the slave quarters, was gutted by the fire. Furnace No. 1 and the Double Furnace were spared, but left useless by the loss of their support facilities.

Two days later, the Selma Arsenal fell to Union forces and the industry that fed the Confederate forces was still. A week later, the Confederacy surrendered to the Union forces.

The furnaces of Tannehill sat abandoned for about a century. In 1969, the Alabama Legislature established Tannehill State Park as a state memorial to the history of iron and steel manufacturing in Alabama.

Today, more than a quarter of a million visitors come to Tannehill Historical State Park - a 1,500-acre historical complex.

The park, along the Cahaba River, is built around the reconstructed furnaces and the furnace yards where iron rolled from the cast sheds. Built in three main sections, the park is interlaced with historic trails including the 1815 Bucksville-to-Montevallo Stage Coach Road. Cool streams, lined with wildflowers and frequented by wildlife, roll along through the woods.

Farm life in early Alabama is re-created at the Tannehill Farm, which includes a working blacksmith shop, a sorghum mill, the 1850 Williams House and a barn dating to 1822 - the oldest structure in the park.

Also at the farm is John Wesley Hall's Mill, a grist mill and cotton gin operation. Hall's Mill operated from 1867 to 1931 on the banks of Mill Creek (one of the creeks flowing through Tannehill Park). This second generation mill replaced the original structure, which operated on Mud Creek above the iron furnaces before the Civil War. That original mill was a victim of the Union forces' raid on Tannehill.

The Hall's Mill that stands today was completely restored in the late 1970s and continues to turn out corn meal for park visitors.

More than 40 restored structures from Alabama's earliest days form another section of Tannehill Park. A school, a post office, a church and a number of houses take visitors back in history to see demonstrations of such skills as quilting, printing and woodcarving. At the old-fashioned photography shop, you can pose in Civil War style garments to have your picture snapped with an 1840s camera. School children who visit the park on field trips spend part of the day in the schoolhouse under the watchful eye of a guide dressed as the typical school marm.

The crowning glory of Tannehill Park may be the Iron and Steel Museum of Alabama. It contains the South's largest collection of iron-works artifacts. Exhibits and photographs in the museum trace the history of the area from time of the Creek Indians—who used the iron they found there for arrowheads—to the day the Union troops arrived at Tannehill. The museum also includes the Walter B. Jones Center for Industrial Archaeology and two other educational centers.

Not far from the museum are the furnaces that started it all, restored now to their original condition. In 1976, Furnace No. 1 roared back to life, put back into 3,100-degree blast. Within a week, more than two tons of pig iron had been produced there. Most of that iron went into the making of a full-size Confederate field cannon and souvenir ingots. The restorations at Tannehill represent the first time a Civil War-era ironworks has ever been put back on blast after lying silent for more than a century.

Recent archaeological excavations at the park revealed what is believed to be the original forge at Tannehill, built in 1830. During that excavation, archaeologists also found a Civil War cannonball, a large machinery wheel, an anvil bottom and an 1842 dime.

Tannehill Park is open daily from 7 a.m. to sundown. Admission is $1 for adults and $.50 for children 6 to 17. There is no charge for preschoolers.

If you want to spend more than one day at Tannehill, there are campsites equipped with water and electrical hook-ups.

OAK MOUNTAIN

Spreading over almost 10,000 acres about 15 miles south of Birmingham and about 20 miles southeast of Bessemer, Oak Mountain State Park in Shelby County is the largest in Alabama's park system.

Open year-round, it has plenty of room for fishing, boating, swimming, hiking, horseback riding and cycling. Set among pine tree covered ridges and lush valleys, the park encompasses Peavine Falls and two lakes. There also are a golf course, tennis courts and spots for picnicking scattered throughout the park.

A demonstration farm at Oak Mountain lets children get close-up looks at horses, pigs, chickens, turkeys and goats.

For overnight visits, there are more than 70 primitive and improved camping sites as well as 10 family cabins. Fees for camping range from $3

---

to $7 for primitive camping and $7.50 to $10 for improved camping. Cabin rental fees are from $45 to $70.

Admission to the park is $1 per person, which includes access to swimming, fishing, boat launch and the demonstration farm. Golf green fees are $13 for 18 holes, $8 for 9. The $1 day-use permit must be purchased by all park visitors 6 years old or older except overnight campers or cabin guests.

On the grounds at Oak Mountain State Park is the Alabama Wildlife Center. Nestled on 10 acres, the center treats injured wild birds and mammals and, if possible, releases them back into the wild.

Begun in 1977, the Nature Center was sort of a "backyard operation," with the animals being cared for in the homes of volunteers. In 1982, the manager of Oak Mountain State Park offered to house permanently some of the non-releasable birds of prey as part of the park's education program.

From that arrangement came a permanent home for the Wildlife Center. A few years later came the Center's Treetop Nature Trail, an elevated boardwalk flanked by cages on stilts. Walking along the trail is a little like journeying by so many tree houses, each inhabited by one to three birds.

The birds who live here each suffered an injury that left it unable to survive in the wild. But the elevation of the Treetop Trail allows the birds to feel at home - high above the ground. Observation windows along the trail are placed so that adults, visitors in wheelchairs and children have viewing spots that are just the right heights.

Among the birds living here is an albino barred owl, an extremely rare bird, found injured along a railroad track.

The Treetop trail spans a small valley and connects to the Eagle Hiking Trail. This 1/3-mile long trail leads up a ridge to the Wildlife Center itself.

At the Center, the "hospital" is divided into two sections, one for injured birds and the other - "The Fur Side" - for injured mammals. Birds treated here have ranged from golden eagles to blue jays. Mammal patients have included raccoons, foxes, squirrels, beaver and deer.

Reports on the animals' injuries and treatments are posted beside one-way observation windows which allow guests to see what's going on inside without disturbing the animals.

Limiting the exposure of the animals to their human guests is essential if they are to be released into the wild after their recuperation.

Public tours of the Wildlife Center are conducted each Saturday from 10 a.m. to 4 p.m. Admission to the center is free, however you do have to pay the admission fee to Oak Mountain in order to reach the center.

Deeper Into Shelby County

When you leave Oak Mountain, go south on I-65 to the Columbiana exit and visit that city, the county seat of Shelby County. One thing you'll want to be sure to see is the Old Courthouse Building there.

Built in 1854, it recently has been saved from a scheduled demolition and restored by the Shelby County Historical Society. In the museum they've created there, are the archives and records from Shelby County's past.

Because of the wills and property records at the museum, there is a constant stream of visitors who are looking for clues to their family histories. A large number of these people come from Texas to Columbiana to do their research. A look at old newspapers in the museum shows why.

"Right after the Civil War, trainloads of people left Alabama for Texas to find their fortune," says one of the museum employees. "Now their descendants are coming back to find their roots."

Montevallo is about seven miles southwest of Columbiana. There, you'll find the University of Montevallo.

On campus at the school are a number of historic structures. Among them is King House, built in 1823, which now is used as housing for visiting lecturers and for receptions. Near King House is the King Family Cemetery.

Reynolds Hall, built in 1851, was used as a Confederate hospital during the Civil War. Today it houses some administration offices as well as the college theater and the Departments of Speech and Drama.

Flowerhill, the president's home, is worth a drive-by look as well. It first was occupied in 1929.

You'll find the entire Montevallo campus an inviting place to stroll. The master plan was designed by the Olmstead Brothers, landscape architects whose other works include New York's Central Park, Jackson Park in Chicago and the grounds at Biltmore (the Vanderbilt estate).

In the city of Montevallo, see the Montevallo First United Methodist Church, which was founded in 1818 by Rev. Ebenezer Hearn. (Hearn also founded Walker United Methodist Church in Birmingham the same year.)

In April, 1818, the Methodist Board of Nashville, Tennessee, sent Hearn - a minister and ex-Indian fighter - to organize churches in what would become Alabama. The church in Montevallo was established before the city was there. At the time, it was a settlement called Wilson Hill.

The congregation built its first church building in 1820. That structure burned in 1847. From that time until 1855, church members met in the town's Masonic Hall. After that, the congregation moved into a newly constructed church building, which also burned.

Once again, the church was rebuilt. That structure was lost to a cyclone in 1874. One more time, the congregation rallied to raise funds and rebuild the church. It moved into the red brick building it now occupies in 1910.

Directly across from the University of Montevallo, the church has long enjoyed close ties with the school, which began as Alabama Girls' Training School in 1896. In fact, 12 of the school's presidents have been members of First United Methodist.

Also in Montevallo is Orr Park. The park has all the usual things - a playground, picnic sites and ballfields - and it has a waterfall and creek as well. Residents say it is one of the loveliest parks they've seen and it makes a wonderful getaway for the whole family.

BIBB COUNTY'S HISTORY

Southeast of Montevallo, just into Bibb County are the Brierfield Ironworks. Brierfield, privately owned until 1990, now is state property and, along with Tannehill Park, forms a multi-site state historic park system whose emphasis is Alabama's early iron industry.

Brierfield Ironworks Park is on the site of Bibb Furnace, a Civil War iron-producing facility. From this furnace came most of the metal for Confederate naval plate and heavy cannons.

Even after the war, the furnace operated. The fires that fueled it were put out on Christmas Eve, 1894, when its owners went bankrupt.

Today, the park has a country store, picnic area and hiking trails. Swimming and cycling also are available here and pets are permitted if they are kept on leashes. The park is open from daylight to dusk daily. Admission charge is $.50 for adults and $.25 for children 7-18. Children 6 and under are admitted free. You drop your admission fee into an "honor box" at the park gates.

There are improved and primitive camp sites at Brierfield, on Alabama 25 eight miles from Montevallo. Fees are charged for use of the campsites.

A little farther down Alabama 25 is Lake Payne Recreation Area. There are more than 80 improved camping sites (Fees are charged for use of the camp sites.) as well as picnic tables and barbecue grills. There are facilities for swimming, fishing and hiking. Pets are permitted if kept on leashes. Boating is permitted at Lake Payne, but only in non-power boats.

Lake Payne is in Talladega National Forest and the best picnicking here can be found at Cahaba Mountain, where the tableside view is a sweeping look at the countryside.

Peachy Chilton County

Turning southeast from Lake Payne and traveling down U.S. 82 East, you come to where this road intersects with Alabama 22. About three miles west on Alabama 22 is the town of Stanton.

Here, you'll find the Ebenezer Baptist Church, where a fierce battle raged as Confederate Cavalry troops attempted to stop the Union assault on the arsenal at Selma. A historical marker at the church dates it to April 1865.

Turning east on Alabama 22 from Stanton, you come to Clanton, county seat of Chilton County. You don't leave Chilton County without trying some of the peaches and pecans grown there.

Along I-65 near Clanton are a number of places to stop and buy - and eat - peaches and pecans. These are not wooden sheds out in the middle of fields. These are air conditioned facilities with homemade ice cream and cake to top with freshly picked peaches. The plan for eating your way through Chilton County is to stop at these places, buy something to eat there and something to take home with you.

Down U.S. 31 South from Clanton is Mountain Creek, a city that sits on the Chilton/Autauga County Line. Near here, there once was a settlement called Old Soldiers Home.

At the turn of the century, this small village was home to former soldiers - Confederate veterans who had served the South well, but who found themselves penniless after the war. This was Alabama's Confederate Veterans' home, established in 1902 and available to any Southern veteran who had no means of support other than the $13 they received each month from the Alabama State Confederate Pension.

The home - really a small village in itself - was started by Jefferson Manley Falkner, a Confederate veteran who donated 80 acres for the facility and spearheaded a drive to raise money for construction. The story goes that Falkner, in his zeal to raise money, enlisted the help of Montgomery's prettiest young ladies to sell tickets to a fund-raising lecture. More than $7,000 was realized from this event.

Money also was raised by selling "memorial logs" to be used in the construction of the home's headquarters building.

Benjamin Bosworth Smith, a Montgomery architect and friend of Falkner, donated the designs for the buildings. Smith chose not to design military-style barracks, a typical design for soldiers' homes, but to construct cottages that would house up to eight people each.

The home complex had its own water and sewage systems, a 25-bed hospital and fire-fighting unit. There were vegetable gardens and a small dairy operation. Often, the veterans would be visited by members of the United Daughters of the Confederacy, who brought gifts and organized ceremonies to mark Confederate Memorial Day each April.

About 100 people lived at the home at any one time and over the almost 40 years that it was in operation, about 650 veterans and their wives lived there.

In 1934, the last veteran living at the home died. Seven widows remained there until October 31, 1939, when the home was closed. The buildings were dismantled and the materials used in the construction of local schools and other structures. Even though there were two cemeteries left at the site of the home, the entire complex was pretty much forgotten for the next 20 years.

In the late 1950s, interest in the home resurfaced as the Centennial of the War Between the States approached. The U.D.C., the Sons of Confederate Veterans and the residents of Chilton County cleaned up the site and began the move to have it recognized as a memorial.

Now the spot that was Old Soldiers Home is Confederate Memorial Park, administered since 1975 by the Alabama Historical Commission. On the grounds are the remnants of the cottages that were home to the Confederate veterans as well as a museum - set in a log cabin - filled with Confederate artifacts such as uniforms, utensils, artillery and money. One of the most unusual things on display is a set of homemade checkers, created from bullets that had been hammered flat.

Visitors can walk two trails, one a nature trail and the other a historic trail that trace the original main road through the village.

Near the picnic pavilion on the grounds are a number of cedar trees. They, too, are a memorial to a Confederate veteran. Among the Rebel expatriates who left Alabama was a Confederate officer and his wife who moved to Rio de Janeiro. The cedars were planted at the home in the early 1900s when the officer's widow wrote from Brazil asking that a tree be planted in her native state in memory of her husband.

And visitors can see the two cemeteries, among the few in the nation that contain only Confederate dead. Though not all the men who died at the home are buried here, there are tombs of more than 200 veterans and 15 wives.

Among the tombstones is that of James Wildcat Carter, an Indian herb and medicine man who preferred to be called "Doctor." He was one of the last veterans to come to the home. On his tombstone is the inscription, "J.W. Carter died March 3, 1927, age 105 years, Chief Scout for General Forrest, Indian, C.S.A."

Also buried here is Charles Driggers, whose gravestone says he was born in 1799 and died in 1912, a lifetime that touched three centuries.

Some of the gravestones tell less about the man, listing only his name and the date he died. Each grave is marked with a footstone that gives the military regiment of the soldier buried there.

In the cemeteries there also is a grave marked "Unknown Soldier, Confederate States Army."

The gates of the park are open daily from dawn to dusk. Museum hours are 8 a.m. to 5 p.m. Admission is free.

GONE FISHIN'

Lake Mitchell and Lay Lake both lie on the Chilton/Coosa county line. The lakes, formed by Lay Dam and Mitchell Dam, provide excellent fishing and boating spots. A 30-minute guided tour of the hydro-electric generating plant is available at Lay Dam daily. There is no charge for the tour.

The Oakachoy Covered Bridge spans the Oakachoy Creek about seven miles northeast of the city of Equality in Coosa County. This modified Queenpost bridge was built in 1916 to give travelers a convenient way to cross the rocky creek and to provide a direct route between the county seats of Coosa and Tallapoosa Counties. To see the bridge, take Alabama 259 North from Equality. Turn left at Mount Sinai Church and follow that road to the bridge.

As long as you're in Coosa County, take the opportunity to see one of the oldest jails in the state. The Old Rockford Rock Jail is one-half block from the County Courthouse in Rockford.

The imposing three-story structure was built of native stones in 1842. Recently, the Coosa County Historical Society has restored the jail and converted it to a museum.

The museum is open from 2 to 4:30 p.m. on the second and fourth Sundays of the month from May to October and there is no admission.

RETURN TO SHELBY COUNTY

The county seat of Shelby County is Columbiana, where you'll find the Smith-Harrison Museum and an extensive collection of George and Martha Washington memorabilia.

The Washington artifact collection here is second in size only to that at

Mount Vernon. Included are portraits, letters, china and silver. Many of these items belonged to a Shelby County resident who was a direct descendant of Martha Washington.

The museum, in the Mildred B. Harrison Library Building on Lester Street, is open from 10 a.m. to 3 p.m. Monday through Friday and there is no admission charge.

Between Columbiana and Calera is the Confederate Cemetery at Shelby Springs. Until recently, this cemetery was forgotten. In fact, it mostly was unknown even to the people who lived in the area.

In the cemetery, there are civilian graves that pre-date the Civil War by as much as 40 years and the graves of 180 Confederate soldiers.

The Confederate veterans buried here died at a makeshift hospital nearby. The Shelby Springs military hospital was established and run by Catholic nuns, members of the Sisters of Mercy. Like all of the military hospitals of the time, this one was filled with soldiers who were wounded and critically ill. Despite the best efforts of the medical staff, many of the patients died. Even if a soldier survived his battlefield injuries, the likelihood of his dying from an infectious disease was great.

In fact, three times as many Confederate soldiers died from diseases as were killed in battle. The Shelby Springs hospital was better than most, but shortages of supplies and the overwhelming numbers of injured took their toll.

When the men died there, their bodies were taken to the burial grounds not far away and, with little ceremony, interred in one of the neatly lined-up graves. Back at the hospital, names of the deceased were recorded, but few of the hospital records were saved.

Nothing remains today of the hospital, but the cemetery recently has been cleaned and restored by the Shelby County Historical Society.

From as far back as the early 1900s, the Society has sponsored efforts to preserve and protect the cemetery. Serious work got underway in 1986, when the society hired a soil scientist to help them pinpoint as exactly as possible the location of graves in the Confederate portion of the cemetery. Several hundred graves were found during this study.

At the beginning of the restoration project, Society members had the names of only 24 men who might be buried in the cemetery. Since then, more than 100 additional names have been found.

One hundred-thirty-four of the graves are marked with white marble stones, put in place by workers from the Shelby County Sheriff's Department, the Shelby County Highway Department and the Historical Society. Only the first 24 names discovered appear on the tombstones. The remaining 110 are marked "Unknown Soldier, C.S.A."

HAIL, MARY

In 1988, a young woman from Yugoslavia came to Birmingham to donate a kidney for her brother's transplant operation and a small community in Shelby County was never the same after that.

Marija Pavlovic, now 24, is one of six Yugoslavian youths who say they began having visions of the Virgin Mary in Medjugorje, Yugoslavia, in 1981. While in Birmingham for her surgery, she recuperated at the home of Terry Colafrancesco near Sterrett. And during her stay, she said she began to have visions of Jesus' mother almost daily.

Overnight, the streets and byways of the Shelby County town were filled with pilgrims, from around the nation - all wanting to visit "The Field," a large grassy area near Colafrancesco's home. Hundreds of cars lined Shelby County 43 and "The Field" ranked as one of the state's top spots for visitors during the winter of 1988. Alabama tourism officials were getting 25 calls a day asking about the site and found themselves mailing out hundreds of Birmingham maps.

With Miss Pavlovic's return to Yugoslavia, the numbers of visitors has lessened, but The Field still sees its share of pilgrims. Across from the field are the offices of Caritas, a non-profit ministry that promotes belief in the visions.

OVER TO ST. CLAIR COUNTY

St. Clair County, just to the east of Jefferson County and northeast of Shelby County, is the latest hot growth spot. For a long time, the growth that resulted from Birmingham's prosperity seemed to be centered in an area south of the city. Now it is spreading to the east.

This county is a rare bird among Alabama counties in that it has two county seats - Ashville and Pell City. If you wonder why, you need only to drive U.S. 231 between the two cities. Once you've crossed Beaver Mountain in an automobile, let your imagination wander to what it must have been like to cross it in a horse and wagon. The mountain runs through the middle of the county and, for a long time, made it very difficult for those who lived in the southern part of the county to get to the courthouse in the northern part. It was simpler to build another courthouse than to move a mountain.

Pell City, the newer of the two county seats, is a town "east of Eden." At least, that's what an Ashville newspaper said in 1844. At the time, there was a St. Clair County town called Eden.

Pell City, which just had been incorporated, would be its eastern neighbor.

The town of Pell City, which started out with less than 40 people now is home to more than 6,000 residents. Fortunately for those who live there, the city cozies up to the Coosa River and the construction of Logan Martin Dam has created an 18,000 acre lake with a 275-mile shoreline for Pell City citizens and visitors to enjoy.

Sailboats, motorboats and pontoons make their way across the lake, which they share with fishermen and water skiing enthusiasts.

In the small community of Cropwell, about three miles southeast of Pell City on U.S. 231, is a monument dedicated to all the men from Pell City who enlisted in the Civil War. Set in an almost triangular park just off Highway 231, the monument site is a quiet place to go and walk or to sit for a while.

ALL ABOUT RAGLAND

About 20 miles northeast of Pell City is the town of Ragland. This community, which now has about 2,000 citizens, came into being as Town Creek in the early 1800s. The name probably was changed in the mid-1800s to honor George Ragland, who operated the town's coal mines.

Coal from the mines in Ragland helped to fuel the Confederate effort during the Civil War. The ore made its way to the arsenal in Selma, where it fed the flames used to turn Bessemer iron into weapons and artillery.

Another industry that came to this city was the Ragland Brick Company. Many structures still standing throughout the state bear the "Ragland Brick Company" mark on their bricks.

And the town gave birth to at least one famous citizen. Rudy York, who holds the major league baseball record for most home runs in one month, was a Ragland native. York's record of 18 runs, set in August, 1937, has stood for more than 50 years.

Though no pre-Civil War homes still stand in the town of Ragland, one of its houses is of some interest. The Van Wie home there is a "Sears and Roebuck" home, purchased from the Sears catalog and shipped to Ragland in pieces for the new owner to assemble.

Northeast of Ragland on Alabama 144 are the remains of Fort Strother, on the banks of the Coosa River. Fort Strother was built and occupied by Andrew Jackson and his troops during Jackson's battle against the Creek Indians in 1813.

Jackson and his men reached the spot where they would build Fort Strother in late 1813. Around the fort, they built a stockade and inside they laid out three parade grounds. Cribs and storage bins were put up to keep the corn and other grains dry and a special storage house for the salt was erected. There was a whiskey storage building, always kept under lock and key. Blacksmith and carpentry shops went up. A sick bay was set up. A safe distance from the fort itself, Jackson's men built an ammunition storage facility.

At times, there were as many as 5,000 men at Fort Strother and at one time there were no more than 150. All that is left of the Fort today are unmarked graves of the many men who died there. A move is underway to preserve the site of the fort and to perhaps build a memorial park there overlooking the Coosa River. A group of Ragland citizens also is working to find out the names of the men who died and are buried at Fort Strother and to have their graves marked at least with a common headstone listing all the names.

Presently, the fort is inaccessible to visitors, but a marker at the start of the road that leads there tells the story of how Jackson and his men lived there.

Just beyond the marker is Henry Neely Dam. Built in 1968 by the Alabama Power Company, the dam impounds a lake that provides fishing, boating and swimming for area residents and visitors.

One of the most beautiful drives in Alabama is the one you can make along St. Clair County Road 26 between Ragland and Ashville. It takes you over

Beaver Mountain and gives you breathtaking views of the valley below. In the fall, there is no better place in the state to see the leaves as they change colors. In the spring and summer, everything around you is green and in the winter, the valley often is shrouded in fog. Any time of year, this 15- to 20-mile drive is like being in a calendar photograph, making worth the time it takes to make it.

GREETINGS FROM ASHVILLE

Ashville is the "official" county seat of St. Clair County and has the traditional white columned courthouse in the middle of the town square. Churches and small stores are clustered around the square, giving the city a hometown feel. But you are as likely to see a video rental shop in one of those stores as you are to see a dry goods emporium.

As you come into Ashville on U.S. 231, you'll see a sign indicating the direction to the "Looney House." Built around 1820, this is considered to be one of the oldest two-story dogtrot homes in the state. The house really is one of two Looney residences built in Beaver Valley. Brothers Jack and Henry Looney came to Alabama in 1813. They were volunteers from Tennessee who served under Andrew Jackson when he had his headquarters at Fort Strother. The men fought at Horseshoe Bend and the Jackson and Looney families had long been friends.

When the brothers came to Alabama, they found the region around Fort Strother a pleasant place and decided to go home, get their parents and return to the area to live.

Each brother built a home on the nearly 800 acres they acquired in this valley. Jack's is gone, but the one built by Henry has stood the test of time well.

The 16-inch logs used to build it were squared perfectly and put together with a "dove-tail lock," fastened with long wooden pegs. The exposed rafters are hand-hewn logs and the two chimneys are of hand-pressed brick.

Well preserved and filled with period furnishings, the house now is a museum of local history. The Looney House is open on the weekends only from noon to 5 p.m. Admission is $3.

Ashville is a city that has a large number of well-cared-for historic homes. Most of them still are private residences, cared for and loved much as they were when they were built.

The Prickett Home, surrounded by a white picket fence, sits near the courthouse. It was built for the Anzi Byers family in 1835 by Richard Crow. Like many of the houses built by Crow, its architecture bears a strong resemblance to tidewater colonial. The one-story white frame building went through a number of other owners after the Byers family left Alabama and, in 1889, was presented to Stella Box Hodges as a wedding gift from her parents. Today it is a private residence.

The Embry-Bothwell-Campbell house also is not far from the courthouse square. Another structure by Richard Crow, it too is a private residence today. When it was built in 1835, it was the residence of Dr. James J.

Bothwell. After Bothwell's death, the house changed hands a number of times and finally was bought by Judge Leroy Box. Like the Prickett House, this one also has been a wedding gift. In 1882, Lula Box Embry received it as a wedding gift from her parents. True to its heritage, today the house, a two-story Classical Revival with the traditional Doric pillars, once again is home to a physician and his family.

On Highway 231, about one-half block from the courthouse, is the John Inzer Home. Built in 1852 by Moses Dean, one of Ashville's first merchants, the house is made of red brick manufactured at the Ashville brickyard. Somewhere in its history, the brick exterior of the home was painted and today, the house is white. The exterior walls and the interior walls that divide rooms are 16 inches thick. The home has two interior chimneys on one side and two on the other.

The front of the one-story Greek Revival house has the obligatory pillars, but these are unusual in that two are Doric and two are square. The pilasters, which should match the Doric pillars, also are square.

The two fluted Doric pillars were carved by slaves of Moses Dean before the Civil War. The war came and work on the pillars was halted. During Reconstruction, it was impossible to find anyone trained in making the classic pillars so the front of the home remained unfinished.

In 1866, John Washington Inzer bought the house. Inzer, a native of Georgia, opened a law office in Ashville in 1856. Well-respected in the community, he was St. Clair County's representative to the Secession Convention in Montgomery in 1861. At 26, he was the youngest delegate to sign Ordinance of Secession. He served as a lieutenant colonel in the Confederate Army and helped to write the new constitution for Alabama in 1875. An Alabama senator, Inzer also was a probate judge in St. Clair County and a circuit judge.

After Inzer bought the Dean house, he decided to settle for square pillars and pilaster and had those made and added to the house.

The house now is owned by the Sons of the Confederacy and is open on special occasions for tours.

HORSING AROUND CHANDLER MOUNTAIN

Huge sandstone formations - as much as 250 million years old - mark the southwestern tip of Chandler Mountain. Though somewhere back in their history these gaps and crevices in the mountain must have had some other name, today they are known as Horse Pens 40. The stone fortress, near Steele in St. Clair County, got its present-day name during the Civil War.

Here, the mountain forms a sort of natural corral with a narrow opening and plenty of room for horses in a rock-encircled area beyond. During the Civil War, settlers drove their horses through the narrow gap and into the "pen" to hide them from Union raiders. The area also served as a place for men to hide. Those who wanted to serve on neither side during the Civil War made their way into the almost inaccessible wooded mountains and let the war pass them by.

Today, the mountain - with its rocks shaped by erosion to look like human faces and animals - is the site of picnic grounds and hiking trails. Heritage festivals and arts and crafts shows are held regularly on the 40 acres here.

Alabama Bureau of Tourism and Travel

Horse Pens 40, Steele

Horse Pens 40 is open from mid-March to Thanksgiving. Hours are from 8 a.m. to 5 p.m. and admission is $5 per person.

WHERE TO STAY

Obviously in a city the size of Birmingham, there will be plenty of chain hotels and motels and other cities in the region provide a number of those facilities as well. There also are privately owned spots, ranging from the extensive and elegant to economy accommodations, for overnight stays.

In Birmingham: Motel Birmingham, Pickwick Hotel, Tutwiler Hotel, Wynfrey Hotel, Rime Garden Inn, Red Mountain Inn, University Inn, Hiway Host Motel and Suburban Lodge.

In Clanton: Alabama Lodge.

In Calera: Parkside Inn.

In Alabaster: Shelby Motor Lodge.

In Brent: Southern Belle

In Sterrett: Twin Pines Conference Center.

Bed and Breakfasts Inns in the region include:

In Ashville: Roses and Lace. Set in the 1890 Victorian-style Robinson Home, the inn has four bedrooms. Breakfasts come in two styles - Southern and New England. The stained glass windows and heart pine wood trim make the house a lovely setting for an evening's stay. The Beeson House, near Horse Pens 40 and usually open only on the weekends.

There are no Bed and Breakfast Inns in Birmingham, but arrangements to stay overnight in private residences can be made by calling Bed and Breakfast Birmingham, 205-699-9841.

Camping facilities, other than those in state parks, include:

Cherokee Beach Kamper Village, Maylene (The facilities include an area for swimming, hiking trails and picnic tables. There also is a carpet golf course), Peach Queen Campground, Jemison, and Sycamore Hill Campground, Trussville.

WHERE TO EAT

Just eating can be a reason to go to Birmingham, the city has so many fine restaurants offering a wide variety of menu choices.

In Birmingham: Andrew's Barbecue, Anthony's, Back Alley, Big L Barbeque, Bombay Cafe, Bombay Connection, Bongiorno, Cafe de France at Botanical Gardens, Botega, Botega Cafe, Buttiker's, Browdy's, Char-House, Christian's Classic Cuisine, Clyde Houston's Five Points South Cafe, Cobb Lane Restaurant, Connie Kanakis' Fine Cuisine, Cosmo's Pizza, Costa's Bar-B-Que, Davenport's Pizza Palace, Dexter's at Chase Lake, Doodle's, El Palacio, El Gringo's, The Fish Market, Formosa Chinese Restaurant, G G In The Park, Gkika Morgan's Fine Foods, Golden China, Golden India, Great Wall, Hamburger Heaven, Highlands: A Bar and Grill, Hopper's, Inverness Oyster Bar and Grill, Irondale Cafe, Jimez, Jim 'N Nick's Bar B Q, Johnny Ray's Bar-B-Que, John's, Joy Young, La-Cocina, Lakeview Deli, Lovoy's, Mauby's, Michael's, Ming's Cuisine, Moneer's Kabob House, Niki's, Niki's West, Pancho & Charlie's, Pat Moon's Full Moon BBQ, Renge Japanese Restaurant, Salvatore's, Sal's Italian, Silvertron, Social Grill (Don't pass up the banana pudding.), Tavern On Cobb Lane, Walker's Restaurant, Zydeco.

In Alabaster: The Meadowlark

In Bessemer: Bright Star (Everybody! eats here).

In Columbiana: House of Plenty.

In Northern Shelby County: Lloyd's (located on Highway 280 South, just below the Jefferson/Shelby County border).

In Montevallo: JeRoe's (This is where everyone in town gathers for lunch.).

In Rockford: Mullins' Grocery Store Deli.

In Clanton: Heaton Pecans (In addition to the obvious, they also have sandwiches here.).

In Centreville: Twix 'N Tween.

In Springville: Laster Sundries (Have coffee and soft drinks here with the very informal local "coffee club.").

In Pell City: Pell City Steak House.

ANNUAL EVENTS

Among the annual events that draw visitors to this part of the state are:

Feline Fanciers Cat Show, Birmingham, January.

Alabama Music Hall of Fame, Birmingham, January.

Unity Breakfast, Birmingham, January.

Alabama Sports Hall of Fame Induction, Birmingham, February.

St. Patrick's Day Parade, Birmingham, March.

Heart Of Dixie Stock Dog Trial, Vincent, March.

Dogwood/Azalea Trail Tours, Birmingham, April.

Fiesta Plant Show and Sale, Birmingham, April.
U.A.B. Weekend of Jazz, Birmingham, April.
Greek Food Festival, Birmingham, April.
Heritage Tours of Pioneer Homes, Bessemer, April.
Battle At Bibb Furance, Brierfield Ironworks, April.
Arts, Crafts And Food Festival, Steele, April.
Birmingham International Educational Film Festival, April. (This
event is one of the nation's most pretigious festivals for
educational films. A number of Academy Award winning films first
won awards at BIEFF. Each year, the Festival also honors a
national figure for his contribution to education with a "Sadie"
Award. Past "Sadie" winners have included Carroll Spinney (Sesame
Street's Big Bird), Bob Keeshan (Captain Kangaroo) and Fred
Rogers.)
Decorator's Show House, Birmingham, April/May.
Birmingham Festival of Arts, April/May. (Another nationally
recognized festival hosted by the city of Birmingham. Each year,
the culture and art of a "guest" country is saluted.)

Birmingham Children's International Performing Arts Festival,
May.
Southern Applachian Dulcimer Festival, Tannehill State Park, May.
Blacksmithing Festival, Birmingham, May.
Magic City Arts Connection, Birmingham, May.
Kennedy Center Imagination Celebration, Birmingham, May.
MayFair, Birmingham, May.
Oak Mountain Barbecue Cook-off, Oak Mountain State Park, May.
Alabama Folk Fair, Bessemer, May.
Brierfield Music Festival, Brierfield Ironworks, May.

Homestead Hollow Springfest, Springville, June.
Confederate Memorial Encampment, Mountain Creek, June.
Vandiver Bluegrass Festival, Vandiver, June.
City Stages, Birmingham, June. (A major downtown music and
heritage festival featuring the best of Alabama talent as well as
national and international performers)

Fireworks From Atop Red Mountain, Birmingham, July.
"I Love America Festival," Birmingham, July.
Function at Tuxedo Junction, Birmingham, July.
Black Powder Muzzle-Loaders Rendezvous, Tannehill, July.

Great Southern Kudzu Festival, Birmingham, August.

Chilton County Fair, Clanton, September.

Oktoberfest, Birmingham, September.
Civil War Re-enactment, Tannehille State Park, September.
Arlington Country Fair, Birmingham, September.
Antique Farm Machinery and Engine Show, Tannehill State Park, September.
Horse Pens 40 Labor Day Arts, Crafts and Food Festival, Steele, September.
Swedish Heritage Fest, Thorsby, September.
"A Day In Old Birmingham," September/October.
Trout Creek Days, Ragland, September/October.

Magic City Classic Parade and Football Game, Birmingham, October
Bluff Park Art Show, Birmingham, October.
Alabama State Fair, Birmingham, October.
Ghost Stories at Sloss Furnaces, Birmingham, October.
Jazz Hall of Fame Induction and Concert, Birmingham, October.
"Taste of Birmingham," October.
Kid's Day, Birmingham, October.
Bonsai Show, Birmingham, October.
Tannehill Heritage Days, Tannehill State Park, October.
Looney House Fall Festival, Ashville, October.

Veteran's Day Parade, Birmingham, November.
Vulcan Run, Birmingham, November.
Homestead Hollow Christmas in the Country, Springville, November.
North Jefferson Quilters Guild Show, Mount Olive, November.
Christmas Market, Steele, November.

Christmas at Arlington, Birmingham, December.
Pioneer Homes Christmas Tour, Bessemer, December.
Christmas Pioneer Dinner, Bessemer, December.
Miss Alabama USA Pageant, Birmingham, December.
North Arts Council Arts and Crafts Show, Gardendale, December.
Bessemer Christmas Parade, December.

Alabama's State Capital Landmarks

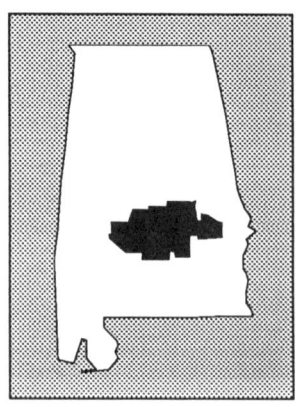

A labama's Black Belt, with its rich, fertile soil, cuts through part of this region. But the region's richest resource is the history that one finds here. Two of Alabama's capitals - the first and the present one - are in this area of the state, the Confederacy found a home here and Civil Rights history was written on the streets and roads, over the bridges and in the churches of this region.

The city of Selma has found itself in the center of many historic events. Its

Alabama Bureau of Tourism and Travel

Marker at Cahawba, near Selma

quiet streets and flowing river hardly give it the look of a place so destined to be a place where history - often violently - was made. Still, Selma's and Dallas County's date with destiny began when the state of Alabama was formed.

ALABAMA'S FIRST CAPITAL

Just southwest of what now is Selma lies the ruins of Alabama's first state capital, Cahawba. When Alabama became a state in 1819, this city on a bluff overlooking the confluence of the Alabama and Cahaba Rivers was chosen as the seat of government.

A copper-domed State House was built and a building boom swept the city. Houses, state buildings and churches went up. Steamboats arrived regularly with Parisian furnishings, chandeliers, china and fabrics.

The city became the social center of the state. Historians record that the dinners were more bountiful, the horses better

146

groomed, the voices gentler in Cahawba than anywhere else in America. Cahawba was so lavish in its entertaining, in fact, that it practically broke the state's bank when, in 1825, it threw a party for General Marquis de Lafayette, the French hero of the Revolutionary War.

Disaster struck the city shortly after that, though, when a flood swept down the rivers and into Cahawba. The state capital was moved to Tuscaloosa at that time, but Cahawba remained the county seat of Dallas County.

Two events sounded the death knell for Cahawba - the Civil War took most of the men from the city and another flood, this one in 1865, left the city crippled. Not long after that flood, Selma became the county seat. The citizens who had remained in Cahawba left and the buildings were razed to make use of the building materials in other places. Many Selma homes were constructed from the brick, board and glass of Cahawba. The copper dome from the State House now is on the Lowndesboro CME Church.

Today, visitors reach the remains of Cahawba by driving down a country road off State Highway 22 south of Selma.

The city's streets still can be traced, though some of them end in a mass of trees and others at the banks of the Alabama River.

Markers designate the locations of the State House and Castle Morgan, a cotton warehouse that was converted into the Confederacy's second-largest prison.

The remains of the Methodist Church and the Perine Well, the deepest known well of its time, still are visible. But the city that hosted Lafayette is gone and now mostly is inhabited only occasionally by fishermen who take advantage of the riverbanks where steamers once docked.

The Capital and Surrounding Counties

Montgomery, the capital of Alabama, lies on the outer fringes of the Black Belt in this region of the state. The counties here are linked geographically and historically.

This region, made up of six counties, cradled not only the Confederacy, but the Civil Rights movement as well. The names of cities that today are population centers - Selma, Montgomery, Tuskegee - sound like a roll call of Civil Rights landmarks. About 400,000 people live in this central section of Alabama.

The region also is where the Coosa and Tallapoosa Rivers meet to become the Alabama.

Up to Selma

Though Selma benefited to some degree from Cahawba's hard times, it too was destined for difficulties brought on by war. With its gracious Georgian mansions and Greek Revival homesteads, Selma hardly looked like the kind of town that would be a major target of the Union forces during the Civil War. But the city wasn't just a social center, it was one of the South's main military manufacturing centers and the Union forces knew that Selma's fall would cost the Confederacy dearly.

To exact that cost, Union General James H. Wilson made his way through Selma on April 2, 1865. More than 2,000 of General Nathan Bedford Forrest's troops were captured and the city's role as a supply depot was ended with the destruction of the naval foundry (where the warships Tennessee, Tuscaloosa and Huntsville had been built) and the powder works.

But the city still retains much of the grace that was part of antebellum Selma, the city named by William Rufus King, vice president of the United States under Franklin Pierce.

It is easy to see what a charming city Selma was during the years before the war when one visits Sturdivant Hall, which has been called by some architects "the finest Greek Revival Neo-Classic Mansion in the Southeast." Sturdivant's architect was Thomas Helm Lee, a cousin of Robert E. Lee. Six massive Corinthian columns support the roof of the house, built in 1852. Sturdivant Hall has been completely restored and hour-long tours of the house are given daily, except Mondays. The house is open from 9 a.m. to 4 p.m. and admission is $4 for adults and $2 for students.

Old Town Selma - and Civil Rights

The Old Town Historic District includes more than 600 structures, making Selma's historic district the largest (in number of houses) on the National Register. There is a self-guided tour through the district. The driving tour uses a cassette tape, for which there is a $5 refundable rental fee, available through the Chamber of Commerce. For the walking tour, there is a brochure. The Joseph T. Smitherman Historic Building also brings the city's past into focus. Built in 1847, the building's exterior and first floor have been restored and it now houses Selma-manufactured munitions, war relics and Indian artifacts. The building is open Monday through Friday from 9 a.m. to 4 p.m. and Sunday from 2 to 4 p.m. Admission is free.

Wilson's trek through Selma left the city and the Confederacy changed, but change wasn't through with Selma. The city was destined at least one more time to be the place where change began.

When the Civil Rights Movement began in the South, the eyes of the world turned to Alabama. While Montgomery often found itself in the spotlight as the movement progressed, the city of Selma was the starting point for those events that would change the South and the nation.

It was from Brown Chapel AME Church on Martin Luther King Street that marchers went to the Dallas County Courthouse for voting rights demonstrations in 1965. Week after week, the demonstrators - sometimes led by Dr.

Martin Luther King - would make the walk to the courthouse to emphasize the fact that less than 1 percent of blacks in Dallas County could vote.

Founded in 1867 as the first AME Church in the state, the Byzantine-style building is the only known structure remaining of the work at A.J. Farley, an early 20th century black builder from Dallas County. The church is open for tours by appointment only Monday through Friday.

Marchers left from this church on one of the most memorable events of the Civil Rights Movement - the march to Montgomery. From the church, they made their way along U.S. 80 toward Montgomery, eventually reaching the Edmund Pettus Bridge which spans the Alabama River.

More than the river, the bridge also spans the civil rights movement in Alabama, marking the end of legal segregation in the state. It was on this bridge that the Civil Rights marchers on the Selma to Montgomery march were confronted by law enforcement officers on Bloody Sunday, March 7, 1965. Driven back in this attempt to reach the state capital, marchers once again left from Brown Chapel two weeks later. This time, they reached Montgomery and opened the door to voting rights for all American citizens.

Outside the church is a monument to Dr. King, bearing the inscription, "The demonstration that led to the most important advance in civil rights for millions of black Americans began here March 21, 1965..."

MORE BLACK HISTORY

So much of Selma's history is linked to the history of the city's black citizens that there is an entire Black History tour of the city. Included in the stops are the Saint James Hotel, managed during the Civil War by ex-slave Benjamin Turner, who later became Alabama's first black Congressman, and First Baptist Church, which gave birth to Selma University, now the oldest black junior college in the nation.

Other stops include the Old Live Oak Cemetery, a National Register landmark and the burial place of Vice President William R. King, Turner and Martha Todd, Mary Todd Lincoln's half-sister. Rose Hill Cemetery on Beloit Road is the burial site for many ex-slaves. The history of the city of Selma, "from Civil War to Civil Rights" is told in the Old Depot Museum. This museum comes by its name honestly - it is in an old depot. Exhibits range from items as large as a railroad boxcar to those as small as mourning pins worn by 19th century widows. The museum is open from 10 a.m. to noon and from 2 to 4 p.m. Monday through Friday. Admission is free.

GRIST STATE PARK

Paul M. Grist State Park is 15 miles north of Selma. The 1,080-acre park offers facilities for primitive and improved camping, picnicking, swimming, boating, fishing and hiking. Pets are allowed if they are kept on leashes. There is a fee for use of some of the park's facilities.

In Lowndes County, southeast of Selma, is Holy Ground Battle Park in Whitehall, one of the largest parks in Alabama in a predominantly black community. At the park - open daily - is a playground and a beach area. There also are facilities for picnicking, swimming, fishing and hiking.

State Capital Region

MONTGOMERY'S BEGINNINGS

What now is Alabama's state capital once was the dwelling place for Alibamu and Creek Indians. Then, in 1871, a group led by Andrew Dexter of Massachusetts founded the town of New Philadelphia there. That same year, a group headed by General John Scott of Georgia established Alabama Town nearby.

In 1818, Scott's group moved its town nearer to New Philadelphia and renamed its settlement East Alabama. The two towns united in 1819 and formed a single city, which the people named Montgomery after Revolutionary War hero Brigadier General Richard Montgomery.

And when Southerners gave birth to a whole new nation in 1861, they hung her cradle in Montgomery. On February 18, 1861, Jefferson Davis took the oath of office as president of the Confederate States in Montgomery. At the same time, the city that had become Alabama's capital in 1846, became the capital of the Confederacy.

It was from Montgomery that the telegram reading, "Fire on Fort Sumter" was issued. It was in this city that "Dixie" was set to music by Dan Emmett. When the war ended and Montgomery's battle song was silenced, the city had to look for some way to rebuild her resources. She had been spared the kind of devastation that took place in other Southern cities, but she still was the victim of much destruction and looting. The war had drained her coffers and changed her way of life forever.

Before the war, Montgomery was a great cotton market. Now she would have to rebuild, this time without an economic base built on slave labor. The state government supplied part of the city's economic base after the war - where there is government, there will be jobs. And the men who had grown cotton picked by slaves now share-cropped the cotton fields out to the Blacks who remained in the South.

The city made such a remarkable recovery from the war that in the late 1800s, a mere 20 years after the war's end, it was boasting the nation's first electrical trolley system, called the "Lightning Route," because its cars obtained phenomenal speeds of six miles per hour.

Today, visitors still can ride the Lightning Route on three heated and air-conditioned buses that travel through much of the downtown area and past many of the places where the city's, Confederacy's and state's history was and still is being written.

The "Lightning Route" buses run Monday through Saturday from 9 a.m. to 4 p.m. and leave the various stops at 20 minute intervals. The cost for a ride is $.25.

One "must-see" on the Lightning Route is Old Alabama Town, a historic district that brings together several structures that give visitors a look at what life was like for the ordinary people who contributed to Alabama's development.

In the district is Lucas Tavern, which provided a popular stopping place for travelers in the early 1800s. The tavern's one "claim to fame" (other than now being a part of a historic district) came in 1825 when Lafayette spent one night as a guest there.

Examples of Southern architecture reconstructed in the district include a one-room log cabin from the early 1800's; a Dogtrot House, with the open breezeway between two identically sized rooms that give it its name, and a two-room Shotgun house, which was typical in black neighborhoods in the late 1800s.

The Old Alabama Town district also includes a grange hall, a barn, a one-room schoolhouse, a corner grocery store, a country doctor's office and a church that housed a black Presbyterian congregation. The most pretentious structure in the district is the Ordeman-Shaw House, an Italianate residence built in 1848.

The buildings in the district are furnished with period pieces and there's even a grape arbor in the center of them all, giving visitors a cool place to rest. The district is open daily, except for January 1, Thanksgiving and Christmas. Hours are 9:30 a.m. to 3:30 p.m., Monday through Saturday and 1:30 to 3:30 p.m. on Sunday. Adult admission is $5.

HANK'S RESTING PLACE

Nearby, at 1305 Upper Wetumpka Road, is Oakwood Cemetery, where Hank Williams is buried. In the cemetery is a gravesite memorial to Williams, the man who gave the world, "Your Cheatin' Heart," "Your Cold, Cold Heart" and "Hey, Good Lookin'."

Not far from Old Alabama Town is St. John's Episcopal Church, where Jefferson Davis worshipped. It is open daily.

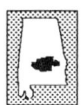

Also along the trolley route is the the Rice-Simple-Haardt House, the last antebellum residence still standing on its original site in the Alabama Capitol complex. It is a combination of several styles - Italianate (overall), Greek Revival (in the Doric columns) and Gothic Revival (in upper level gingerbreading). In this house is the Lurleen B. Wallace Museum, containing important memorabilia of Alabama's only woman governor. The house is open daily, except January 1, Thanksgiving and Christmas. Hours are 8 a.m. to 5 p.m. Monday through Friday and 9 a.m. to 5 p.m. Saturday and Sunday. Admission is free.

ALABAMA'S CAPITOL

For truly exploring Montgomery's history, there's no place like the Capitol Complex, around Washington and Bainbridge Streets and Dexter Avenue.

The centerpiece of the complex, of course, is the State Capitol itself. The Capitol building holds the history of the state as well as the Confederacy within its Alabama marble walls. It has been the seat of the state government for more than 100 years and it was here that the State Convention passed the Ordinance of Secession and the Confederate government was formed. The building, which for some time has been undergoing extensive interior renovation, is scheduled to reopen to the public in mid-1991.

State Capital Region 151

Alabama's State Capitol Building, Montgomery

The First White House of the Confederacy, a two-story frame house on Washington Avenue across from the Capitol, was the residence of President Jefferson Davis and his family while the Confederate capital was in Montgomery. Moved from its original location in 1921, it now houses a Confederate museum with many personal belongings of the Davis family. It is open daily, except January 1, Thanksgiving and Christmas. Hours are 8 a.m. to 4:30 p.m. Monday through Friday, 9 a.m. to 4:30 p.m. Saturday and Sunday. Admission is free.

Also across from the Capitol Building is the Alabama Department of Archives and History. The nation's first Department of Archives and History, this one houses a historical museum and artifact displays detailing Alabama history. There also is a genealogical research library, which houses Alabama and Southeast history documents as well as family records. The museum is open daily except for holidays. Monday through Friday, museum hours are 8 a.m. to 5 p.m. On Saturday and Sunday, the museum is open from 9 a.m. to 5 p.m. The reference room is open Monday through Saturday.

CIVIL RIGHTS MEMORIAL

At the corner of Decatur Street and Washington Avenue is the Southern Poverty Law Center and the city's new Civil Rights Memorial. The memorial - designed by Maya Lin, designer of the Vietnam Veterans Memorial in Washington, D.C. - is cast in black granite.

A circular black table and curved wall form the focus of the memorial. The granite table, Ms. Lin explains, "records the names of 40 martyrs of the civil rights movement and chronicles the history of the times in lines that radiate like the hands of a clock." Water flows from the table's center over the inscriptions.

Behind the table, water also flows across the nine-foot high wall that bears the words from the Bible chosen by Dr. King for his first speech during the Montgomery Bus Boycott, "(We will not be satisfied) until justice rolls down like waters and righteousness like a mighty rushing stream."

Alabama Bureau of Tourism and Travel
Civil Rights Memorial, Montgomery

Less than a block from the Capitol is Dexter Avenue King Memorial Baptist Church, where Martin Luther King Jr. was pastor in the 1960s. A mural here depicts the major events in his life. The church is open Sunday through Friday and on Saturdays and holidays by appointment.

Not far away is Centennial Hill, an area that was developed in the late 1870s as a prominent black residential area. Most of the buildings in the

district are closed to the public, but are worth a look from the outside. Within the National Historic Register-listed district are the John W. Jones House (341 South Jackson), a large two story house built in 1900 by the Reconstruction-era state senator; the Moore House (754 South Jackson), built in 1900 by Marshall Moore and his wife, who were in the first graduating class of State Normal school; the Nathan Alexander Home (503 Union Street), where the Reconstruction republican and vice president of the Alabama Penny Prudential Savings Bank of Montgomery lived until his death in 1915, and the Dorsette-Phillips House (422 Union Street), which was purchased in 1886 by Dr. Cornelius N. Dorsette, Montgomery's first black physician.

Not far away, at 1524 St. John Street,

Alabama Bureau of Tourism and Travel

Dexter Avenue Baptist Church, Montgomery

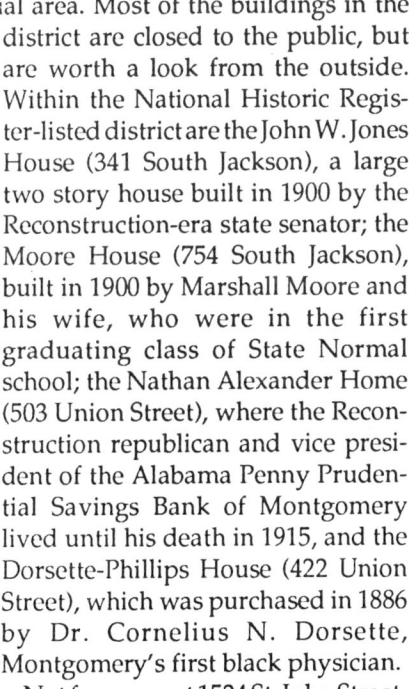

is the Cole-Samford House, the birthplace and early childhood home of Nat King Cole. It is a private residence, closed to the public.

Also near the Capitol complex and the Cole-Samford House is Oak Park and W.A. Gayle Planetarium. There are shows at the planetarium on Sunday at 2 p.m. Admission is $2 for adults and $1 for children.

SCOTT AND ZELDA'S PLACE

A few blocks south of Oak Park is the Scott and Zelda Fitzgerald Museum, the nation's only museum devoted to the lives and works of the talented couple. The two-story home at 919 Felder Avenue is the only house in which Zelda Fitzgerald lived left standing in Montgomery. She and husband, F. Scott, moved into what then was 819 Felder in October, 1931, and left six months later.

"We knew this was a short period of time for them to have lived there, but it was the only home of Zelda's left and, really, they never lived anywhere for very long during their marriage," explains Julian McPhillips, one of the key people involved in getting the house converted to a museum. "My wife and I travel a lot and always have loved `little' museums. We were amazed that there was no museum anywhere devoted to F. Scott Fitzgerald."

Since Zelda Fitzgerald was a Montgomery native, the house where she and her husband lived seemed like the natural place to have the museum. It was in this house that Fitzgerald worked on one of his best known novels, "Tender Is the Night." And while they lived in the home, Zelda wrote her one published book, "Save Me The Waltz."

The 7,000-square foot home set on one and a half acres has been restored and furnished much as it was during the Fitzgeralds' residency. Throughout the house are artifacts, mementos and paintings of the Fitzgeralds. Many of the books that line the shelves are inscribed by Fitzgerald. A video shown in the house tells the story of the Fitzgeralds and their lives together.

The museum is open from 10 a.m. to 2 p.m. Wednesday through Friday and from 1 to 5 p.m. on Saturday and Sunday. Admission is free.

THE RIVERFRONT

On the Riverfront, where Montgomery streets meet the Alabama River, is the Lower Commerce Street Historic District. Once an area of railroad and commercial warehouses, the district now has been restored and the Victorian buildings - dating from the 1800s to the turn of the century, now house offices. The Riverfront Tunnel to Riverfront Park dates from the days when cotton was king in Montgomery. The riverboat "Betty Ann" is docked at Riverfront Park. Mostly for charter, the riverboat does have one dinner cruise per week on Thursday night.

Two other spots to see near the downtown area are The Teague House, at 468 South Perry Street and the Governor's Mansion at 1142 South Perry. The Teague House, a Greek Revival antebellum mansion, served as headquarters for Union General James H. Wilson after April 12, 1865, and now houses the offices of the Business Council of Alabama. The Governor's Mansion is a neo-classical mansion set on beautifully landscaped grounds. Free tours are available by appointment.

LEAVING DOWNTOWN

Not everything there is to see in Montgomery is right downtown. You have to venture out a little for some of the treasures the capital city holds. North of downtown is the Montgomery Zoo, which offers almost 150 species of animals - from a miniature cow to African lions. The zoo is open every day except Christmas and New Year's from 9:30 a.m. to 4:30 p.m. Admission is $1.50 for persons 13 years and older and $.25 for children 2 to 12.

Northwest of downtown Montgomery is Maxwell Air Force Base, which has been an airfield since 1910 when Wilbur Wright began the world's first flying school on this site. Orville Wright made his first flight in Montgomery on March 26, 1910, and underscored Maxwell's place in aviation history. Named for Lt. William C. Maxwell of Atmore, who was killed while serving with the Third Aero Squadron in the Philippines, the base now is the home of the Air University, which includes the largest military library in the Department of Defense. Daily tours (except for holidays) are available by appointment.

SHAKESPEARE'S HOME

Southeast of downtown Montgomery are the Alabama Shakespeare Festival and the Montgomery Museum of Fine Arts. The art and drama complex is set in the quiet atmosphere of the Wynton Blount Cultural Park, where the buildings surround a lake, complete with swans guiding peacefully by. At the Shakespeare Festival, housed in the Carolyn Blount Theatre, are two stages and classic and contemporary theatrical productions both have

Alabama Bureau of Tourism and Travel

Alabama Shakespeare Festival, Montgomery

Montgomery Museum of Fine Arts

found a home in what has been designated as "The State Theatre."

The art museum houses the Blount collection of 41 paintings by 32 American artists as well as collections of European art and regional and decorative arts. Filled with skylights and windows, the museum lends itself to "staying a while" and enjoying the works on exhibit there.

One portion of the museum is devoted to a children's hands-on art area, where youngsters can discover how perspective, lighting and colors can change the look and feel of a piece of art. Adults seem to like the area as much as the children and are just as likely to spend a lot of time there.

The museum is open from 10 a.m. to 5 p.m. Tuesday, Wednesday, Friday and Saturday and from 10 a.m. to 9 a.m. on Thursday. Sunday hours are noon to 5 p.m. Admission is free.

UP TO AUTAUGA COUNTY

Northwest of Montgomery, in Autauga County, is Buena Vista Mansion. Buena Vista, located on County Road 4 between U.S. 31 North and Alabama 14, was built in the early 1800s by Major William Montgomery. Montgomery spared no expense in constructing his home. Materials for the house were prepared in Birmingham, England. When the materials came from England with them came English craftsmen hired by Montgomery to complete the elaborate construction on site.

Buena Vista is open Tuesdays from 10 a.m. to 2 p.m. Admission is $2.

Many visitors to Montgomery plan a side trip into nearby Shorter to take in the greyhound racing at VictoryLand. The track is about 20 miles east of Montgomery off I-85 and is open daily except Sundays. Monday through Saturday, there are races beginning at 7:20 p.m. There are matinees at 3 p.m. on Monday, Wednesday, Friday and at 1 p.m. on Saturday. Admission is limited to those 19 years old and over and if you plan to have dinner at the track, you'll need to make reservations in advance. Admission to the track is $.50 general admission and $2 for a clubhouse seat.

THE TOWN OF TUSKEGEE

A little farther to the east is the city of Tuskegee and even those who aren't familiar with the name of the town are bound to recognize the names of the two men who made Tuskegee their home - Booker T. Washington and George Washington Carver.

For a relatively small town, Tuskegee has a lion's share of landmarks and historic sites. Tuskegee Institute National Historic Site, for example, includes more than 27 landmarks associated with Booker T. Washington and George Washington Carver on its 4,500 acres.

Tuskegee University (first called Tuskegee State Normal School and then Tuskegee Institute) began in a church and a shanty on July 4, 1881, with 30 students. Today, the school sprawls across a large campus filled with museums and monuments.

On campus, you'll find the Carver Museum, where you easily can spend a couple of hours. Carver Museum was established by Tuskegee University in 1938 as a tribute to the former slave who, as a young man, was called "the plant doctor." As a youngster, Carver was fascinated by rocks and plants, a fascination that later earned him his nickname. A native of Missouri, he came to Tuskegee in 1896 at the urging of Booker T. Washington. At the school, he continued the research he had begun at Iowa State College and revolutionized agriculture in the South.

The museum on the Tuskegee campus houses many examples of Dr. Carver's contributions to science, including samples of some of the more than 500 products he developed from the peanut, the sweet potato and the

Alabama Bureau of Tourism and Travel

Carver Musuem, Tuskegee

State Capital Region

pecan. It was Carver's demonstration of the uses of these crops that encouraged Southern farmers to grow more than just cotton and opened up new agri-industries in the area.

The museum is open daily from 9 a.m. to 5 p.m. except Thanksgiving, Christmas and New Year's and no admission is charged.

Also on Tuskegee's campus is The Oaks, Washington's home, which was designed by Robert Taylor and built by Tuskegee students. It is one of the few surviving structures of the late 1800s designed and built by blacks. You can arrange a tour of The Oaks while you are in the Carver Museum. Tours are conducted every hour on the hour for small groups. Larger groups need to make arrangements ahead of time.

Among the other sights to see on the campus are the Booker T. Washington Monument, the Old Administration Building, which once was Washington's office,

Alabama Bureau of Tourism and Travel

Booker T. Washington Monument

and the Washington Collection and Archives. Again, check at the museum for tour information and arrangements.

Another structure on the campus is the Chapel Building, constructed in 1969. The original chapel, designed by Paul Randolph, was built in 1896 by Tuskegee students. That structure burned in 1957 and the one built in 1969 was designed by Robert R. Taylor. Beside the chapel are the gravesites of Carver and Washington. Tours of chapel can be arranged through the University Public Relations Department.

Also on campus is the Daniel "Chappie" James Center for Aerospace Science and Health Education. The center honors James, an outstanding student at the university and the nation's first black four-star general. James learned to be a pilot from one of the best - C. Alfred "Chief" Anderson, who was instrumental in forming the aviation school at Tuskegee's Moton Field. It is appropriate that another student of Anderson's, architect Tarlee W. Brown, who also graduated from Tuskegee, designed the James Center. Arrangements for a tour of this facility can be made through the university's Public Relations office.

Near the main campus is Grey Columns, the home of Tuskegee's president. The house was built by William Varner in the mid-1800s. Miss Lou Varner, who lived in the house, is credited with having saved the home and the city of Tuskegee from being torched by Union forces. The story goes that when the Raiders arrived to burn the house, Miss Lou, who was 11 years old, met the soldiers and told them her brother was sick and could not be moved. When the commanding officer learned that her brother was a Harvard schoolmate, he ordered the troops to spare the city.

One hint for touring these sights in Tuskegee - when visiting during May, arrange these tours as far ahead of time as possible. The tours are led by students and during May, escorts usually have to schedule their tours around final exams.

You can visit Moton Field in Tuskegee, where Anderson worked to turn civilian volunteers into some of the best fighter pilots of World War II. Today the field serves as the city's airfield but during World War II, it was the only place in the United States for blacks to train as military pilots.

Seven miles east of Tuskegee on U.S. 80 is Tuskegee National Forest. This is the smallest of Alabama's national forests, but that doesn't mean it's short on beauty. The forest covers more than 11,000 acres, 125 of which are devoted to a wildlife viewing area. There also is an 8-1/2 mile hiking trail and two picnic areas, Atasi and Taska. There is no charge for admission to the forest facilities.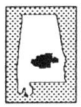

JASMINE HILL

Jasmine Hill just sounds like the name of something you'd find nestled near some Alabama town and, sure enough, it is. What you might expect to see when you get there is a plantation house with white columns and horse-drawn carriages out front. What you'll find in reality is an outdoor museum filled with copies of some of the finest classical Greek sculpture.

Jasmine Hill is 17 acres of gardens hidden away in a wooded area off U.S. 231 near Wetumpka and just northeast of Montgomery.

The gardens were the idea of Mary and Ben Fitzpatrick, who were childhood sweethearts. Fitzpatrick, the grandson of Alabama's Governor Fitzpatrick, left the South to attend Yale. When he returned in 1907, he married Mary, a Birmingham schoolteacher at the time. The Fitzpatricks spent the first years of their married life building a chain of stores across the South. They sold their holdings in 1927 and retired to Jasmine Hill and their little cottage set on the southernmost outcropping of the Appalachians.

The Fitzpatricks spent part of their time in the Gardens of Jasmine Hill, reading poetry to one another. They also spent part of their time traveling, especially to Greece, which they loved. Over the next few decades, the Fitzpatricks made more than 20 trips to Greece to purchase art objects, to study at the American Classical School and to enjoy Greek culture.

Not entirely content to just enjoy the culture while in Greece, the Fitzpatricks determined to bring some of it back with them. On their trips, they would commission copies of classical sculptures and return the next year to pick them up. Among the copies that found their way to Jasmine Hill are Girl Playing Knuckle Bones, Venus de Melos and the Lions of Delos. All of the art works at Jasmine Hill are set among gardens that bloom year-round with everything from winter blooming azaleas in January to crepe myrtle in July to sasanquas in December.

Also on the grounds is a copy of what remains of one of the oldest Greek temples, The Temple of Hera. The original temple sat in one of the most sacred precincts of ancient Greece, adjoining the site of the Olympic games. The only way the Fitzpatricks' temple varies from the original is the inclusion of a pool of water in an area used for worship in the Greek temple.

Two areas have been added to Jasmine Hill since the Fitzpatricks' deaths - a wedding garden and an open-air amphitheater where entertainment is presented during the summer.

Today visitors wander through the gardens where the Fitzpatricks lived in their own "little corner of Greece." The gardens are open daily from 9 a.m. to 5 p.m. Tuesday through Sunday. Admission is $3.50 for adults, $2 for children.

Fort Toulouse

For the fan of military history, a visit Fort Toulouse/Jackson National Historic Landmark, also near Wetumpka, is in order. Fort Toulouse was built by Bienville in 1717 to establish trade in the heart of Creek Indian Territory. Andrew Jackson reopened the fort in 1814 after the Battle of Horseshoe Bend. Fort Toulouse has been reconstructed and Fort Jackson has been partially reconstructed.

The park also is the site of Indians mounds dating from around 1100 A.D. Park facilities include a boat ramp, nature walks, camping sites, picnic areas and a museum. A living history program is presented there on the third weekend of each month, April through October. The park is open daily (except January 1, Thanksgiving, Christmas Eve and Christmas). Hours are from 6 a.m. to 9 p.m., April to November, 8 a.m. to 5 p.m. the rest of the year. Admission is $1 for adults, $.50 for children 6 to 12. Camping fees range from $6 to $8 per night.

Take a Ride on a Riverboat

To see the countryside from a different perspective, take a cruise down the Coosa River on the "Shirley Jean" sightseeing boat.

The boat leaves from Gold Star Memorial park in Wetumpka each Sunday at 2 p.m. for a 90-minute trip. Price for the trip is $5 for adults, $2 for children 12 and under. To arrange for a trip on the "Shirley Jean," make reservations at 569-BOAT.

WHERE TO STAY

Because this region encompasses the state capital, there naturally are any number of chain hotels and motels. In addition, there are independent facilities, bed and breakfasts and private campgrounds.

Independent hotels and motels include:
In Montgomery: Capitol Inn, Hotel Monticello, Governor's House, Riverfront Inn, the Madison and Villager Inn.

Bed and breakfasts here include:
In Selma: Grace Hall. Built in the mid-1800s, this antebellum mansion now is a bed and breakfast inn with six guest rooms. A tour of the mansion is included in the cost of an overnight stay.

In Montgomery: Red Bluff Cottage, Old Parsons Lot, East Fork Farm, Cloverdale, Hillwood, Ford Haven and Grand View Pines. Reservations for a stay in any of these bed and breakfasts can be made by contacting Red Bluff Cottage.

Private campgrounds in the area include Six Mile Creek, Lake Lanier Travel Park, Selma, and Kountry Air and K&K Campground, Prattville.

WHERE TO EAT

In addition to a number of chain restaurants and fast food eateries in the area, there also are several independently owned restaurants. They include:
In Selma: Major Grumbles (located on the river in a cotton warehouse that was built in 1850), Pagoda and Tally-Ho (The entrance and waiting area of this restaurant are located in an old log cabin.), Hancock's Bar-B-Q and The Downtowner.

In Montgomery: Vintage Year, Sahara, Martin's and Martha's Place (There's usually a line at the door of the two-story clapboard house at 431 on predominantly black Sayre Street. And in the line you're likely to see businessmen, tourists and politicians - sometimes even the governor himself. Food here is cooked the Southern way with fresh ingredients. Martha's Place is open for lunch from 11 a.m. to 3 p.m.)

In Prattville: Pratt Village Inn (Set in one of the structures in Prattville's historic district on First Street, the restaurant is open for lunch from 11 a.m. to 2:30 p.m. Monday through Friday and Sunday.)

ANNUAL EVENTS

Annual events in this part of the state include:

Martin Luther King Jr. Birthday Celebration, Selma, January.

Art and Music Festival, Tuskegee, February.
Dixie Jamboree (Square dancing), Montgomery, February.
Zoo Weekend, Montgomery, February.

Spring Arrives at Jasmine Hill, Wetumpka, March.
Hullabaloo, Montgomery, March.
Southeastern Livestock Expo Rodeo and Livestock Show, Montgomery, March.
Historic Selma Pilgrimage and Antique Show, Selma, March.

Tuskegee University Founders Day, April.
Calico Fort, Fort Deposit, April.
Cityfest, Prattville, Late April, early May.
Battle of Selma Re-enactment, Selma, April.
Alabama Private School State Track Meet, Selma, April.

Memorial Day Fly-In, Tuskegee, May.
Autauga County Heritage Pilgrimage, Prattville, May.
Jubilee, Montgomery, May.
NCAA Division II World Series, Montgomery, May.
Jaycee Speed Boat Races, Selma, May.
Cahawba Festival, Selma, May.
Alabama High Athletic Association Track Meet, Selma, May.

Concert at The Zoo, Montgomery, June.

History Hurrah, Montgomery, June. Summerfest, Selma, July.
Dixie Majors State Baseball Tournament, Montgomery, July.
Jaycees Southeast Championship Rodeo, Selma, July.
African Extravaganza, Selma, July or August.

Keeping Cool, Montgomery, August.
Grassroots Rally, Tuskegee, August.
Living For America Award Ceremony, Selma, August.
Performance on the Green, Montgomery, August.
Women's Class A Slow Pitch National Softball Tournament, Montgomery, August.

Governor Lurleen B. Wallace Birthday Memorial Service, Montgomery, September.

Central Alabama Fair, Selma, October.
Sweet Potato Festival, Tuskegee, October.

South Alabama State Fair, Montgomery, October.

Festival in the Park, Montgomery, October.
Tale Tellin' Festival, Selma, October.
Riverfront Market, Selma, October.

Turkey Day Classic Football Game, Montgomery, November.

Holiday Festival, Selma, December.
Tuskegee University Christmas Concert, December.
Old Alabama Town Christmas, Montgomery, December.
Blue-Gray All-Star Game, Montgomery, December.

Alabama's Wiregrass & The Valley

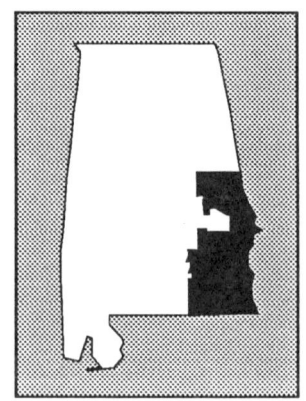

A bout halfway between Tennessee and Florida, the Chattahoochee River becomes the Alabama-Georgia border. In some spots extremely narrow, in others massively wide, the river twists, turns and tumbles as it heads toward the Apalachicola River and the Gulf of Mexico.

This link to the Gulf, historians tell us, long has been a border - between Indian nations, between frontier settlements and the unknown land that lay west and finally, between states. The river also has served as a source of power, a means of transportation and a provider of food. All the things the river offers made it attractive to the Creek Indians and to early settlers. Its strategic position made it a stronghold for Confederate armies and a target for Union attack.

The counties that lie near the river are a history lesson, easily learned as visitors lose themselves in stories of famous battles, well-known residents and ordinary people. And the area is filled with some of Mother Nature's nicest handiwork, all tucked just off the beaten path along highways and byways.

One of the delights of touring the area is that you can take as much or as little time as you want.

Given only a day, you can squeeze in glimpses of several sites. Or, given more time, you can linger, see more and get a real feel for the nostalgia and beauty of the Old South.

Logically, the best way to get the most out of a trip to this part of the state is to pick several cities as "base stations" and to venture out to surrounding cities and sights on day trips.

For seeing the best of the upper counties, you might choose Alexander City, Auburn, Opelika or Phenix City for your "home port" and do your exploring each day around those cities.

HORSESHOE BEND

If you choose Alexander City, you'll get a big dose of history and also be able to enjoy what has been called one of the South's finest inland recreation areas.

Andrew Jackson made his way into history at Horseshoe Bend, about 20 miles from Alexander City. The Creek Indians, divided by their relationship with the white man into the Lower Creeks of Georgia and the Upper Creeks of Alabama, were warring among themselves in the spring of 1813. By summer, the settlers were involved in the Indians' differences and soon became the victims of the Upper Creeks' wrath.

Militias from Georgia, the Mississippi Territory and Tennessee were sent to put down the Indian uprising and stop the massacre of settlers. Jackson and his men moved south from Tennessee and confronted the Upper Creeks on March 27, 1814, in what would be the final battle of the Creek Indian War of 1813-1814. The Indians had gathered for this last stand against an army that included both Jackson and Sam Houston in the spot where the Tallapoosa River took an unusual horseshoe-shaped turn. Jackson and his men soundly defeated the Upper Creeks during this short-lived battle at the bend of the river. The battle brought national attention to Andrew Jackson and brought an end to the Creek Confederacy. After the Battle of Horseshoe Bend, the Creeks were forced to sign most of their land over to the United States.

Today, the battle site is Horseshoe Bend National Military Park. On the grounds are a

Alabama's Wiregrass and Chattahoochee Valley Regions

This region encompasses Alabama's Wiregrass region, named for the tough grass that grows across the land in this part of the state.

Made up of 11 counties, this region winds its way down the eastern border of the state, hugging both Georgia and Florida.

Population centers in this part of Alabama - where more than 440,000 people live - include Phenix City, Dothan, Auburn, Lanett and Ozark.

museum with exhibits and artifacts telling the story of the battle. There also is a three-mile tour road, which winds its way around the river's bend. The self-guided tour has six stops at important sites of the battle. There are 13 miles of trails, a picnic area and a boat ramp in the park.

Because the park contains more than 2,000 acres of forest, there is an abundance of trees, flowers and animals to be seen during a drive or walk through the area. Fall offers an especially spectacular scene as the leaves change colors and provide a bright backdrop for the scenes from history.

At various times during the year, the park hosts living history programs

Alabama Bureau of Tourism and Travel

Horseshoe Bend, near Alexander City

and special events. The grounds are open daily from 8 a.m. until dusk. The Visitors' Center is open every day except Christmas and New Year's. The museum is open from 8 a.m. to 4 p.m. There is no admission charge.

Martin Dam in neighboring Elmore County creates Lake Martin on the Tallapoosa River. With its 760-mile shoreline, the lake was the largest of its kind when it was created in 1926. Wind Creek State Park, seven miles southeast of Alexander City, offers a place for family outings as well as campouts. Among the largest camping facilities in the Southeast, Wind Creek offers a beach complex, hiking and cycling trails, picnic areas, a marina and a boat launch. An observation tower overlooks the area.

The park has about 650 improved camping spaces. Also at the park are a concession area, a camp store and grills. Pets on leashes are allowed.

LAFAYETTE, WE ARE HERE!

From Alexander City, it's an easy day trip to Lafayette, where the town's depot has been converted into the Chambers County Museum, filled with relics once used by the people whose roots run deep into the city. When Lafayette's original depot burned in 1907, residents were quick to rebuild that hub of the city where the likes of drummers, lawyers and out-of-town relatives once had pulled into town.

The warehouse section of the depot still bears names of local businesses whose signs have been painted on brick walls and sliding doors. The large freight weighing scales, built into the warehouse floor, still weigh accurately. To the people of Lafayette, it has been important to preserve remnants of their past so that today's children will have some idea of what life used to be like in the small town which in 1833 was named the County Seat of Chambers County.

The depot museum has blacksmithing tools, medical and dental displays including instruments and overstuffed examining tables, logging equipment, early schoolhouse furnishings, clay churns and water jars and turn-of-the-century fashions.

The museum is open each Wednesday and Saturday from 9 a.m. to noon. Admission is free.

Lafayette's 62-building business district has been named to the National Register of Historic Places. In the center of the city square is a turn-of-the-century courthouse. Inside, the wood floors lead to offices and a courtroom that so perfectly represents hundreds of such Southern places of justice it looks like it was lifted from a Hollywood backlot.

Moviegoers did, in fact, see this tiny Alabama hamlet in a film set in Mississippi. In 1988, film crews rolled into the city to film "Mississippi Burning," starring Gene Hackman as an FBI agent trying to solve the murder of three civil rights workers.

Not far from Lafayette is Valley, where historians and genealogists can find a wealth of information at the H. Grady Bradshaw Chambers County Library and Cobb Memorial Archives. In the library, there are reference materials, which frequently are updated to meet the requests of patrons doing research. The archives also are the headquarters for the Chattahoochee Valley Historical Society. Among the items housed in the Archives is an excellent collection of local history and genealogical material. Much of this was donated by the Historical Society when the Archives were built in 1976. An archivist is on duty Monday through Friday to assist researchers.

The exhibits at the archives, which feature historical and folk life items of local interest, are changed quarterly.

The library and archives are on Alabama 29 about one mile south of Interstate 85. The library is open 10 a.m. to 8 p.m. Monday through Thursday, 10 a.m. to 6 p.m. Friday and 10 a.m. to 5 p.m. Saturday. The Archives are open from 10 a.m. to 6 p.m. Monday through Saturday.

Fishermen will find much to love about this area of the state. Among the spots to try and catch "the big one" are Chambers County Lake and City Lake, both about three miles from LaFayette.

AUBURN: WAR EAGLE, USA

For the football fan living in Alabama, Auburn is half of the name of "the game." The annual Auburn-Alabama clash brings droves of visitors to whatever city is hosting the event (depending on the season, the coach and the home team, it's Auburn or Birmingham). Just about everyone in Alabama knows Auburn as one of the places to see the Tigers play. In fact, the city plays host to about 80,000 fans a game.

But Auburn and her sister city Opelika both have lots to offer visitors that has nothing to do with football. Stories of kissing bridges, poetry read for sweethearts, eight-track tapes and swamplands that don't exist all are part of the stories of these two cities. The two were among the top 50 cities in the nation in the 1990 book "The Rating Guide to America's Small Cities."

Judge John J. Harper founded the city of Auburn in 1836. He had thought of naming the town Geneva, but his son's girlfriend, who had read a poem that spoke of "Sweet Auburn, loveliest village of the plains," suggested that as a name for the spot instead.

Whether you're there for a football weekend or not, see the campus at Auburn University. Among the earliest land grant colleges and the first four-year educational institution in the state to admit women on an equal basis with men, the school was founded in 1856.

While seeing the campus, be sure to visit the Donald E. Davis Arboretum, which is open daily to the public. The arboretum is on South College Street. Also on that street is the chapel, the oldest building on campus. It was built in 1850.

South College also is part of Auburn's Historic District. The district, added to the National Register of Historic Places in 1976, encompasses the earliest section of what now is Auburn University. Buildings in the district, which date from the 1880s to early 1900s, are built in the revivalist styles of that architectural period.

The President's Mansion, on the corner of Samford and South College, and Auburn's landmark Samford Hall, at Thach and South College, both are nearby. Samford Hall, built in 1888, is the location of the president's office.

On Roosevelt Drive, you'll find the coliseum. (You didn't really think you'd get out of Auburn without seeing something that had to do with sports, did you?). Also on Roosevelt - when he's not at football games - is War Eagle, the university's golden eagle mascot. If you want to see Jordan-Hare Stadium, you'll need to go to Donahue Drive, which isn't far from the coliseum.

At the corner of Samford and Donahue, you'll find the new Auburn University Athletic Facility. It's "home" to two Heisman trophies - one belonging to Pat Sullivan, the other to Bo Jackson.

Once you've seen the sights on campus, venture into the city itself. Much of the history of the area is seen through the homes, churches and cemeteries of Auburn.

The Dillard-Lane House, a one-story frame structure that dates from 1853, was the home of Brig. Gen. James Henry Lane, an aide to Gen. Stonewall Jackson. It now houses the Auburn Women's Club. For tours of the house, call the Auburn/Opelika Convention and Visitors Bureau. The Old Main and Church Street District has 52 structures that date from 1847 to 1927. The architectural styles of the buildings vary and include Greek Revival, Victorian and early 20th century styles.

The Ebenezer Missionary Baptist Church on East Thach Street is one of the area's early black churches. It was built in 1870 by the congregation.

Pine Hills Cemetery on Armstrong Street was begun in 1830 and is the final resting place of a number of Confederate soldiers.

For one more quick look at history, take a brief side trip to Loachapoka, about seven miles west of Auburn on Alabama 14. The historic district there includes the building that houses the Lee County Historical Society Museum. The building, which was an induction center for recruits and volunteers during the Civil War, was being used as a dwelling some 50 years ago, according to one of the city's residents.

"And one of the boys who was raised there swears it is haunted," she adds. Haunted or not, the exterior of the building can be seen anytime and you can get an appointment to see the inside as well.

Also in Loachapoka is an oak tree, hundreds of years old, that is believed to be the site where many Indians tribes would gather for meetings.

OPELIKA

On the other side of Auburn, about seven miles to the northeast is Opelika, a city whose Creek Indian name means "Big Swamp." Why the Indians named it that is a mystery, according to local residents, since the area where the city sits is the highest point on a direct line from Atlanta to New Orleans.

The city was founded in 1854 at a point where two railroad lines crossed. The original railroad intersection today is part of the Railroad Avenue Historic District.

On Ninth Street is the Museum of East Alabama, which pays tribute to the city's textile industry. Included in the displays there are such items as an 1890s sheeting loom, a spinning wheel and other pieces of machinery used as Opelika became a textile center.

Also on display in the museum are "tapettes," forerunners of the 8-track tape. The tapes, and the first automobile tape player, were invented by Opelika resident J.H. Orr Jr.

In Opelika, go by the Lee County Justice Center for a look at the granite memorial that honors veterans of four wars. Designed by Kit Conner, the memorial is circular, with a pie-shaped wedge - each set on a different level - designated for each war.

Spring Villa Park in Opelika is the location of "The Big House," an antebellum Carpenter Gothic home which is on the National Register of Historic Places. The original home on this spot was built in 1850 by William Penn Yonge. That home burned in the late 1920s, but was rebuilt in 1934 to duplicate Penn's plantation estate.

Legend has it that the place is haunted. According to the tale, Yonge was a gracious host, but a harsh master to his many slaves. One of the slaves is supposed to have hidden on the 13th step of the spiral staircase and stabbed Yonge as he came up the steps for the night.

Whether a ghost still pays calls on the house or not is a matter of question. What's for sure is that William Penn Yonge and his son Joseph are buried on a hillside about 100 yards from the "Big House," their graves marked with simple white marble stones.

The 300-acre park at Spring Villa has 25 sites in the family campground area as well as several family picnic units, a picnic shelter, a nature trail and a playground.

Opelika also has given the state two governors - William J. Samford and

Forrest Hood (Fob) James. The Ellington-James Home, on North Ninth Street is where the future governor lived when he was a young engineer.

About eight miles east of Opelika, just off U.S. 280, is the Salem-Shotwell Covered Bridge. Located on a dirt road, the bridge, built sometime between 1865 and 1900, is Alabama's southernmost remaining covered bridge. Experts on such structures have called this bridge "the Alabama bridge to see" for those interested in how such bridges were built. White oak pegs, handhewn for the job, join the lattice-work, roof trusses and the substructure of the Town-truss bridge. This fine example of covered bridge construction makes it easy to see why they were called "kissing bridges." In a much more modest era, wooden siding on the outside of the bridge gave courting couples an opportunity to steal a kiss without being seen by others. The bridge presently is being historically restored and future plans include creating a county park around it.

Near the bridge, on County Road 77, is the Dr. A.D. McLain Museum. This facility, which includes the doctor's office, a drug store with a soda fountain and a pharmacy, honors the memory of a country doctor who served the area for more than 50 years. Appointments to tour the museum can be made through the Auburn/Opelika Convention and Visitors Bureau.

One of the state's more than 20 state parks is near Auburn and Opelika. Chewacla State Park, which has been called one of the states "hidden treasures," really isn't that hard to find once you know you should be looking for it. It is four miles south of Auburn, just off Interstate 85. Chewacla gives visitors a chance to get close to nature with its more than 650 acres of woodland, filled with nature trails, and its streams that tumble across rocks and waterfalls. The park is open year-round and has 18 improved camping sites as well as 13 sites for primitive camping. There are six family cottages in the park as well. Chewacla has picnic facilities, barbecue grills, a playground. The 26-acre lake there has a swimming beach and you also can fish and boat. Pets are allowed in the park on a leash. There are fees for use of some of the park facilities.

PHENIX CITY

Sitting directly across the Chattahoochee River from Columbus, Georgia, Phenix City is in the heart of an area rich with history.

The City of Girard, which now is part of Phenix City, was established sometime before 1820. The city was a trading post in the Creek Indian Territory. The settlement grew as more people acquired land there and especially as a railroad made its way through the town. Phenix City itself was established as Brownville in 1883, but the new town seemed to be having a hard time deciding what its name really was. The U.S. Post Office serving it was called "Lively" and the railroad called the depot "Knight's Station." The name Phenix City was decided on in 1889 and the town was consolidated with Girard in 1923.

Today, Phenix City and the area around it reflect both the history and beauty of this area of the state.

Two markers in Phenix City tell the story of the close relationship between an artisian and his apprentice. The teacher, John Godwin, was a bridge builder, and his student, Horace King, was a slave in Godwin's service who learned the art of bridge building as he worked side by side with Godwin. King was construction foreman for the first Dillingham Street Bridge, built in Phenix City in 1832. That year, he and Godwin introduced the "Town Lattice" bridge design into the Chattahoochee Valley. King built most of the early wooden bridges spanning the river, including those at West Point, Eufaula and Fort Gaines-Franklin. King was freed by an act of the Alabama Legislature in 1846 and later served in the Alabama House of Representatives. A historical marker at the corner of Dillingham and Broad Streets commemorates King's accomplishments.

King's acknowledgment of the education Godwin gave him in bridge building can be see at Godwin's grave in Godwin's Cemetery. After Godwin's death in 1859, King raised a monument to mark Godwin's grave. Inscribed on the pillar is King's tribute "in lasting remembrance of the love and gratitude" for his "lost friend and former master."

FORT MITCHELL

Ten miles south of Phenix City on Alabama 165 is Fort Mitchell and Fort Mitchell Park. Fort Mitchell, a National Cemetery, was named in honor of Georgia Governor David B. Mitchell, who served as an Indian agent from 1819 to 1821.

Established in 1813, Fort Mitchell was known as the gateway to the West and for many years was the site of the U.S. Agency to the Creek Indians. The fort was built as one of the first semi-permanent U.S. military garrisons in the region. Today, the historic area includes the fort, the fort hospital, the home of Creek Indian Agent John Crowell and the Cantey Plantation.

The Cantey Plantation, about a half mile north of the fort, was the home of James Cantey, a wealthy planter and veteran of the Mexican War. Cantey also served in the Confederate Army during the Civil War. He was a colonel of the 15th Alabama Regiment and later was promoted to Brigadier General.

Fort Mitchell is open from 8 a.m. to 5 p.m. seven days a week and from 8 a.m. to 7 p.m. on Memorial Day. The fort is not regularly staffed on the weekends, but is open to the public. Visitors are asked to remember that there is a cemetery on the fort complex and to behave accordingly.

Also near Phenix City is Fort Gilmer, a gun emplacement that was part of the area's Civil War defense lines. The fort has been described as "possibly the best example of preparations made in 1863" to protect against invasion of Federal troops. Plans are in the works to clear the way to the pentagonal-shaped breastworks, located on a hill in the northwestern part of the city.

There is one thing you should keep in mind when visiting Phenix City. Because the city is directly across the river from Columbus, Georgia, it's natural that some of its citizens work in Columbus. Even though Phenix City is in the Central Time Zone, many of the people there operate on Eastern Time. If you ask about the hours attractions are open or when an event begins, be sure you're talking the same language as the people giving you the information. Double check whether the time given to you is Central or Eastern.

The city of Seale, about 15 miles southwest of Phenix City on U.S. 431, is the location of the old Russell County Courthouse. The third oldest standing courthouse in the state and the oldest standing public building in the eastern section of the state, the courthouse was in use from 1868 until 1943 when Seale was the County Seat.

Three historical markers in the county help spell out how the area was explored and developed. On U.S. 431 near Seale is a marker indicating the area where the oldest route from the Atlantic Ocean to the Southwest passed. In 1805, it became the Federal Road. About 13 miles south of Seale on U.S. 431, a marker pinpoints the location of the town of Glennville, one of the earliest white settlements in the Old Creek Nation. Twenty-one miles south of Phenix City on Alabama 165 is the plaque marking the route traveled by naturalist William Bartram as he journeyed through the Southeast from 1773 to 1777.

BARKING IN BULLOCK COUNTY

If you are a sportsman or a student of history, you'll want to be sure to include a trip to Bullock County on your itinerary. Union Springs in that county plays host to a number of National Field Dog Trials each year. For many of those who follow the art and sport of training these dogs and watching them perform, a trip to Union Springs is an annual tradition.

For the history buff, Union Springs offers the Bullock County Courthouse Historic District. The district, listed on the National Register, offers a group of commercial buildings from the late 19th and early 20th Century. The buildings are clustered around the courthouse building, which dates from 1871.

DEEPER IN SOUTHWEST ALABAMA

Once you've seen upper counties in this region, its time to explore those counties that make up the lower half, extending from Eufaula down to Florida.

For seeing the lower portion of the region, you might choose Eufaula, Troy or Dothan as your "home port."

ENCHANTING EUFAULA

When you go to Eufaula, prepare to be enchanted by a city. For this is a city filled with homes that have stood for more than a century and city streets with businesses housed in buildings almost as old as the town.

One of the homes, Shorter Mansion, houses the Eufaula Historical Museum and Eufaula Heritage Association. The Neo-Classical Revival mansion was built in 1884 and remodeled in 1906. Shorter is open from 10 a.m. to 4 p.m. Monday through Saturday and from 1 to 4 p.m. on Sunday. Admission is $3 for adults and $.50 for children.

If you are lucky, there will be someone available to play the rosewood piano at Shorter during your visit. The melody you're most likely to hear played is the haunting "Eufaula Waltz." The tune was composed in the 1860's and was dedicated to a Miss Carrie Caruthers.

A hostess at the mansion says there is a story that a blind man used to play this tune on his accordion on a street just outside the windows of the mansion. Such romance as a blind man writing tunes for lost loves seem appropriate in Eufaula, a town that is the epitome of the Deep South as people know it in books and movies. It is a city of lovely old homes set against the backdrop of azaleas and dogwoods. It even comes complete with a river and Spanish moss hanging from the trees that line it.

And Eufaula truly is a town born of the trademark of the South - cotton. Cotton once was king in Eufaula. The city, located on a bluff above the Chattahoochee River, offers water access to Alabama, Georgia and Florida. In the early days of the town, steamboats regularly docked there to take on bales of cotton.

It was that crop that made many early Eufaulians well-to-do, according to a representative of the Eufaula Chamber of Commerce. And their wealth was reflected in the houses they built. Many of the magnificent homes built in Eufaula in the mid-1800's still stand. They often are open to welcome visitors during annual pilgrimages. Eufaula escaped the destruction that befell many other Southern cities during the Civil War. In April, 1865, 4,000 Union troops marched through the city, but the Confederacy had surrendered two weeks before and most of the city was spared.

You might want to call on the Eufaula Chamber of Commerce, located in the Sheppard Cottage, the oldest residence in Eufaula still in existence. There's no charge to see this raised Cope Cod cottage, built in 1837. The  Chamber of Commerce is open from 8:30 a.m. to 4:30 p.m. Monday through Friday. The Historic Chattahoochee Commission is in the Hart House, a house in the Greek Revival style. The one-story white frame building, constructed in the early 1800s, features a front porch with six fluted Doric columns. The Hart House is another of Eufaula's lovely homes you can enjoy at no charge. The Hart House is open from 8 a.m. to 5 p.m. Monday through Friday.

Eufaula has street upon street of such homes, many of them with cupolas that afford a view of the river and most of them with either ghost tales or enchanting back-fence talk about the builders. A number of the homes are in the Seth Lore and Irwinton Historic District, the second largest such district in the state with more than 550 registered landmarks. The homes there feature a mixture of Greek Revival, Italianate and Victorian styles. Churches and commercial buildings also are part of the district. Many of the homes and other structures are private residences now, but they can be seen on a bus tour. There also is a driving tour. You can get a brochure for that at either the Chamber of Commerce or the Eufaula Heritage Association.

While in Eufaula, be sure to see The Tavern. If ever there's a place that makes you wish you had been born in a different time, it's this building on

---

Wiregrass and Valley   173

the bluff overlooking Lake Eufaula. It was built in the 1830's to accommodate Chattahoochee River traffic and you'll swear you still hear tavern music drifting from behind the doors as you stand in front of it today. The Tavern is Eufaula's oldest frame structure and now serves as a business/residence.

There's much more to see in Eufaula - churches, monuments, depots, cemeteries and historic districts. Set aside at least a couple of days if you plan to do this city justice.

It won't be easy, but tear yourself away from the city of Eufaula proper and stop by Tom Mann's Fish World for a treat of a different kind.

For starters, Fish World houses the world's largest bass aquarium. The main aquarium, 38,000 gallons in size, allows viewing of huge largemouth bass and many other native fish as they swim in a completely natural setting. Call ahead and find out about feeding times. You won't have to be told more than once to keep your hands back when the bass answer the dinner bell. When you've seen them break the surface of the water, grab the food and thump back under, you'll be sure the wife and kids aren't leaning too far over the edge of the tank.

Also at Fish World is the plant where Mann's company produces what it says are some of the finest fishing lures ever to cast a come-hither wiggle in a bass's direction.

At one time, all of the lures were personally approved by Leroy Brown, Mann's "pet" bass. If Leroy would nip at a lure, it would go into production; if he ignored it, the lure wasn't worth the trouble to market.

Leroy's gone to the giant bait shop in the sky, but there's a monument to him on the grounds at Fish World and it's worth seeing. From March to September, Fish World is open from 8 a.m. to 5 p.m. Sunday through Saturday. During the other months, it is open from 9 a.m. to 5 p.m. Monday through Thursday and from 8 a.m. to 5 p.m. Friday through Sunday. Admission is $2.25 for adults and $1 for children in grades 1 through 12 as well as senior citizens 55 and over.

EUFAULA'S WILDLIFE

If you're in Eufaula during the bird migratory season, visit the Eufaula National Wildlife Refuge. The Refuge is a dual-purpose area. The land is farmed during the growing season and flooded during the migratory seasons to provide a resting place for birds making their annual journeys to and from the South. Even when the water and birds aren't there, visitors can catch a glimpse of an occasional deer bounding across the fields. The Refuge is open from 8 a.m. to 4:30 p.m. Monday through Friday. One of the nicest times to go is on a spring morning.

Lakepoint State Park Resort is a few miles north of Eufaula. At Lakepoint, there are both hotel and cottage facilities available. If you are lucky enough to get a hotel room facing the lake, you'll be able to watch a variety of birds as they come to the water. And the sunrises and sunsets alone are worth the price of admission.

The resort also has a golf course, tennis courts, swimming pools, camp grounds, beaches and a marina. The motel has a restaurant, coffee shop and lounge.

The lake itself is, of course, among Eufaula's top attractions. Lake Eufaula is one of America's top bass fishing lakes. Fish camps, marinas, tackle and bait shops, fishing guides and equipment rentals are readily available along the shore. Since the town's main thoroughfare also parallels the lake, nothing is very far away.

Nature - the human kind - is the emphasis in Clayton. It's there that you can see the Whiskey Bottle Tombstone in the Clayton Baptist Church Cemetery. It marks the final resting place of W.T. Mullen.

Mullen, a bookkeeper who was born in 1834 and died in 1863, was a heavy drinker. His wife was as devoted to temperance as Mullen was to the bottle and tried to reform him. When she failed, she vowed that when he drank himself to death, she'd make his gravesite a testimony to the kind of life he lived.

Mullen's vice is preserved for eternity in the head and foot stones of his grave - granite whiskey bottles complete with removable stone corks.

THE EIGHT-SIDED HOUSE

Though it doesn't have a particular moral lesson to teach, the Octagon House in Clayton is worth a visit while you're in the town. The Octagon House is the only antebellum example of this unusual architectural style in Alabama and one of the few surviving examples of the mid-nineteeth century architectural style in the nation.

The house, an octagonal-shaped structure, is constructed of 18 inch stone and gravel walls. Four chimneys start in the basement and rise above the home's cupola. The rooms inside the home are rectangular, with odd, pie-shaped "mini-rooms" between them to accommodate the house's unusual exterior design.

The house is open by appointment and all you have to do to get one is call the number on the sign in the window of the Octagon House.

CLIO: WALLACE'S HOMETOWN

While in Barbour County, you may want to drive through Clio, if for no other reason than to say you've been to George Wallace's home town.

Blue Springs State Park, with its more than 100 acres, is about 10 miles southeast of Clio on Alabama 10. Fed by a crystal clear underground spring, the swimming pool is the center of attention at the park. Accommodations include 50 improved campsites and primitive camping areas. Recreation facilities include picnic areas, playgrounds, swimming and fishing areas and tennis courts.

DOWN TO DOTHAN

If you choose Dothan as your home away from home, you'll find yourself in the heart of Alabama's Wiregrass Country. The region is named for the tough, wiry roots of the grass that grows there and that name says a lot

---

about the land itself as well as the hardiness of region's early settlers. The "official" Wiregrass Region stretches along Houston, Geneva and Covington counties along Alabama's boundary line with Florida, then heads north to Butler County. From there, it travels due east to the Georgia border, encompassing Pike, Coffee, Dale and Henry Counties.

Dothan is one of the largest cities in the Wiregrass region. There's plenty to do in Dothan, so plan to spend a couple of days at least. Otherwise, you won't be giving yourself a fair chance to enjoy all that the city has to offer.

If you're there during warm weather, you can cool off with a visit to Water World. Waterslides, water bumper boats and a giant wave pool provide wet fun for the entire family.

Water World is in the Westgate Recreational Complex and right down the road is Westgate Softball Complex, with five softball fields that host local, regional, state and national tournaments. Water World opens in late May on the weekends only and is open daily from Memorial Day to Labor Day. Hours are 10 a.m. to 6 p.m. Monday, Wednesday and Friday, 10 a.m. to 9 p.m. Tuesday and Thursday, 10 a.m to 7 p.m. Saturday and noon to 7 p.m. on Sunday. Admission is $5 for adults, $3.50 for children 3 to 12. Senior citizens are admitted free.

If you go to Dothan during the early fall, you can enjoy a salute to the area's main crop - the peanut. The National Peanut Festival each year means dancing, parades and peanuts, cooked or raw, added to more recipes than you even imagined could accommodate the peanut.

During any season of the year, the Dothan Opera House is something you have to see when you visit the city. The white marble of the lobby and the velvets of the parlors take you back to the elegance and grace that highlighted life in the turn-of-the-century South. The Opera House, on North St. Andrews Street downtown, was built in 1915 and is on the National Register of Historic Places. Several times each year, the Opera House is host to theatrical productions, symphony performances and ballets. Tours of the facility are available free of charge.

A quiet place to begin - or end - the day in Dothan is Landmark Park. Part of the park is designed to be a "living history museum," with a working farmstead. On the farmstead, there is a 1908 farmhouse where visitors can peek inside at rooms decorated with period furnishings. Behind the farmhouse is the barnyard, where goats, sheep, turkeys, roosters, pigs and mules wander inside a split-rail fence. A cotton crop grows on the farm which also has a blacksmith shop and a corn crib.

In the middle of the farmstead is a white gazebo, used during the summer for band concerts. Across from the farmhouse is the Headland Presbyterian Church, which was relocated at the park from nearby Headland. The white clapboard church, with stained glass insets in its doors, was built without the congregation incurring any debt.

But that's only part of the park. There also is a boardwalk through the woods, over beaver dams and across streams. To stroll this trail at twilight is to forget the cares of the day and simply enjoy the nature that surrounds you.

Visitors seem to fall silent as they make their way farther into the forest and begin to listen for the sounds of birds and other animals around them. The boardwalk was built around the trees, to preserve the natural beauty of the area and has several rest stops along the way.

The park is open from 9 a.m. to 5 p.m. Monday through Saturday. On Sunday, hours are noon to 6 p.m. during Daylight Savings Time, noon to 5 p.m. when DST isn't in effect. Admission is $1 for adults; $.50 for children. The price of an adult ticket may be higher during special events.

A POWERFUL VISIT

From the wonders of nature in Dothan's Landmark Park, it's only a short hop to the wonders of modern technology at Farley Nuclear Visitors Center. At the Center, located on the plant site of the Joseph M. Farley Nuclear Electric Generating Plant, there are hands-on exhibits and computer games explaining fission, nuclear energy and other subjects.

A wise-cracking robot who converses with visitors provides information and entertainment and a mini-theatre presents movies with an emphasis on energy education. The Visitors Center is open from 8 a.m. to 4 p.m. Monday through Friday. In June, July and August, it also is open from 2 to 4 p.m. on Sundays. There is no admission charge.

Campers who like to rough it will want to visit Chattahoochee State Park, 11 miles from Gordon, tucked into the southeastern corner of the state. There are a number of primitive camping sites on the banks of the 35-acre lake in the park as well as picnic spots. Boats are available for rent and the lake is a popular fishing spot. Pets are allowed if they are kept on leashes.

FORT RUCKER

Northwest of Dothan and Houston County is Dale County, where helicopters and history mix. Fort Rucker, which the U.S. Army Aviation Foundation calls home, is the world's largest helicopter training center. And right down the road, just outside Ozark, is Claybank Church, a long-standing piece of the area's history.

The Fort Rucker military complex, with its museum and Aviation Hall of Fame, sprawls across more than 63,000 acres just a few miles off U.S. 231 on Alabama 249 South. Students from more than 60 countries have received their training in the skies over Ozark and Dale County.

Also at Fort Rucker is the newly remodeled U.S. Army Aviation Museum. The 87,000-square foot facility tells the tale of Army aviation from the first military planes of the Wright Brothers to the latest in technology. The museum collection contains more than 100 aircraft and one of the largest helicopter collections in the world. Among the aircraft on display there are the R-4, the Army's first helicopter; the YO-3A "Silent" aircraft, one of the first attempts at designing an attack helicopter and a prototype of the AH-64 Apache helicopter, one of the newest entries in the Army's company of helicopters. There even are a couple of heli/planes which combine the

Claybank Church, Ozark

features of airplanes and helicopters into rather strange looking birds that are interesting to look at even if the practical applications are over the head of the observer. Admission to the museum is free and hours are from 9 a.m. to 4 p.m. seven days a week.

Claybank Church and Cemetery is one mile southwest of Ozark on Alabama 149. One of Dale County's earliest settlers, Rev. Dempsey Dowling, came to Ozark in 1826. He and his descendants took part in the building of the first Claybank church in 1829. The structure that stands today was built  in 1852 and is the oldest log church of its type in Southeast Alabama. Claybank Church is the oldest extant structure in Dale County. The cemetery beside the church is the location of graves of many early settlers as well as many Civil War soldiers.

If you'd rather fish or boat than look at helicopters or if you like tennis, baseball or picnicking, don't cross Dale County off your itinerary. There are lakes and parks all around. Dale County Lake is just one of the places where you can try to catch a record-breaking catfish or bass. Steagall Park has facilities for softball, baseball and basketball as well as a playground for the children. It also is the site each June for the All-American Softball Tournament with teams from four Southern states. A nature trail, with 20 exercise stations, winds its way through the park.

Next to Dale County Lake is Sam Dale Monument and Park, named in honor of General Samuel Dale, a pioneer and Indian fighter known as the "Daniel Boone of Alabama."

A STOP IN ABBEVILLE

Abbeville, the county seat of Henry County, is about 30 miles northeast of Dothan on U.S. 431. This town, older than the state of Alabama, is the oldest remaining colonial settlement in east Alabama from Florida to the

Tennessee line. Fortunately, the city has preserved much of this history and many turn-of-the-century commercial and residential buildings can be seen here.

About 16 miles northeast of Abbeville is the Walter F. George Lock and Dam, which spans the Chattahoochee and, since it does, is sort of in Alabama and sort of in Georgia. The facility is the second highest locklift in the nation and can be toured by appointment. Access to the dam and lock is on the Alabama side.

HISTORIC TROY

A visit to the area around Troy will remind you of the Wiregrass region's dependence on the crop. Like most Southerners, the people of the Wiregrass grew cotton. The appearance of the tiny Mexican boll weevil in 1915, brought disaster to this portion of the state. For two years, the cotton crop was ravaged. Then, in 1917, farmers learned to diversify their crops and they found a new prosperity.

The farmers' battle against the boll weevil and other adversity is one of the aspects of Wiregrass history explored at the Pike Pioneer Museum, three miles north of Troy on U.S. 231. One part of the nine-museum complex is devoted to rows of plows, saddles, carts, cultivators and planters. Tools such as these fill the farming area and speak eloquently of life on the Southern farm in the 19th and early 20th centuries.

But life wasn't all farming, even for rural Alabama families, during that period of history and all the parts that went into writing the history of that time are explored at the musuem.

One area contains items used in the preparation of food, while another is filled with objects used by dairy farmers of that time. Still another is devoted to the chore of laundering. Here are heavy irons that were heated in the fire before they could be used and displays of fluting irons, used to press pleats into collars and cuffs.

One display case at the museum is devoted to samples of embroidery and tatting done by women who made sewing, decorating and mending an art form. The equipment used to manufacture everything from turpentine to moonshine (In some cases, it was hard to tell the difference.) line another wall.

So that farmers would know what was going on in their communities as well as in the world, there was the weekly newspaper. The museum contains a Chandler and Price letterpress, the type used to print those newspapers.

Outside the museum proper are a number of buildings that made up the towns and cities of rural Alabama. A tenant house, typical of the stuctures tenant farmers called home in the late 1800s and early 1900s, sits with its interior walls papered with newspapers. Not only did the farmer find his newspaper a way to communicate, but a way to keep out the draft as well. Behind the tenant house sits a "privy," another necessity of rural life.

The two-pen split log house sitting on the museum grounds orginally was located in a rural area of Pike County. It was carefully dismantled and reconstructed at the museum site. Its two rooms are separated by a dog trot (an open hallway without walls at either end). The kitchen adjoins one main room; the other served as a bedroom for the family.

Also relocated to the museum is a country store, crammed with the necessities of life in the 1920s - from bolts of fabric to tins of snuff. Outside, there's a hand-operated, gravity-fed gasoline pump. The museum is open Monday through Saturday from 10 a.m. to 5 p.m. and Sunday from 1 to 5 p.m. Admission is $2 for adults and $.50 for children.

Once you leave the museum and rejoin the late 20th century, you may want to tour the campus of Troy State University. The school hosts a number of band concerts and competitions throughout the year and is the location of the National Hall of Fame of Distinguished Band Conductors.

ENTERPRISE: HAIL TO THE BOLL WEEVIL

About 40 miles south of Troy is Enterprise, the location of what probably is the only statue in the world erected in honor of a bug. After

Boll Weevil Monument, Enterprise

Shoals to Sand Dunes

the boll weevil destroyed the cotton crop and peanuts became the major crop of the area, people there realized that they had needed the pest to give them a little nudge into a new era of farming progress. That's why, at the corner of Main and College Streets in Enterprise, you'll find a 10-foot high statue - the Boll Weevil Monument - looking a little like a Greek goddess holding an enormous bug over her head. You wouldn't want to get to this part of the state and go home without being able to say you had seen the monument erected "in profound appreciation of the boll weevil and what it has done as the herald of prosperity."

Also in Enterprise, be sure to see the Enterprise Depot, which contains a very good collection of genealogical materials and collections of Indian artifacts, early 20th century medical equipment and farm tools. The depot is open Monday through Friday from 10 a.m. until 4 p.m.

On U.S. 85 Bypass, just north of Enterprise, is the Enterprise Welcome Center and the Little Red Schoolhouse. The Welcome Center is housed in a replica of an early 19th century log home. The schoolhouse, fully furnished with desks, school books and even a pot-bellied stove, is a look back at early American schools.

WHERE TO STAY

There are any number of chain hotels and motels throughout this part of the state. In addition, there are locally owned and operated facilities and a number of Bed and Breakfast facilities. Camping also is available at a number of the area's parks and there are a number of private campgrounds as well.

Among the other hotels and motels in the area are:

In Alexander City: The Horseshoe Bend.

In Dothan: Motel Leon, Olympia Spa, Town Terrace Inn, Walker's Deluxe Motel, the Adams Motel Traveler's Motor Inn.

In Enterprise: The Boll Weevil Inn, the Colony and the Enterpriser.

In Ozark: The Motel Alternative (This all-suite facility is in a residential area of the city and the complex has a pool and outside barbecue grills.)

Bed and Breakfasts in the area include:

In Ozark: The Steagall House. This bed and breakfast, located in an antebellum home on East Broad Street, is owned by Mr. and Mrs. Rod Marchant.

In Auburn: The Crenshaw Guest House. Located in the middle of the Historic District and set in a restored Victorian home, this Bed and Breakfast has two suites in the main building and a cottage in the carriage house.

In Lafayette: The Hill-Ware-Dowdell Mansion Bed and Breakfast.

Private campgrounds in the area include Lake Eufaula Campground in Eufaula, Bluff Creek Park in Phenix City, Deer Run RV Campgrounds in Troy and Lazy Louse Ranch Campgrounds in Opelika.

WHERE TO EAT

Again, there are a number of chain restaurants and fast food eateries scattered throughout the area. And there are some special places you might want to work into your eating schedule. Among the restaurants you may want to try are:

In Alexander City: Cecil's Public House.

In Dothan: King's Inn, Garland House (located in a charming Southern home), Mrs. Boomer's (a neighborhood pub), Bosun Joe's, Atlantic City Cafe and Sports Bar, Grate Things, The China Star, Popular Head Mule Company Pub and Grill (in a historic building) and Old Mill Restaurant.

In Eufaula: The Dogwood Inn (The building is a former boarding house, built in 1905. The food's good and the atmosphere is warm and friendly.), the Airport Restaurant and White Oak.

In Opelika: The Greenhouse (There's a Victorian atmosphere at this restaurant, which is set in a restored home from the early 1900s.)

In Troy: The Pines Restaurant and The Mossy Grove Schoolhouse Restaurant (it's in an old schoolhouse, naturally).

In Enterprise: The Lobby (in the Historic Rawls Hotel), Miss Mattie's, Josephine's and Steamers.

ANNUAL EVENTS

Some of the annual events in this area of the state include:

Southeastern U.S. Band Concert Weekend, Troy, February.
National Free-For-All Championship (Field trials for hunting dogs), Union Springs, February.

Spring Farm Days, Dothan, March.
Azalea-Dogwood Trail, Opelika and Dothan, late March or early April.

Eufaula Pilgrimage, April.
Kaleidoscope (A celebration of the arts for young people), Dothan, April.
Alabama Air Fair, Dothan, April.
Troy State University Band Concert, April.
Jazz Fest, Auburn, April.
Auburn Village Fair, April.
Little Britches Rodeo, Clayton, April.
Piney Woods Quilt Show, Enterprise, April.
Geneva Festival on the Rivers, April.

Jean Lake Festival, Troy, May.
Medieval Fair, Dothan, May.
Wiregrass Charity Horse Show, Dothan, May.
May Day, Phenix City, May.

Summer Swing (series of concerts), Opelika, June-August.

Liberty Day Festival, Eufaula, July.
Old Fashioned Fourth of July in the Park, Phenix City, July.
Troy State University Symphony Concert, July.

East Alabama Pine Tree Festival, LaFayette, August.

Old Russell County Courthouse Country Fair, Seale, September.
Bike Trek for Life and Breath, Eufaula, September.
Claybank Jamboree, Ozark, late September, early October.

Pike County Fair, Troy, October.
Pioneer Peanut Days, Dothan, October.
Alabama Chitlin Jamboree, Clio, October.

Lee County Historical Fair and Loachapoka Syrup Soppin' Festival, Loachapoka, October.

Alabama State American College Theater Festival, Troy, October.

American Flag Run, Phenix City, late October, early November.

"Christmas City," Ariton, late November, early December.

Christmas Parade, Opelika, November. Bi-City Christmas Parade, Phenix City, December.

Lights Beautiful, Opelika, December.

Christmas on Moon Lake, Phenix City, December.

"Luminaries," Opelika, December.

Touring Southwest Alabama

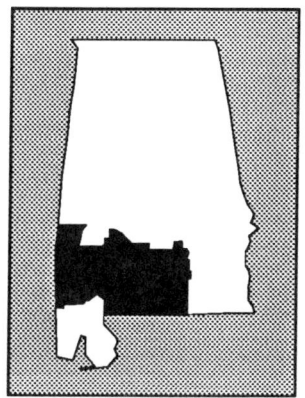

I n this part of the state, where the Black Belt ends and the land begins to
stretch toward the sea, Alabama truly reaches into its past. There still are
Indians here and antebellum homes tell of a time when cotton plantations
were scattered across the countryside.

The Tombigbee River cuts its way southward through Choctaw and
Washington Counties, providing the area with an abundance of natural
resources. The river also made it easy to send such goods as cotton to
Mobile, so antebellum towns and homes are clustered here as well.

STARTING IN CHOCTAW COUNTY

While cotton may have reigned for a while in Choctaw County, there was
another commodity that brought attention to the area. You still can see the
state's first oil producing well in Gilbertown. And oil wells, many of them
still active, dot the countryside around that city.

Gilbertown also soon will be the location of the Choctaw County Historical Museum. The museum will be housed in what once was the Farmers' Co-
op Building. That structure is being renovated for the museum's use. In
addition to being a place where the history of Choctaw County is traced, the
museum has been a "community project" as well, according to one of the
museum officers. "It's been almost miraculous how it has shaped up," she
said. Since a museum committee was formed and work began about two
years ago, people have been donating artifacts and relics - many of them
more than 100 years old - for display. People of the county also have pitched
in on fund-raising projects and, as a result, the museum is being opened
almost debt-free. Among the items visitors will be able to see is the press on
which the first newspaper in Choctaw County was printed.

Mount Sterling Methodist Church, about five miles east of Butler, was
built in 1859. In 1980, the Choctaw County Historical Society began having
the church structure restored. That restoration should be completed in
spring, 1991. Although regular services no longer are held at the church, it
is used for special events. The church is the only structure in Choctaw
County listed on the National Register of Historic Places.

If you've never traveled across - or even seen for that matter - a dual use highway/railway bridge, you'll get your chance in Choctaw County. Near Pennington, where the Tombigbee River divides Choctaw and Marengo Counties, is the Naheola Bridge. Local historians say that the bridge, which spans the river, was at first only a railroad trestle. It was built for the M&B Railroad, acquired by American Can Company when it bought a paper mill nearby. The railroad carried goods to and from the mill, one of largest paper mills in the American Can Company holdings (American Can's paper mills have since been bought by another company.). Someone - perhaps American Can - decided to add a second deck to the bridge to accommodate automobile traffic. Historians speculate that the deck was added so that paper mill employees who lived on the other side of the river could get to work more easily. Whatever the reason, the extra "layer" was added to the bridge and still is in use today. Automobile traffic across the span is one-way and you have to wait for a light to signal that it's your turn to cross. There aren't many bridges like this in the South and not many anywhere that were constructed in stages, according to the Historical Society.

Bladon Springs State Park is in southeast Choctaw County. Located on the site of a pre-

Southwest Alabama

This 11-county region is laced with waterways. The Alabama, the Tombigbee and the Mobile Rivers all flow through this southwestern part of the state. Indians lived here when the white man came and still live here today.

Population centers in this region, where almost 275,000 people live, include Andalusia, Opp, Brewton and Greenville.

Two counties in this region border Mississippi - Washington and Choctaw. Escambia and Covington border Florida.

Civil War spa, the park covers 357 acres. On the grounds are four mineral springs, which were a vital part of the resort when it was visited by the pampered antebellum set. Picnic shelters and barbecue grills in the park make it a popular place for day outings. Primitive camp sites are available for those who would like to stay overnight. The park is open year-round and pets are allowed if they are kept on leashes.

NEXT STOP - WASHINGTON COUNTY

Just south of Bladon Springs is Washington County. Healing Springs here once was a popular spa, where visitors went to "take the waters." Some of the springs still are active and accessible if you are willing to take a short

walk to them.

About 16 miles southeast is the St. Stephens Historical Site. St. Stephens was a fort that sat on a river bluff near the present-day town of St. Stephens. The fort and St. Stephens Historical Site are on privately owned land, but the Washington County Historic Society hopes to develop at least part of the area. Near the location of the fort are what the people in the area call "Indian bathtubs." They actually are indentations that the Indians apparently made in the rock formations in order to catch rainwater.

In the town of St. Stephens, drive by the Masonic Lodge. Built in 1852, the structure also served at one time as the county courthouse. The Masons have repaired and restored the building and replaced the original exterior porches. Upstairs in what was the courtroom, the Masonic meetings are held. The downstairs is used as a meeting place for other community groups.

In Chatom, the county seat, is the Washington County Museum. Housed in the basement of the courthouse building, the museum has a wealth of artifacts from the county's past. Among the items on display is an Indian dugout canoe, created from a single log. The canoe was found on the riverbanks and brought to the museum. Also at the museum is part of an antique glass collection, which belonged to one of the ladies of the town and was donated after her death. The mother of an attorney from Chatom created lavishly decorated eggshells in the tradition of the Faberge eggs. Several examples of her work have been donated to the museum as well. The museum is "open anytime the courthouse is open. If it (the museum) is locked, just find somebody in the courthouse to let you in," according to a member of the county's Historical Society.

In the works in Chatom is a city museum to be located in the family home of one of the town's founders.

The McIntosh Bluff Log Church in the southern part of Washington County is one of the few remaining log churches in Alabama. Constructed in 1860, the interior still has the original pews and pulpit furnishings. Located on U.S. 43 near McIntosh, the church is among the oldest buildings in the county. Inside the church are framed pictures of several of the congregation's early members. Services still are held at the church on special holidays and the Methodist Church next door to the structure has information about the log church and its members.

Near McIntosh, in Calvert, is a Choctaw Indian Reservation. At the tribal offices, open from 8:30 a.m. to 4:30 p.m. Monday through Friday, you can get information about the catfish farm, the truck farms and horticulture project that are on the reservation.

CLARKE COUNTY

Parts of Clarke County's borders are formed by two rivers - the Tombigbee on the west and the Alabama on the east. The history of this county is told through exhibits at the Clarke County Museum in Grove Hill. Housed in the 1854 Alston-Cobb House, the museum is open on Tuesday and Thursday from 1 to 4:30 p.m. and on Saturday from 8 a.m. to noon. Admission is free.

The Kimbell House in Jackson is Clarke County's other historic building open to the public. The house was built in 1848 by Isham Kimbell, a survivor of the Kimbell-James Massacre near Fort Sinquefield during the Creek Indian War of 1812. The house, one of the few pioneer dwellings left in Jackson built in the Plantation Plain style, is made of heart pine and cypress.

Kimbell House has been restored and is furnished with antiques donated by various individuals and groups. Located on Mayton Drive, the house is open by appointment (Call the Jackson Chamber of Commerce to set up one.) and there is no admission charge.

During the mid-1800s, Hal's Lake in Clarke County was a stopping place for runaway slaves from Mississippi. The slaves would stop at the lake, named for an ex-slave who aided them, then continue on their journey to the north.

Nearby is the Mount Nebo Baptist Church and Cemetery, also known as the Effigy Cemetery. This cemetery contains several grave markers that bear the likenesses of the persons buried beneath them. Isaac Nettles cast the death masks and made the markers for many years. Nettles is buried in the cemetery, but ironically, his grave is not marked even by a simple slab.

STOPPING OFF IN CAMDEN

Camden, the county seat of Wilcox County is more than 150 years old. A number of the buildings in the town were there before Camden was formed and the downtown business district now is on the National Register of Historic Places. Because it is close to the Alabama River, the picturesque community plays host several times each year to B.A.S.S. Club outings as well as to a number of hunters' groups.

Once a year, in September, one of Wilcox County's communities is chosen to host a tour of homes and the antebellum structures that have housed  citizens of the area for decades open their doors to the public. Many of the houses still are occupied by descendants of the original owners and are furnished with family heirlooms.

They still hold services a few times a month at Oak Hill Presbyterian Church in Oak Hill, about 15 miles southeast of Camden. The structure standing today was built in the late 1800s, but the congregation was established several years before that.

Six miles northeast of Camden is Roland Cooper State Park, where you can fish, play golf, swim, boat or cycle. There are picnic areas and a playground at the park, where the Dannelly Reservoir provides 22,000 acres of water for visitors' enjoyment. The nine-hole golf course at the park not only challenges the golfer, but also provides a look at some of the area's nicest scenery. For those who might like to stay for more than just one day, there are more than 40 improved campsites, about 10 primitive campsites and five cabins at the park.

It is open year-round; there are some fees for camping there and pets are allowed if they are kept on leashes.

MONROE COUNTY'S FAMOUS COURTHOUSE

If you are a Gregory Peck fan, you probably feel that you know Monroe County, Alabama, which sits cozied up to the Alabama River just south of Wilcox County. But long before Peck made it famous with his portrayal of a small-town Southern lawyer, Monroe County had found favor with other people.

The old settlement of Fort Claiborne, which sits on a bluff overlooking the river, was the county seat when Monroe County was formed. During the 1820's, the bustling town had about 5,000 residents, and when LaFayette toured in the state in 1825, he visited the home of the Dellet family home in Claiborne. During the Civil War, Claiborne was headquarters for part of Sherman's Army.

A fierce outbreak of yellow fever and the decline of riverboat transportation combined to cause the decline of Claiborne and only a few structures, such as the Dellet home, stand today.

One of the earliest structures built in Claiborne was the Masonic Lodge, which also served as the county courthouse. In 1884, the lodge was moved by ox cart two miles from Claiborne to Perdue Hill. Today it sits in that town beside U.S. 84. Beside the lodge is the home of South Carolina native William Barrett Travis, who originally moved to Claiborne to teach school. Travis eventually practiced law in Perdue Hill. When he left Monroe County in 1831, he went to Texas. Travis was the commander of the Texas patriots who died defending the Alamo in 1836. Although the buildings are not open regularly to the public, an inquiry at Broughton's Store nearby should net you a chance to see inside the buildings.

Monroeville became the county seat in 1832. Although county business today is conducted in the courthouse built in 1963, it is the 1903 courthouse that people know best. The old courthouse, designed by Andrew J. Bryan, is a three-story brick structure with octagonal dome and central oval section. The courthouse gained fame when it was used as a model for the courthouse in the mid-1960s film "To Kill a Mockingbird." The novel of the same name - written by Monroeville native Harper Lee - won a Pulitzer Prize. Peck took home an Academy Award as Best Actor for his portrayal of Atticus Finch and the courthouse became a part of American literary and movie history.

Today the courthouse is the site of a museum, filled with artifacts from the county's history and also is the location of Monroe County Chamber of Commerce and Historical Society offices. The courthouse is being restored with plans for the newly refurbished structure to house a theater, the museum, office space and a reception area. When the work is finished, the plans are to use the theater for summer productions of Miss Lee's work and Christmas productions of "A Christmas Memory," written by another former Monroeville resident Truman Capote.

Presently, the museum is open to the public Monday, Wednesday and Friday from 10 a.m. to noon and from 1 to 3 p.m. Admission is free.

Southwest Alabama

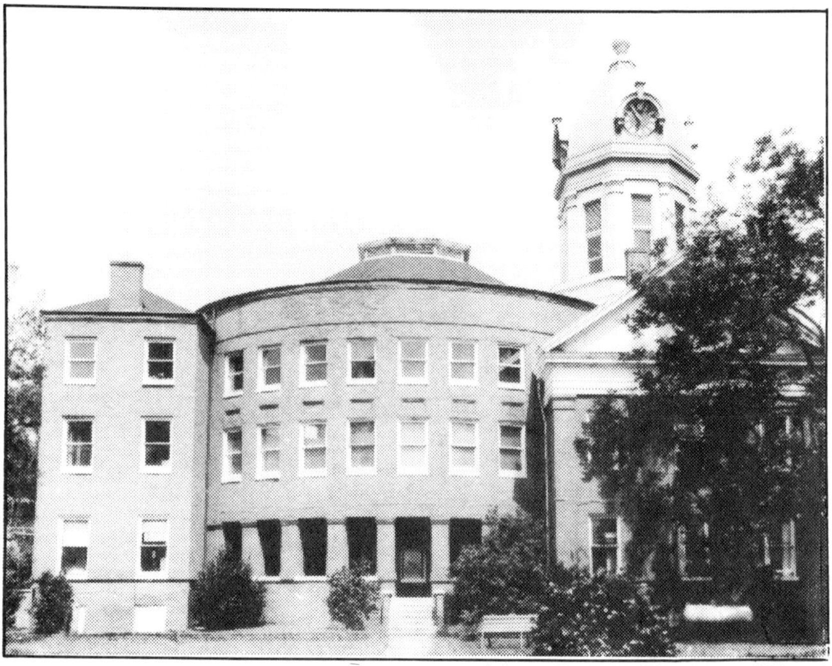

Alabama Bureau of Tourism and Travel

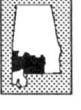

Monroe County Courthouse, Monroeville

It's not only Gregory Peck fans who know about Monroeville. Careful shoppers can tell you all about the city as well. On Drewry Road in Monroeville are more than 30 outlet shops, carrying everything from ribbons to toys. A number of clothing manufacturers have outlets here as well.

About 10 miles north of Monroeville is Tunnel Springs, a town that got its name from the railroad tunnel there. On Alabama Highway 21 North near the city is the 150-year-old Philadelphia Baptist Church.

Northwest of Monroeville in Claiborne is the Old Claiborne Cemetery, one of the oldest in the county. It is located just before the Alabama River bridge on U.S. 84 West.

Claiborne Lake, part of Alabama's River Lakes System, reaches 60 miles from Claiborne Lock and Dam to Millers Ferry Lock and Dam. Almost a million people each year enjoy the fishing, boating, swimming and skiing there. There also are sites for picnicking, hiking and camping. One of the hiking paths, a rather rugged foot trail over Gullet's Bluff leads to a spectacular waterfall.

Much of the park land around the lake is being allowed to go back to its natural state, providing a habitat for wildlife of the area, including the Red Hill Salamander - an endangered species that lives only in this portion of Alabama.

The lake area does, however, provide 11 developed sites with such recreational facilities as beaches and boat launches.

BURNT CORN, ALABAMA

On the Monroe County/Conecuh County Line is the town of Burnt Corn, a city that local people say is a lot like a place frozen in time. The past always is alive in Burnt Corn. Dr. John Watkins, one of the first physicians in this part of the state, made his home near Burnt Corn. Dr. Watkins treated those who survived the massacre at Fort Mims in 1813. He is in the Burnt Corn Baptist Cemetery.

There are a number of historic homes around Burnt Corn, established in the early 1800s. One of the most interesting places in town, however, and the place where you can get information about the historic sites of the town is Sam Lowery's store. Stop in the store for directions and "not only can you find out about seeing Burnt Corn, you'll spend some time with one of the best storytellers in this part of the state," says a Monroeville resident.

CONECUH COUNTY

Turk's Cave, near the town of Brooklyn in Conecuh County, is said to have been used by Spanish pirates to hide their treasure chests. But that's not the only story about Brooklyn. The locals like to talk about when, in the mid-1900s, a former governor of Alabama was campaigning for re-election and kicked off his campaign in Brooklyn, which sits on the Sepulga River. The river was dredged then and was navigable for at least part of the way to Florida. The politician, it is said, promised that if he was re-elected, he would keep the river dredged and make it navigable all the way to Pensacola. Excited about the prospects, some of the town's citizens formed a shipping company and had a vessel built. They hoped to use their ship to carry such goods as cotton southward when the governor kept his promise. The big day arrived for the ship's maiden voyage and the dignitaries all went aboard. The boat left the dock and promptly sank, necessitating the rescue of a number of soggy bigwigs. The politician was re-elected, but the company never got its chance to send Conecuh County goods to the sea.

ESCAMBIA COUNTY

Just south of Conecuh County, lying horizontally along the Florida border, is Escambia County. East Brewton, technically, is a city that predates Escambia County, where it is located. The city originally was Fort Crawford. The fort, built by order of Andrew Jackson and constructed by troops under his command, was a supply base for federal troops fighting against Indians in the early 1800s. The fort got its name from William H. Crawford, Secretary of War under James Madison.

Escambia County was created in 1868 and the first county seat was Pollard. The city of Brewton, which became the county seat in 1880, first was called Crossroads because two early roads intersected there. Later the name was changed to Newport, noting the fact that the town was a landing for two large creeks. It became Brewton, named after William Troupe Brewton, the

---

first Louisville and Nashville Station agent there, when the L&N opened a station in the town in 1861. Brewton also was a great-nephew of one of the first settlers of the area.

As Brewton and Fort Crawford grew, Fort Crawford took the name East Brewton because of its location in relationship to the other city.

As you make your way through South Alabama, the Jefferson Davis Junior College in Brewton should be one of your stops. On its campus is Thomas E. McMillan Museum. This county museum has permanent displays such Civil War relics and a complete set of dental tools from the late 1800s as well as a number of traveling exhibits. It also is well known for its genealogy museum and files. The museum is open from 1 to 5 p.m. Monday through Friday. Admission is free.

ATMORE'S INDIANS
Sitting in the corner of Alabama, just above Florida is Atmore. If you go to the town for relaxation and sports, visit Tom Byrne Memorial Park. There are ballfields and tennis courts in the park, which often is the location of arts and crafts shows.

The Poarch Band of Creek Indians' Reservation is in Atmore. On the reservation, which really is a small town in itself, are the tribal offices, housing, a health clinic, the Pow-Wow Grounds and a museum. The museum, which exhibits tribal artifacts from this area of Alabama, is open Monday through Friday from 7:30 a.m. to 4:30 p.m. Admission is free.

The reservation also has a bingo parlor.

ONE GREAT FOREST
Located partly in Escambia County and partly in Covington County is the Conecuh National Forest. Several state and county road go through the forest so it's easy to take a pleasant drive surrounded by trees and forestland. If you want to get a little closer to nature, take the Conecuh Trail. This 20-mile hiking trail winds through the forest past dogwoods, holly, pine and magnolia. Cypress ponds spring up throughout the forest. Don't take the hike without your camera. You'll want to have it along. The easy entry points to the trail are at Open Pond Recreation Area and at Blue Pond Recreation Area.

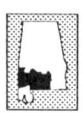

COVINGTON COUNTY
Andalusia is the county seat of Covington County, which also sits just on the Florida border. Created in 1821, the county was named for Wailes Covington of Maryland, an officer in the Creek Indian War and the War of 1812, who was killed in 1813. For a few months in 1868, it was Jones County, named for Josiah Jones, a political leader in the county. Jones politely refused the honor of having the area named after him, however, and it became Covington County again.

The first county seat was called Covington, but that city was renamed Montezuma to honor the emperor of Mexico in 1821. When the town flooded in 1844, the people looked for a new site for their county seat. When they found it, they called the town, appropriately enough, New Site. In 1847, it was renamed Andalusia, after a region in Southern Spain.

People come to this city for lots of reasons - the county fair draws exhibitors and visitors, the Pecan Festival and the Farmers' Market are treats for those who like to eat. And there are those who come to Andalusia because of the recreation facilities available there.

Because there are a number of lakes in the area, fishermen and boaters are finding plenty of fresh water to enjoy in Andalusia. North of the city is Point A State Park, a 70-acre facility with boating, camping, swimming and picnicking along the banks of the 700-acre Point A Lake. Open Pond has fishing and picnic sites and offers overnight camping for tents and trailers. To get to Open Pond, take U.S. 29 South from Andalusia about 10 miles, then turn left on Alabama 137 South for about five miles. Turn left on County Road 24 East for about one-half mile, then turn right on Forest Service Road 336 east for one mile. Fishing, swimming and boating all are available at Blue Pond Recreational Area There also is a hiking path that connects it to Open Pond. To get to Blue Pond, take U.S. 29 South from Andalusia about 10 miles, then turn left on Alabama 137 South for about four miles. Turn left on Forest Service Road 347 East for one mile.

The city itself has seven parks. Johnson Park probably is the one visitors see most often since it is the home of the District Babe Ruth League Baseball Play-Offs. Johnson also has a gymnasium, football fields, soccer fields and tennis courts. Lurleen B. Wallace Junior College offers residents and visitors a golf course, nature trails and jogging paths. The college also brings with it plays and other cultural events that draw visitors to the area.

On the Alabama-Florida line in Covington County is Florala State Park. Open year-round, the park has facilities for primitive and improved camping. Swimming, fishing, boating and hiking all are offered at the park, which also has barbecue grills and picnic areas. Pets are allowed in the park if they are kept on leashes. There is a fee for camping at the park.

More Places to Go

Butler and Crenshaw Counties sit just north of Covington County and only about 30 miles south of Montgomery. Greenville, the county seat of Butler County, was settled in 1819 when a wagon train of emigrants from Greenville, South Carolina, camped for the night in the area. They obviously found the land appealing and decided to stay. As Alabama began to grow and the cities started to flourish, transportation from one spot to the other became important. A stagecoach road from Montgomery to Mobile went through Greenville and later the railroad was built on the same route.

Today, Greenville still is a place that welcomes visitors with its "down home" type atmosphere. Near the center of town is Confederate Park, a town square kind of park with statues of various dignitaries and heroes. Scattered throughout the town are historic homes and structures and to see them one only has to drive through the streets of the city. Signs along the way direct visitors and each building is marked as an historic site.

About 15 miles west of Andalusia is Opp, which got its name from Henry Opp, an attorney who was the settlement's principal promoter. Just a few miles outside the city proper on Alabama 134 West is C.C. Bess' Store. The store, which has had a number of different names, dates back to the late 1800s. In its early days, the store was the place where the earlier citizens of the area came once a month to do their grocery shopping. Open seven days a week from "daylight to dark," the store still has old metal advertisements tacked to the outside and people on the front porch playing dominoes.

LUVERNE'S MUSEUM

Luverne, in Crenshaw County, is about 30 miles north of Opp. It is the location of a rather unusual museum complex, Southern Museums. Made up of five small buildings, the museum houses exhibits of "popular culture, from the 1960s to the 1990s," according to its owner. Right now, the museum still is being completed and is open only by appointment. By 1992, it should be open to the public all the time. Southern Museums is on Ninth Street, just off Forest Avenue near downtown Luverne.

WHERE TO STAY

In addition to chain hotels and motels in this area, there are a number of independent facilities. Among them are:

In Butler: Butler Hotel and Reid's Motel.

In Andalusia: Charter House Inn, The Gables, J&B Motel, Town Line Motel and Key Motel.

In Opp: Opp Motor Lodge.

In Monroeville: Monroe Motor Court South, Sunset Motel and Western Motel.

In Camden: The Southern Inn.

In Brewton: Brewton Motor Inn and Colonial Manor.

Bed and breakfasts inns in the area include:

In Franklin: The Rutherford-Johnson House.

Camping facilities in the area, in addition to those in state parks include:

In Millry: J. Emmett Wood Lake Campgrounds (open from February to November).

In Franklin: Claiborne Lake, Bells Landing Park, Isaac Creek Park, Silver Creek Park.

In Coffeeville: U.S. Army Corps of Engineers Service Area. Located four miles west of Coffeeville on U.S. Highway 84, this camping area has 32 improved camping sites. The area was closed for renovation in March, 1990, but will reopen as soon as renovations are completed. For information, contact the U.S. Army Corps of Engineers Headquarters in Demopolis.

In Camden: Chilatchee Creek Park, East Bank Park Campground.
In Beatrice: Monroe County State Lake.
In Greenville: Sherling Lake Campgrounds.
In Opp: Opine Campgrounds.

WHERE TO EAT

There are a number of chain and fast-food restaurants scattered throughout this part of the state. In addition, several locally owned dining spots are gathering places for visitors as well as residents. Among them are:
In Butler: Butler Cafe, Ezell's Fish Camp and Bobby's.
In Gilbertown: Bonner's Restaurant.
In Silas: Bobby's Fish Camp and Petromales.
In Andalusia: The Market Place, The Lobby, Covington Ice Cream Parlor, and The Hickory House.
In Camden: Gainesridge Dinner Club (The restaurant is located in an 1850s plantation house that is furnished with period antiques. On the grounds, there is a lake and horses roam about the surrounding pastures. The setting gives a meal here a definite plantation flavor.) and Boone and Crockett Restaurant, which is known for its fresh seafood dishes.
In Monroeville: David's Catfish House, City Cafe, Martinee's, Radley's Deli, Radley's II, Southwind Restaurant, Sweet Tooth Bakery, M.A.C's Bar-b-Que, Kat's Restaurant, Chick-A-Dee's and Mel's Dairy Dream.
In Thomasville: Alabama Grill and Delmar Rock Restaurant.
In Greenville: Giuseppi's and Alabama Grill.
In Luverne: Chicken Shack, Annie's and The Hickory Pit.
In Atmore: Sweet Shop, Buster's Restaurant, Plantation House and Ponderosa.
In Brewton: Ole Willie's.
In Opp: Barr's Seafood (This is a popular restaurant with people from all over the area. It only seats 30 or 40 people, so the advice from the local folks is to "come early if you're hungry.") and B&B's Steak House.

ANNUAL EVENTS

Opp Rattlesnake Rodeo, Opp, March.
State Turkey Calling Contest, Jackson, March.
All-Youth Choctaw Indian Pow-Wow, McIntosh, March or April

(Easter Weekend).Civiettes' Country Fair, Butler, April.
Gilbertown's Arts and Crafts Show, Gilbertown, April.
Old Home Folks Day, Opp, April.
Mayfest, Atmore, May

Hank Williams Memorial Celebration, Evergreen, June.
MOWA Choctaw Indian Pow-Wow, McIntosh, June.
Alabama Blueberry Festival, Brewton, June.

World Championship Domino Tournament, Andalusia, July.

Watermelon Jubilee, Greenville, August

Fall Festival, Atmore, October
Forestry Capital of Alabama Celebration, Monroeville/Monroe
County, October.
Octoberfest, Brewton, October

Veterans Day Parade, Greenville, November.
Forestry and Wildlife Festival, Jackson, November.
Poarch Band of Creek Indians Thanksgiving Pow-Wow, Atmore,
November.
Jackson Arts and Crafts Show, November
Southwest Alabama Forestry and Wildlife Festival, Jackson,
November.
Andalusia Kiwanis Covington County Fair, November.
Conecuh Heritage Festival, Evergreen, November.
Fall Craft Festival, Greenville, November.
Business and Professional Women's Arts and Crafts Fair,
Andalusia, November.
Peterman Station Arts and Crafts Festival, Peterman, November.

 Christmas Parade, Atmore, December.

Mobile & Baldwin: The Dunes

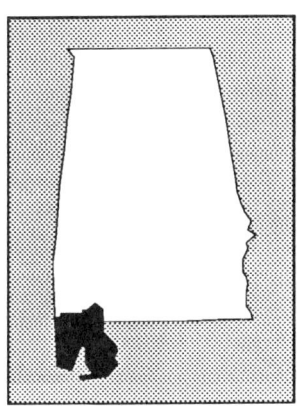

I t is in this region where Alabama meets the sea. Visitors usually come here for the sun and the sand. Once they get here, though, they quickly find that - as wonderful as Alabama's Gulf Coast is - there's much more to this part of the state than just the water and the beach.

Because Mobile is the oldest city in Alabama and one of the oldest in the Southeast, the area around Mobile Bay is filled with historic sites that take visitors from the early 1700s through the present. And nature puts on some of her very best shows here. The region around the bay takes in two counties - Mobile on the west side of the bay and Baldwin on the east. The two counties form a sort of "wishbone" around the bay. And it wasn't lost on early settlers that anyone wanting to come into the bay would have to sail between where the "feet" of the wishbone extend into the Gulf of Mexico and turn to almost touch one another.

The largest city on the west side of the bay, of course, is Mobile. Along the eastern side, smaller cities dot the coastline. There's so much to see and do in these two counties, that visitors have to allow themselves several days, enjoying the Southern hospitality and the taste of the Old South, mixed with dashes of French, Spanish, English and Cajun spices.

Take More Than a Day in Mobile

Since it is the largest city in the area, perhaps Mobile is the logical place  to start when sampling all this region has to offer. A word of warning - there's a lot to see in this part of Alabama and it can't all be done in a day. In fact, you need to plan to spend several days if you hope even to begin to see everything that's here.

Think of Mobile as your great-aunt from the South - the scandalous one who forced your family into the era of Women's Lib.

She still wears hoop skirts the color of azaleas and shawls of Spanish moss draped across her shoulders, yet she bobs her hair and never has married, preferring instead to be independent and self-supporting. She looks every bit the Southern belle on the outside, but inside beats the heart of a very modern woman.

One has only to look at the city's center to see how her past and present combine. Nestled amid Mobile's businesses, hotels and churches is Fort Conde, for more than a century the center of the town's activities.

The fort was headquarters for the military rule of this coastal area by the French, the English and the Spanish. At one time, it was the home base for the entire French Louisiana Territory. It also served Mobile's citizens well as protection from Indians.

In 1711, the fort was built of 14-inch cedar stakes that stood 13 feet high. In 1724, the French made it a more permanent structure of brick and mortar. In 1820, the fort was declared "surplus" by an act of Congress and was sold at public auction. Its walls were blasted down with gunpowder and the rubble used to fill in low-lying riverfront areas.

Fort Conde stands again on its original site, though, after the City of Mobile spent more than $2 million reconstructing it from drawings in French archives. The "soldiers" there today are guides, showing visitors the fort and giving demonstrations of cannon and rifle firings. The fort now serves as the city's Welcome Center, giving visitors a taste of the past along with the latest in tourist information. It is open from 8 a.m. to 5 p.m. daily except Christmas and Mardi Gras.

Alabama's Dunes: Mobile & Baldwin Counties

This two-county region juts into the Gulf of Mexico and takes Alabama to the sea. Almost 500,000 people have chosen to make this part of the state, so rich in both history and recreational opportunities, their home.

Population centers here include Mobile, Prichard, Bay Minette, Chickasaw and Saraland.

More people will arrive if Mobile becomes a Navy Homeport.

THE STATE DOCKS

If you're looking for recent Mobile history, the Alabama State Docks should be on your itinerary. Located at the Port of Mobile, the docks have berths for 34 ocean-going vessels and a 1,000-foot-wide turning basin. Tour lines in the Mobile area arrange tours of the docks.

THE MANSIONS

Of course, no one thinks of Mobile without thinking of antebellum Mobile - with mansions, mint juleps and lavish parties. The city doesn't disappoint visitors looking for this aspect of the city - a number of Mobile's mansions are open to the public. These homes, restored and turned into museums, give visitors a perspective on antebellum life. The oldest of the historic house museums in Mobile is the Condé-Charlotte House, a Federal style structure built in the early 1800s. It began as the city's first official jail and became a private residence in 1845. Jail doors still can be seen in the building, along with a jail floor, exposed when the Historic Mobile Preservation Society purchased the house in 1940 and began renovating it. The Condé-Charlotte House is at 104 Theatre Street, adjacent to Fort Conde. It is open from 10 a.m. to 2 p.m. Tuesday through Saturday. Admission is $2 for adults and $.50 for children.

Oakleigh Mansion, the city's official antebellum period house museum, is built in the Greek Revival style and is noted for the graceful curves of its exterior stairway and its beautiful grounds, filled with azaleas and live oaks. Bricks for the first story of the mansion were made on the site and the main upper portion of the house is of hand-hewn timber.

Perhaps one of the nicest times of year to see Oakleigh is during the annual Christmas tours, usually given in early December. "Candlelight Christmas at Oakleigh" has become a Mobile tradition. Each year, the opening ceremony for the Christmas tours re-enacts an event that took place on Christmas Day, 1885.

On that day, according to reports in the "Mobile Daily Register," the Mobile Rifle Company halted on parade in front of the home to offer a salute to their sponsor Miss Daisy Irwin, whose family owned the home. For the re-enactment, a local teenager is chosen for the part of Miss Daisy each year and an ROTC unit plays the part of the Rifle Company.

During the Christmas season tours, the pathways leading to the home are lighted with candles. Inside, Mobile's official Christmas tree, trimmed with handmade and antique ornaments, sparkles in the parlor.

On the 3-1/2 acres that make up Oakleigh also are the Cox-Deasy House and the Minnie Mitchell Archives. The Cox-Deasy House, built in the mid-1800s, is a raised Creole cottage, typical of the modest homes of middle class residents of the Gulf Coast.

The Mitchell Archives contain books, records, documents and pictures pertaining to the history of Mobile. It is open to the public for research.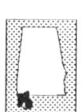

The Oakleigh complex is open from 10 a.m. to 4 p.m. Monday through Saturday and from 2 to 4 p.m. on Sunday. Admission is $4 for adults and $1 for children 6 to 18.

The Richards-DAR House is an Italianate mansion noted for its elaborate "iron lace," which decorates the front facade of the home. The home was built in the 1800s by steamboat captain Charles G. Richards, who came from Maine to Mobile. At the Claiborne Port of Call, he met and married Caroline Elizabeth Steele. Together, they built the home at 256 North Joachim Street.

The Ideal Cement Company bought the house in 1946 from the descendants of Captain and Mrs. Richards and renovated it for offices. In 1973, the home was presented to the City of Mobile, which leased it to the Daughters

Alabama Bureau of Tourism and Travel

House Museums of Mobile include (clockwise from top left) Richards DAR House, Condé-Charlotte House, Bragg-Mitchell Mansion, Oakleigh.

of the American Revolution. The DAR administers it as a museum.

The elaborate ironwork on the outside of the house is an introduction to the lavish interior. Carved Carrara marble forms the mantelpieces, etched panes of ruby Bohemian glass frame the doorway and the front gallery floor is made of gray and white marble squares. In each room, there is a silver "pull-bell," once used for calling the servants and from the ceiling hang brass and bronze chandeliers whose designs are mythological figures holding etched glass globes. In the dining room is one of the largest crystal chandeliers in the city.

The mansion is open Tuesday through Saturday from 10 a.m. to 4 p.m. and Sunday from 1 to 4 p.m. Admission is $2 for adults and $.50 for children.

The Bragg-Mitchell Mansion on Springhill Avenue is one of the grandest antebellum mansions of the Gulf Coast. It was built in 1855 by Judge John Bragg and today is the most photographed building in Mobile. When Judge Bragg was living in his Greek Revival-Italianate mansion, it was the center of social life in the Port City.

When the mansion was restored a few years ago, workers discovered elaborate Victorian stenciling beneath the many coats of paint. The stenciling has been painstakingly restored and the color schemes of the house as it was in the 1870's recreated.

During the Civil War, Judge Bragg moved all of the mansion's elaborate furnishings to a plantation he owned up river from the city, thinking he would save them from the ravages of war. But the country house fell victim to Wilson's Raiders and the house and furnishings were burned. The exquisite mirrors in the mansion's double parlors are among the few original furnishings remaining with the house.

The Bragg-Mitchell House is open from 10 a.m. to 4 p.m. weekdays and 1 to 4 p.m. on Sunday. Admission is $3 for adults and $2 for children.

The Bragg-Mitchell House is part of Mobile's Exploreum, a 12-acre museum center. Also there are one of Alabama's oldest schoolhouses and the Museum of Discovery, a children's hands-on museum, offers youngsters more than 80 science exhibits and hands-on experiments. The museum is open from 9 a.m. to 5 p.m. Tuesday through Friday and from 1 to 5 p.m. Saturday and Sunday. Admission is $3 for adults and $2 for children 2 through 17.

The Carlen House, at 54 Carlen Street, is an excellent example of the Creole cottage. Located on the campus of Murphy High School, well within the city now, the home was a day's wagon ride from town when it was built in 1842 by Michael Carlen. It is decorated with 19th century furnishings and has displays of period fashions throughout. Among the most interesting features of the house are the random-width pine floors in which one still can see the saw marks. The home is open Tuesday through Saturday from 10 a.m. to 5 p.m. and Sunday from 1 to 5 p.m. Admission is free.

MOBILE'S MUSEUMS

The Museum of the City of Mobile, in the century-old Bernstein-Bush House, has exhibits spanning the history of the city. In addition to displays of Indian artifacts, antique carriages and Civil War documents, there are the "Queens of Mardi Gras Mezzanine," saluting the city's annual funfest, and the Hammel Collection of fine women's fashions of the early 20th century. Also at the museum is the world's second largest collection of Boehm porcelains. The museum, at 355 Government Street in the Bernstein-Bush House, is open Tuesday through Saturday, 10 a.m.-5 p.m. and Sunday from 1-5 p.m. Admission is free.

Nearby is the Phoenix Fire Museum at 203 South Claiborne Street, which occupies the home station house of the Phoenix Steam Fire Company No. 6,  organized in 1838. It contains fire engines and fire-fighting equipment from the time of the first Mobile volunteer fire company, founded in 1819, until the present. On the second floor are paintings of volunteer fire stations and members in uniform. The museum is open Tuesday through Saturday, 10 a.m. to 5 p.m. and Sunday from 1 to 5 p.m. Admission is free.

For the art lover, there is the Fine Arts Museum of The South (FAMOS), located in a peaceful setting beside a lake in Langan Park. The permanent collection here includes Southern furniture, decorative arts and American and European 19th-century paintings and prints. The museum is open Tuesday through Sunday from 10 a.m. to 5 p.m. and admission is free.

Mobile's Colleges

Nearby are Spring Hill College and the University of South Alabama. A group of French Catholics donated 38,000 francs, an uncle of Napoleon Bonaparte gave another 25,000 and the City of Mobile provided 380 acres of land so that Spring Hill College, the oldest chartered college in Alabama, could be built. The school still occupies the site chosen by Bishop Michael Portier in 1830 and campus tours are available upon request.

On the campus of the University of South Alabama, you can see Seaman's Bethel Theatre (1860), the Plantation Creole Home (1828), another reconstructed Creole cottage and the Mobile Townhouse (1870), a Federal-style building showing Italianate and Greek Revival influences.

An Ancient Cathedral

Almost as old as the city of Mobile is the Catholic parish here. The Bishop of Quebec formally established the first parish on the Gulf Coast at Mobile in 1703. In 1829, the Diocese of Mobile was established and the parish became the Cathedral of the Immaculate Conception. In 1980, the diocese became an archdiocese and the Cathedral the seat of the diocese.

The cornerstone for the Cathedral building itself was laid in 1835, the building consecrated in 1850. Several renovations and improvements have changed the building over the years, but it remains an awe-inspiring structure.

The exterior of the cathedral, at Dauphin and Claiborne Streets, has a rather severe classic look, but inside, the structure fairly explodes with the beauty of stained glass, burnished bronze and carved wood. At the front of the cathedral is a marble altar, topped with a magnificent bronze canopy. Along the side aisles are 12 windows of German art glass depicting New Testament scenes.

Two other churches in the city tell the history of another group of Mobile's early residents. State Street AME Zion Church at 502 State Street was constructed in 1854. One of the most imposing structures to be built for a black congregation in Alabama during the Reconstruction period, it is the oldest Methodist church building in Mobile and is one of only two black Methodist churches established in the city prior to the Civil War. Stone Street Baptist Church at 311 Cleveland is the oldest black church in the state. It was built in 1820, but the congregation first met under a brush arbor near Government Street.

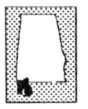

A Cemetery to Behold

While touring cemeteries may not seem like the kind of thing most people do on their vacations, there is a cemetery in Mobile you need to see. Magnolia, Mobile's third oldest municipal cemetery, was opened in 1836. An epidemic of yellow fever had filled Church Street Cemetery and the new cemetery had to be opened at once. The small parcel of land that was designated for the cemetery now is part of Magnolia's more than 100 acres.

Laid out in 36 squares on a grid pattern, the cemetery is oriented from east to west, a standard Western burial practice. Magnolia offers a wide variety of funerary art and tomb sculpture.

At Colonel John Hinson's burial site (1821), for example, a three-dimensional hand-carved weeping willow is presented in the traditional "bed board" marker. The Hinson family plot contains several other hand-carved markers, signed by Jarvis Turner, a local stonecarver who is himself buried in Magnolia.

In Magnolia, there are a number of "group association" plots. These may have been common because such groups, predating insurance companies, arranged for the burial of their members. Among those in Magnolia are the Baymen's Benevolent Association, whose monument features a sailing ship and cotton bail; Woodmen of the World, with a monument of various tree forms and timbering tools, and the Cotton Benevolent Association's full scale figure of a cotton gin.

The cast iron industry, active in 19th-century Mobile, is represented in the cemetery in fences, markers and even in full scale sculpture. Among the cast iron figures in the cemetery are the cast iron setter, representing watchfulness and fidelity, in the Anderson plot, and the statue of a woman, the origin of which remains a mystery.

Confederate Rest, where 1,100 war dead are buried, is a major part of Magnolia. A prominent element in this section is a statue of a Confederate soldier, completed by Matthew J. Lawler in the late 1800s. The statue, a full figure, was damaged by lightning and the upper portion of the figure was reinstalled on a pedestal base.

The Jewish Cemetery within Magnolia is marked primarily with traditional stone bearing Hebrew inscriptions. Near this section is a group of mausolea. The Tardy Mausoleum, is one of the very early brick structures built by local artisans. A later one, the Owen Farley Mausoleum, is of roughly textured blocks. The Caldwell Mausoleum is done in Gothic Revival style, while the Wilson Family Mausoleum illustrates Egyptian revival style.

In the National Cemetery area is the grave of Chappo Geronimo, son of the Apache leader. The Bellingrath-Morse monument, a classic-style colonnade, is here.

A number of Mobile's black citizens are buried in Magnolia. One of them, Bettie Hunter, was a prosperous Mobilian. Also buried here are the black soldiers of General Hawkins' First Division, Union soldiers who died during an attack on Fort Blakeley on April 9, 1865.

A brochure detailing a walking/driving tour of the cemetery is available at the Fort Conde Welcome Center. Remember when visiting Magnolia that it is an active cemetery with funeral services being conducted regularly. Visitors are expected to respect others at the cemetery. And even though the markers in the cemetery are tempting subjects, stone rubbings are not allowed.

Also worth a visit while in the downtown area is the Church Street East Historic District, Mobile second oldest existing neighborhood. Within the district, you'll find Christ Episcopal Church (115 South Conception Street), where the Tiffany and Cenzo stained glass windows are outstanding examples of this art form; the Church Street Cemetery (Scott and Church Streets), established in 1819; City Hall (111 Royal Street), one of the oldest municipal buildings in the United States still in use; Barton Academy (504 Government Street), Alabama's oldest public school and a Union hospital following the fall of Mobile in 1865; Spanish Plaza (Hamilton and Government Streets), which honors Mobile's sister city, Malaga, Spain, and Bienville Square (St. Francis and St. Joseph Streets), commemorating the city's French founders.

A Few More Historic Districts

A city with this much history obviously has a number of historic districts. Church Street is just one. DeTonti Square, built in the 1850s during Mobile's "Golden Era" is another. Homes here belonged to cotton brokers, merchants, river pilots and maritime traders. Common Street Historic District, a small one-block area, is in the Old Dauphin Way Preservation District, which was built during the mid-1800s to the early 1920s.

The USS *Alabama*

Military history floats serenely in Mobile Bay in the hulking shape of the Battleship "USS Alabama."

When the keel of the battleship was laid at the Norfolk Navy Yard in Virginia on February 1, 1940, Europe already was involved in World War II. Two years later - two months after Pearl Harbor - the $200 million ship was launched, given the official numerical designation BB-60 and christened the "USS Alabama."

The gray lady glided into the water that day weighing more than 35,000 tons. She measured 680 feet from bow to stern and 193 feet from keel to mast, with a breadth of 108. Her side armor was a foot thick above the waterline, tapering to one inch at the bottom. Her four golden propellers, each weighing more than 18 tons, could drive her through the seas at speeds up to 28 knots - more than 32 miles per hour.

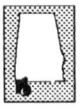

During her years of service, the battleship saw 37 months of active duty during World War II. The "Lucky A" downed a total of 22 planes and earned nine battle stars, but never suffered casualties or significant damage in enemy attacks.

After the war, she was placed in mothballs in Bremerton, Washington. When the Navy announced in 1962 that the battleship would be scrapped, it seemed as if the luck had run out for the "USS Alabama."

But the Navy hadn't counted on 3 million determined Alabamians. A campaign was launched to bring the ship "home" as a memorial to Alabama's sons and daughters who had served in World War II and in Korea. The Navy abandoned plans to scrap the "Lucky A" and donated the ship to the cause. Then it was up to the Alabamians to raise the money to bring her to her final port. From all over the state, funds poured in. School children, contributing nickels, dimes and quarters to the cause, raised almost $100,000 for the ship.

The USS Alabama, Mobile Bay

The "USS Alabama" sailed into Mobile Bay in September, 1964.

Today, the battleship welcomes more than 300,000 visitors to her decks each year. Taking a self-guided walking tour, those who come to see her can look close-up at the ship from stem to stern, from top to bottom.

Also at Battleship Memorial Park are the submarine "USS Drum" (also open for tours), a marine Corsair (the airplane known as "Whistling Death"), "Calamity Jane," a B-52 bomber, an Army Air Corps fighter plane and a number of tanks and guns. There also is a bit of Alabama pride from Huntsville. A Redstone rocket, like the ones first used to launch men into space, towers above the exhibits at the park.

The most important things to remember when planning a visit to Battleship Park are the words "walking tour" and the number "680" - as in feet in the ship's length (and that's if you just walk from one end to another, not taking into consideration weaving among turrets, crew's quarters and the bridge or going up and down several flights of stairs). In other words, wear your walking shoes.

To reach Battleship Memorial Park, take the Bankhead or George C. Wallace Tunnel under the bay to Battleship Parkway.

The park is open every day (except Christmas) from 8 a.m. to sunset. Admission is $1 per car for parking and $5 for adults, $2.50 for children 6-11.

If seeing the "Alabama" makes you want to take to the sea, you might try a cruise on the "Commander," a 150-passenger vessel that leaves Battleship

---

Mobile and Baldwin Counties   **205**

Park for Harbor Tours and Dinner Cruises. The 90-minute Harbor Tour Cruise takes you by the "Alabama," then by Little Sand Island out into Mobile Harbor. The Dinner Cruise takes a little over two hours and includes a buffet and music for listening or dancing. You don't need reservations for the Harbor Tours (prices range from $6 to $8) but you do for the Dinner Cruises ($22.95 for adults, $14.95 for children).

OUTSIDE OF TOWN

Once you've seen the city of Mobile, make it a point to see Mobile County. Just north of Mobile on I-65 is Prichard, where you'll find AfricaTown U.S.A. State Park.

The park salutes the passengers of the "Clotilde," the last known vessel carrying a cargo of Africans intended for slavery to this country. The passengers never became slaves because federal authorities thwarted the attempt to smuggle and enslave them.

The freed passengers settled in the community of Plateau and called it AfricaTown U.S.A. Many of their descendants live there today. It is the oldest African community in the state. As you drive through AfricaTown U.S.A., you can see the Scott Paper Company, which is on the site of the shipyard of William Foster. It was from this place that the "Clotilde" sailed. Also in the area is the grave of Foster, who was the builder and captain of the ship. Timothy Meaher commissioned the sailing of the ship in 1859 and later established AfricaTown U.S.A. His gravesite is in the area as well.

Plateau Cemetery is the burial site for Cudjoe Lewis, the last survivor among the passengers of the "Clotilde." Many of the other slaves who sailed on the ship also are buried here. Across the street is Union Baptist Church and the Cudjoe Lewis Memorial. The church was attended by many passengers of the "Clotilde" and their descendants. The Lewis Memorial stands in front of the church.

Southwest of Mobile, off I-10 at the Theodore-Dawes exit, is the Mobile Greyhound Park, where they race from January 15 through December 15. You can't take the kids with you to this one - no one under 18 is allowed. But it's a fun "grown-ups only" outing. The park has a dining room and two lounges and you can watch the races from an air-conditioned grandstand. Admission is $1 for the grandstand, $2.50 for the clubhouse. Races on matinee days - Monday, Wednesday and Friday start at 1 p.m. Night racing, daily except for Sunday, begins at 7:30 p.m.

BELLINGRATH GARDENS

As you head south from Mobile, plan to spend a while at Bellingrath Gardens. To get there, take U.S. 90 West to Theodore. In Theodore, take Bellingrath Highway to the Gardens. The estate once was the residence of Coca-Cola bottling pioneer Walter D. Bellingrath and his wife Bessie. In 1919, Bellingrath purchased the land for a retreat, a place, he said, where he could "lie down with my feet on the sofa."

And Bell Camp was that place for him for a few years. Then he and his wife began the landscaping of their fishing camp and Bellingrath Gardens was born. Before long, friends of the couple were asking if they could come and see the gardens, patterned after those of England, France and Italy. From there, it was only a short step to abandoning the name Bell Camp and opening the gardens to the public.

Among the gardens on the grounds is the Oriental-American garden, with tea houses and a moon bridge. This area is a bird sanctuary where more than 200 species either live or spend part of the migratory season.

At the center of the gardens is the Bellingrath Gallery of Boehm Porcelains, among the largest public displays of these porcelains in the world.

Mobile Area Chamber of Commerce

Bellingrath Gardens, Theodore

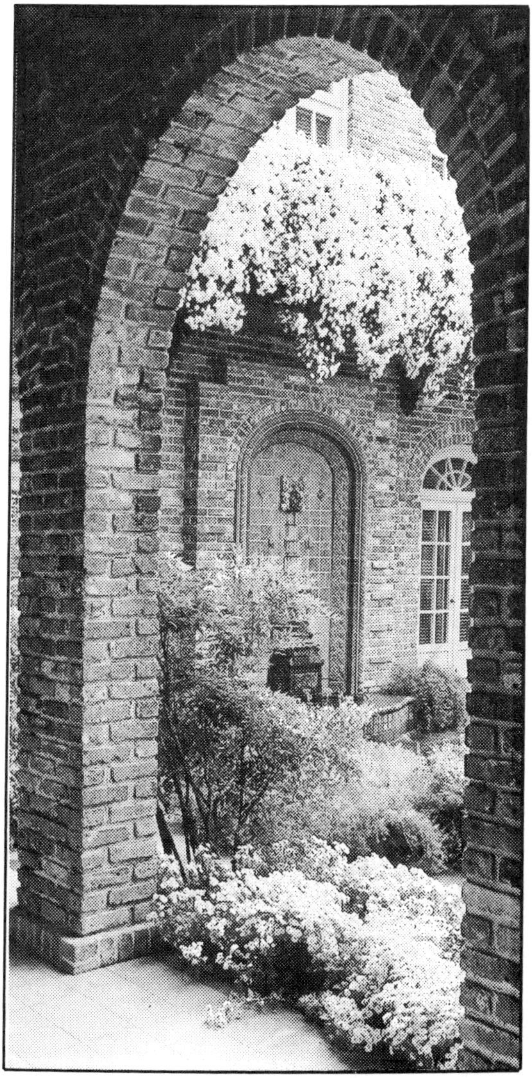

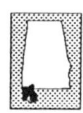

On the 800-acre estate is the Bellingrath Home, which houses the Bessie Morse Bellingrath Collection of antique furniture, fine china and rare porcelain. Within the home, which combines French, English and Mediterranean architectural styles, are three dining areas, a drawing room and an upstairs accented with galleries of iron lacework and windows that open onto the gardens.

Because the gardens are filled with more than 200,000 plants of various

types, something is in bloom every month at Bellingrath. It takes at least half a day to see the gardens and home, which are open daily. Admission to the gardens is $5 for adults and $2.50 for children 6 to 12. Admission to the home is an additional $6.25 per person.

OVER TO THE BAYOU

When you leave Bellingrath Gardens, you can drive west on Alabama 188 as it loops around near the coast and then back upward to Bayou La Batre, one of the top seafood producing areas in the nation. Here you can tour the local seafood plants and chat with the locals, many of whom are direct descendants of the Acadians who came to the area from Nova Scotia at the turn of the century.

If possible, you want to time your visit to this city during June when the Catholic community - in fact, the whole city - celebrates The Blessing of the Fleet. The traditional ceremony is stretched into a weekend of fun and food. Gumbo is the main course. After St. Margaret's Church almost ran out of gumbo during the festival a few years ago, the church acquired a 250-gallon stainless steel cookpot that stands 61 inches high, is 35-1/2 feet in circumference and weighs 525. This pot, they say, will cook up enough gumbo to serve any crowd. Because this is a seafood festival, it makes sense that the gumbo is stirred with an oar as it cooks.

If gumbo isn't your dish, the folks in Bayou La Batre also cook up fish, shrimp and crab. For landlubbers, there are hamburgers and hot dogs.

Saturday, while the cooking's going on, there are games, arts and crafts exhibits and children's events. On Sunday, there are a land parade and the crowning of the Fleet Blessing Queen. Then the decorated shrimp and oyster boats parade in the bayou as they are blessed.

DAUPHIN ISLAND

After you've eaten your fill, get back on Highway 188 and head east until it intersects with County 193, where you'll turn south and cross the four-mile-long high-rise bridge and causeway to Dauphin Island. The island, rich in history, long has been a favorite recreation area. Now more and more people are going there to live. And human visitors aren't the only ones finding the island a nice place to be. A 60-acre bird sanctuary on the island is home to a number of local species and a stopover for several migratory birds.

On the east end of the island is Fort Gaines, one of two forts that played an important part in decisive sea battles during the Civil War.

The five-sided fort was begun in 1821 and completed in its present form in the 1850s. This brick fortress guarded the western approach to Mobile Bay. Across the bay sat Fort Morgan. The Confederate forces began occupying the fort in 1861, hoping that with these two defenses they could hold off an approach from sea by the Union army.

Despite heavy cannon fire from the forts, Admiral David Farragut's fleet fought and won the Battle of Mobile Bay in August, 1864. It was during this battle that Farragut is said to have shouted, "Damn the torpedoes. Full speed ahead." The fort fell to Union land forces later that month.

Today visitors tour the fort, amazingly untouched by the battle, and a Confederate museum on the site. The fort is open daily (except for Christmas) from 9 a.m. to 5 p.m. and admission is $2 for adults, $1 for children.

BALDWIN AND THE EASTERN SHORE

When you've seen Mobile County and the western side of Mobile Bay, you're ready to take in the sights of Baldwin County and the "Eastern Shore." You have a choice about how to get there.

If Fort Morgan, the other guardian of the entrance to Mobile Bay, is your destination, you can make the trip from Dauphin Island by water. The Mobile Bay Ferry runs year-round between the two forts. About every 80 minutes, the boat leaves on its route, which takes you on a sightseeing voyage to Fort Morgan Park. Rates for the trip vary, depending on whether you're walking, riding a motorcycle or driving a car, truck, trailer or motorhome. The 30-minute trip saves about 100 miles of driving between the two shores. The park sits on land explored by the Spanish in the early 1500s. Over the next 300 years, the site was held by the Spanish, the French, the British and, finally, the United States. It was the location of two engagements of the War of 1812. Today the park is more peaceful, offering swimming, fishing and picnicking. Concessions are available from a shop located in restored Senior Staff Officers' Quarters.

On the reservation is Fort Morgan, a star-shaped, brick structure. It was one of the last Confederate strongholds to fall to Union forces, It was begun in 1819 to replace the one captured by the British in 1812. In addition to its part in the Civil War, the fort was activated in the Spanish-American War and World Wars I and II.

FORT MORGAN MUSEUM

Fort Morgan Museum, patterned after a 10-sided Citadel, has displays tracing the history of the fort as well as local history. Fort Morgan is open from 8 a.m. to 5 p.m. Monday through Friday and from 9 a.m. to 5 p.m. on Saturday and Sunday. Admission is $2 for adults and $1 for children 6 to 18.

When you get to Fort Morgan, you're in Baldwin County and it won't take you long to discover that there's as much to see and do on this side of the bay as on the other.

HEAD TO THE BEACH

As you drive east away from Fort Morgan, you can't miss the beaches - they're all around you. All along the Alabama Gulf Coast are opportunities to swim, fish, boat, shrimp or sail. Take Alabama 180 east until it intersects with Alabama 59 South. When you get to Alabama 182, take that road east from Gulf Shores toward Orange Beach. Along the way, you'll enjoy more than 30 miles of coastline, with blue seas and white sands.

Along the way, you'll see Gulf State Resort Park, a 6,000-acre playground for kids and grown-ups. The resort inn, with more than 100 rooms, is right

---

on the beach and near the 825-foot pier that takes fisherman out where they want to be - over the salt water, out into the Gulf.

Set back from the beach, around a fresh water lake, are more than 400 improved camping sites and 21 cottages. When they aren't at the beach, campers can enjoy fishing, swimming and skiing in the lake.

Also at the resort are tennis courts, an 18-hole golf course, a marina and hiking and cycling trails. Pets are allowed if they are kept on leashes.

Bon Secour Wildlife Refuge

A nature preserve at Gulf State Park is one of two in the area. The other, Bon Secour Wildlife Refuge, is on Bon Secour Bay, just north of the figure of land that divides Mobile Bay from the Gulf of Mexico. Both are open year-round and offer fresh water lakes, nature trails, picnic areas, visitor centers and miles of undeveloped beaches.

Endangered species, including Loggerhead Turtles and American Alligators, make the preserves their home. Songbirds, pelicans, herons and ospreys are found in abundance in the area. In September and October, wildflowers mix with migrating Monarch but-

Alabama Bureau of Tourism and Travel

Fort Morgan, Gulf Shores

terflies to bring breathtaking color to the preserves.

The Gulf Shores area itself offers many different types of marine experiences. Those who enjoy snorkeling and scuba diving take advantage of the clear Gulf waters to explore shipwrecks and natural and artificial reefs.

Waterville, U.S.A.

In the city of Gulf Shores itself is Waterville, U.S.A. While it may seem odd to have a water park practically within sight of the beaches and the Gulf,

---

these facilities are increasing in popularity - perhaps with visitors who prefer their waves man-made and without passing crabs and fish.

Waterville, U.S.A. offers just that. Set on 17-acres, the park offers a 500,000-gallon wave pool that generates three-foot waves, five body slides, white water tube riding, a slow moving 1300-foot "river," a children's play area and 36 holes of miniature golf. The water park is open from Memorial Day to Labor Day from 10 a.m. to 8 p.m. Admission is $10.95.

Zooland Animal Park, also in Gulf Shores, offers another opportunity for a family outing. The park has more than 100 exotic and endangered species on display in facilities resembling their natural habitats. Also at the park is an 18-hole mini golf course, where the obstacles - naturally - have animal themes. Hours at the animal park vary according to the season. During the summer, the park opens at 10 a.m. and closes at 7 p.m. Opening time during the fall, winter and spring moves up to 9 a.m. and closing varies from 6 p.m. to 4 p.m. as the season changes. Admission is $5 for adults, $3.50 for children 3 to 11.

ORANGE BEACH

Farther east on the coast is Orange Beach, the place to go if you want to charter a boat of any shape, size or description. There are more than 50 boats available at marinas and charter centers for fishing expeditions. In addition, there are party boats, pontoons, jet skis and sailboats just waiting to take visitors out into the waters of the Gulf or the back bays.

One charter service, Island Sailing Center, offers trips on classic Chesapeake Bay bug-eye ketches.

The ketches once dredged for oysters in the Chesapeake Bay and because they are "shallowdraft" vessels, they are perfect for exploring the back bays of the Gulf area. You can just relax and enjoy the trip or participate in the sailing aboard the fully restored ketches, which make afternoon, sunset and Dinner Cruise trips.

Other saltwater enthusiasts like to try their hand at shrimping and the opportunity is nearby in the form of the "Daedalus," a 50-foot sailboat. Those who charter the boat can travel the waters with seining nets and not only capture the shrimp, but enjoy the company of dolphins who swim along side the boat. The sailboat leaves from Pirate's Cove.

In Orange Beach, you'll find Main Street, an "amusement mall and park." The air-conditioned interior of the mall looks like a Victorian street with two-story storefronts, street lamps and trees.

Behind the storefronts, you'll find party rooms, a billiard parlor, a skating rink, video games, kiddie rides, a deli and a teen dance club. Outside in the park, there are mini-speed boats, go-carts and a skateboard run.

Main Street is open daily during Alabama Education Association Week and during the week-long Mobile City School break. After that, it is open weekends only from late April to late May.

Hours are 10 a.m. to 11 p.m. From late May to early September, Main Street is open daily from 10 a.m. to 11 p.m. Admission is $1 and ride tickets

---

deal on "PassPorts," a package of ride tickets and tokens.

Even though you may think first of the beach when you think of heading to South Alabama, that's not all there is to see there. From Gulf Shores, you can drive north on Alabama 59 to explore the inland areas of Baldwin County as well as the "Eastern Shore" portion of Mobile Bay.

POINT CLEAR

About 11 miles north of Gulf Shores, turn west on U.S. 98. In Barnwell, get on Alternate U.S. 98 (Farther north along the shore, this will become U.S. 98.) and head up the coast to Point Clear, where the Eastern Shore area officially begins. Scattered along the coast of Mobile Bay, from Point Clear northward to Spanish Fort, the cities of the Eastern Shore pop up about every three miles. Each city, despite its grouping with the others, has its own flavor and its own attractions.

Years ago, wealthy Mobilians summered in Point Clear and nearby Battles Wharf and they've left a legacy of charm that's visible in the antebellum homes ringed with magnificent gardens.

THE GRAND HOTEL

Since 1847, the Grand Hotel has played host to guests from around the world. Today, the resort retains the secluded, elegant atmosphere that has made the hotel a favorite getaway for more than a century. The Grand Hotel, on 550 landscaped acres, offers houses, cottages, bungalows and hotel rooms. Guests can play tennis, golf or lawn games, sun on the beach, go horseback riding, cycling sailing or yachting, windsurf, dance or exercise. Even if you bring the family, you can plan to spend some "adults-only" time with your spouse. Supervised children's activities are available free to the guests.

While in Point Clear, stop by Punta Clara Kitchen to stock up on homemade goodies from candy to pickles - all made from family recipes. The kitchen is located in Miss Colleen's House, a sprawling Victorian home in the historic district of Point Clear. Punta Clara Kitchen is open from 9 a.m. to 5 p.m. Monday through Saturday and from 12:30 to 5 p.m. on Sunday. Miss Colleen's House is open the same hours and there is no admission charge.

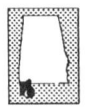

Also in Point Clear, you'll find another opportunity to charter a boat and head for the waters of the bay. The "Southern Comfort," a 111-foot vessel with seven staterooms, offers a number of cruise options - cocktail and dinner cruises and pleasure cruises and cruises to Bellingrath Gardens.

FAIRHOPE

Fairhope, about five miles north of Point Clear, is the largest of the Eastern Shore communities. It was founded in the 1890s by Iowans who hoped to show that Henry George's single-tax theory was workable. The Fairhope Single Tax Colony office leases all the land in the town for a single tax based on an annual assessment. From this tax comes the money for all community services as well as county and state taxes.

Fairhope is a sort of art center as well. The Eastern Shore Art Association is here and the city seems to be a gathering place for artists, writers and other creative types.

Montrose, the next spot up the coast, was the location of a British camp where soldiers were sent to avoid malaria when that disease stalked the troops in Mobile. Montrose is a National Historic District and veterans of seven wars are buried in the old Montrose Cemetery. The post office building in the city is owned by the Historic District of Montrose, making it one of very few post offices not owned by the federal government.

Greek mythology comes to the Eastern Shore in the city of Daphne. Apollo is said to have changed the nymph Daphne into a laurel tree and the city got its name because of the many laurel trees in the area.

The United States Sports Academy, "America's Graduate School of Sports," is in Daphne. The complex houses a number of laboratories studying such things as human performance, rehabilitation and strength conditioning as well as a library learning center said to be one of the best in the country in sports education. Also on campus is the American Research Institution for Substance Abuse.

Students here can gain their Masters of Sport Science Degrees in Sport Coaching, Sport Fitness, Sport Management, Sports Medicine and Sport Research. In addition, the school offers coaching certification on any level from elementary school to Olympic team.

The American Sport Art Museum and Archives on the academy campus is crammed with sports memorabilia, history, art and literature. The gallery is open from 10 a.m. to 2 p.m. Monday through Friday. There is no admission charge.

MALBIS: IT'S GREEK TO US

Near Daphne is Malbis, a Greek community where you'll find the Malbis Plantation and the Malbis Greek Orthodox Church. Jason Malbis, who left the reality of his native Greece at the end of the 19th century to search for the land of his dreams, is responsible for this sampling of Greece which rises above the Alabama countryside.

When Malbis reached the states, he purchased a small tract of land across Mobile Bay from the city of Mobile. From this simple beginning grew the  Greek community, which originally consisted of a cannery, an ice plant, a power plant, a bakery, a nursery and a motel.

During the first few years in this remote area of Alabama, Malbis and his companions were barely able to make enough money to survive. As time passed, however, the community grew and prospered and more Greek immigrants arrived to fill the ranks of residents and to pool their resources.

Shortly before World War II, Malbis returned to Greece for a visit. Unfortunately, before he could return to Alabama, the war had come to his homeland. In 1942, the leader of Malbis Plantation died far away from the land he had come to love. But Malbis' dream - a cathedral opened to all faiths - didn't die with him. Nearly five years in the construction and built at a cost

---

of more than $1 million, the Greek Orthodox Church was dedicated in 1965. The Church, built following the exact details of Byzantine architecture, serves as the nation's first mission center of the Greek Orthodox faith.

The church is a copy of a stately one in Athens, Greece. Marble was brought in from the same quarries that provided stone for the Parthenon. A master painter and his assistants were brought from Greece to paint the murals on the church's walls and panels and the ceiling of the rotunda.

Though he died far from his adopted home, Malbis has found a resting place there. His body now rests in a shrine inside the church he dreamed of, but never saw.

SPANISH FORT

Sitting on a bluff almost at the top of Mobile Bay is Spanish Fort, a city of tall pines, magnolias and oaks. Just north of Spanish Fort on Alabama 225 is Blakeley, a spot that just seemed to lie in the path of history. Some 4,000 years ago, it was a prehistoric Indian village, in the 18th century, it was a French settlement and in 1814, it was settled by New Englanders and named for Josiah Blakeley. It was Baldwin County's first county seat until yellow fever swept through and killed the booming riverfront town.

But history came back to Blakeley during the Civil War, when the last major battle of that conflict was fought at Fort Blakeley on April 9, 1865. The battle ended after the surrender of General Lee, hundreds of miles away in Virginia.

Today, Civil War breastworks wind their way through the woods of Blakeley and the remains of earthen forts, old rifle pits and battery sites are spread across the area. Historic Blakeley Park, listed on the National Register of Historic Places, is the largest such site east of the Mississippi River.

The park is open in the winter from 9 a.m. until sunset and in the summer from 9:30 a.m. until 6:30 p.m. Admission is $1.50 for adults and $.75 for children six to 12.

From Spanish Fort and Blakeley, continue north on Alabama 225 to its intersection with Baldwin County 138. This road takes you to Bay Minette and Peacock Valley Vineyards. The largest winery in the state, Peacock Valley offers tours of the facility.

TENSAW AND FORT MIMS

Return to Bay Minette and take Alabama 59 North back to Alabama 225. Take that road north into Tensaw and Fort Mims Historic Site. The fort, which sat on the Alabama River, was built around the home of settler Samuel Mims. When Mims built the fort, he probably never expected it to be the site of an event that would launch a war.

In 1813, a party of several hundred Creek Indians returning from a trading mission was attacked by settlers at Burnt Corn Creek (in what now is Baldwin County). Fearing a vengeful attack by the Indians, settlers came to Fort Mims for protection. On August 13, 1813, warriors led by William Weatherford (Red Eagle) attacked the fort and killed more than 500 people.

Weatherford (Red Eagle) attacked the fort and killed more than 500 people. The bloody massacre there triggered the beginning of the Creek Indian War and settlers and soldiers shouted the battle cry of "Remember Fort Mims" as Andrew Jackson and his forces made their way from Indian village to Indian village, defeating the Creeks and burning their homes.

Today at Fort Mims, there is only a monument to mark the site of the fort, but Baldwin County is developing the area in order to give visitors better access to the site. Plans call for completion of the project in about two years.

WHERE TO STAY

There are any number of chain hotels and motels in the area, some of them housed in historic buildings and others overlooking the bay.
In addition, there are independent facilities. Among them are:

In Mobile: The Drury Inn, Malaga Inn (Located in restored antebellum twin townhouses) and the Warren Inn.

In Elberta: Donrovan (This B&B has three guests rooms and serves a full breakfast.).

In Gulf Shores: Gulf Shores Plantation (Six condominiums here provide 300 suites with fully equipped kitchens. The complex has five outdoor pools and one indoor, heated one. There also are eight tennis courts, a game room and a fitness center.), Island Winds East, The Phoenix, Seaside Beach and Racquet Club, Summerchase, Summerhouse on Romar Beach, Island Winds West, Island Sunrise, Island Shores, Boardwalk, Hardwick House (two-bedroom kitchen apartments), Lighthouse, Port of Call and Gulf Shores Surf and Racquet Club.
Bed and Breakfasts in the area include:
In Mobile: Church Street Inn and Stickney Hollow. In Fairhope: Mershon Court Bed and Breakfast Inn, The Guest House, Marcella's Tea Room and Inn and (Doc and Dawn's) Garden Cottage Bed and Breakfast.
In addition to camping facilities at Gulf State Park, there are a number of other campgrounds in the area. Among them are:
In Dauphin Island: Fort Gaines Campground (private path to beaches, hiking trail to bird sanctuary). In Mobile: I-10 Campgrounds and Chickasaboque Park.

WHERE TO EAT

Almost any restaurant you choose in this area is going to offer a variety of seafood dishes. In addition to chain restaurants here, there are a number of independently owned ones.

Among them are: In Mobile: Roussos, Weichman's All Seasons, Wintzell's Oyster House (a Mobile landmark), John Word's (in an old warehouse across the street from the Cathedral of the Immaculate Conception), Tiny Diny and Tommie's Terminal Restaurant. There are a number of barbecue restaurants in the area. One of them, Fletcher's Skyline Family Restaurant, has been family owned and operated for more than 50 years.

In Daphne: Malbis Restaurant, Nautilus, Andree's Wine and Cheese and Pier Four.

In Gulf Shores: Mikee's, Sea 'n' Suds, Hazel's Nook (Try breakfast here. By gubernatorial proclamation, it's the home of the official biscuits of Alabama), Coconut Willie's, the Original Oyster House, The Shrimp Boat Restaurant, A La Carte, Adolph's and the Pink Pony Pub.

In Orange Beach: Zeke's, Doc's Seafood Shack and Oyster Bar, Perdido Pass Restaurant, Hemingway's (Until his death in 1988, Eddie Prudhomme was master chef here.), Voyagers, Cotton's and Shirley and Wayne's (It boasts of being "the Gulf Coast's only supper club.)

In Fairhope: Dusty Rhoades (Northern Italian cuisine), Gulwin's, Gambino's (Southern Italian cuisine), Mary Ann's Deli, Original Ben's Jr. (barbecue and, according to some Fairhope residents, "the best hamburgers you can get anywhere"), Twin Oaks (Oriental cuisine), The Wine Merchant, the Yardarm and Wintzell's Old Bay Steamer. In Point Clear: The Wash House. In Spanish Fort: Bates House of Turkey.

ANNUAL EVENTS

Among the annual events in this part of the

Camellia Display, Bellingrath Gardens, January.
Surrender of the Fort, Fort Gaines, (Re-creation of the 1861 surrender of Fort Gaines to the Republic of Alabama at the onset of the Civil War), January.
Senior Bowl, Mobile, January.

AfricaTown Folk Festival, AfricaTown U.S.A. (Prichard), February.
Civil War Encampment, Fort Gaines, (Re-creation of Civil War camp life), February.
Spring Flowering Bulb Display, Bellingrath Gardens, February.
Mardi Gras, Mobile and Gulf Shores, late February, March or April.

Mobile Historic Homes Tour, March.
Azalea Masterpiece, Bellingrath Gardens, March.
Arts and Crafts Festival, Fairhope, March.
Renaissance Festival, Fort Gaines, (Re-creation of Medieval life), March.

Elberta German Sausage Festival, Elberta, March and October
Azalea Trail Festival, Mobile, March.
Craft Bugs Pre-Easter Extravaganza, Mobile, March or April.
Blakeley Battle Festival, Spanish Fort. Late March or early
April.
Easter Chocolate Festival, Mobile, March or April.

Chickasaboque Open Frisbee Golf Tournament, Mobile, April.
Crawfish Boil, Fort Gaines, April.
Taste of Mobile, April.
Mobile Expo, April.
Gulf of Mexico Seafood Culinary Competition, Mobile, April.
Dauphin Island Sailboat Regatta, April.

Strawberry Festival, Loxley, May.
"A Day at the Fort," Fort Gaines, May.
Art-in-the-Park, Foley, May.
Sea Oats Festival, Gulf Shores, May.
Jazz Festival, Mobile, May.

Confederate Fort Gaines, Fort Gaines, (Re-creation of a day in
the life of a Confederate soldier), June.
Alabama/Mississippi High School All-Star Shrine Classic, Mobile.
(Annual football game between Alabama and Mississippi all-star
players), June.
Honey Bee Festival, Robertsdale, June.
Blessing of the Fleet, Bayou La Batre, June.

Grand Bay Watermelon Festival, Grand Bay, July.
Fourth of July Fireworks Display, Gulf Shores.
Alabama's Deep Sea Fishing Rodeo, Dauphin Island, July.
America's Young Woman of the Year Finals, Mobile, July.

Battle of Mobile Bay, Fort Gaines, August.
Civil War Encampment, Gulf Shores (Fort Morgan), August.
Re-enactment of the Massacre at Fort Mims, Tensaw, August.

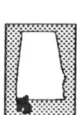

A Taste of the Fort, Fort Gaines, September.
Alabama Port Volunteer Fire Department Crab Festival, Coden,
September.
Baldwin County Fair, Robertsdale, September.
Greater Gulf State Fair, Mobile, September.
Bayou Area Expo and Seafood Festival, September.
Outdoor Arts and Crafts Show, Mobile, September.
Mobile Jazz Festival, September.

Greater Gulf Coast Family Fishing Rodeo, Gulf Shores, September.

Tropical Foliage Display, Bellingrath Gardens, October.
Blakeley Cajun/Bluegrass Festival, Spanish Fort, October.
Shrimp Festival, Gulf Shores, October.
Haunted Fort, Fort Gaines Historic Site, October.
Exploreum Haunted House, October.

Christmas Jubilee, Mobile, November.
Taste 'N Tee Off, Bayou La Batre, November.
Confederate Camp of Instruction, Fort Gaines, November.
Heritage Day Festival, Silverhill, November.
Pecan Festival, Theodore, November.
Chrysanthemum Extravaganza, Bellingrath Gardens, November.
Christmas Open House, Daphne and Fairhope, November.
Linda Zoghby Christmas Concert, Mobile, November.
Alabama-Auburn Scholarship Golf Classic, Gulf Shores, November.
Christmas Trees Around the World, Elberta, December.
Oakleigh Candlelight Christmas, Mobile, December.

Candlelight Christmas at the Richards-DAR House, Mobile, December.
Christmas Fest, Bay Minette, December.
Christmas Parade, Fairhope, December.
Christmas in the Park, Foley, December.
Christmas at The Fort, Fort Gaines, December.
Christmas in the Park, Silverhill, December.
Poinsettia Extravaganza, Bellingrath Gardens, December.
Decemberfest and Taste of the Tropics, Gulf Shores, December.
Kwanzaa (African-American Year-end Celebration), Prichard, December.

The Night Stars Fell on Alabama

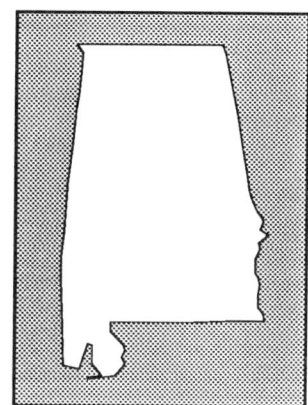

"Stars Fell on Alabama" - it's been a big band standard for years and some people believe it's the state song. It's not the state song, but it is a rather romanticized account of something that really happened in the state.

There was a meteor shower on the night of November 13, 1833, filling the sky with fiery sparks and whirling wheels of light. Alabamians on that night got a particularly good view of the shower, seen in Europe and North America.

In truth, meteors - or falling stars - can be seen somewhere on Earth on almost any clear night. A shower of them that's big enough to cause a noticeable stir among viewers usually consists of about 50 an hour.

On this night, though, the sky literally blazed with meteors, falling at the rate of 200,000 per hour.

When the phenomenon began, frightened spectators thought Biblical prophecy was coming true and the world was ending. In a Huntsville tavern, all drinking and gambling stopped as soon as the stars began to fall. Coins and beer bottles clattered to the floor as tavern patrons scattered. Some of them ran to the stables for their horses and a quick getaway. Others fell to their knees in prayer and repentance. One man even confessed that he had come to Huntsville to rob a bank.

In St. Clair County, young couples were dancing at a pavilion near Greensport. The singing, dancing and music stopped as the night sky suddenly became as bright as day. Ladies screamed and men prayed. Almost as suddenly as it had begun, the shower of stars ended. Subdued by what they were sure was a religious experience, dance pavilion owners in St. Clair County closed up shop. And, it is reported, the small churches that dotted the surrounding valleys experienced a surge in attendance.

Even though there never has been a night to compare with that one in November, 1833, Alabamians are reminded often of that evening. Many homes or events are dated from that one - someone might say, for example,

"That house was built 20 years after the stars fell."

A book, "Stars Fell on Alabama," was written by Carl Carmer in 1934 and became a best seller of its time. Carmer's book told of his experiences in Alabama as a Northerner who came to teach at the University of Alabama.

Then there is the song, also composed in 1934. Mitchell Parish wrote the lyrics and Frank Perkins, the music. Parish, a native of Massachusetts, counted a number of songs with Southern themes among his successes. Perkins, from Louisiana, wrote a number of hit songs - many of them star-struck - including "Stairway to the Stars."

The tune became a signature piece for Big Band Leader Jack Teagarden, and pop singer Jimmy Buffett, a Mobile native, regularly delivers his own version of the song at his concerts.

And what happened to the stars that fell on Alabama that night?

The story is that they plunged into the Gulf of Mexico, just off Alabama's Southern shore. The starfish that wash ashore there are said to be the stars from that night, changed to this new form by the passing of time.

Index

Index

Author Thanks

W riting this book has been a wonderful learning and exploring experience for me. I've met and talked to people from all over the state. And, just as I suspected when I started out, those people have been gracious, helpful and patient. They've answered questions they probably have heard hundreds of times with the same kindness they used when they answered the sometimes less than intelligent questions no one else would have dared ask.

There are a number of people who have been my resources, my support group, my proofreaders, my reference book carriers and my friends while I was so wrapped up in "the book." I want to take this opportunity to thank them.

Many thanks to Susann, who always had the answers or knew where to get them; to Vickie, who "loves research" and wouldn't give up on my question; my husband and children, who put up with a crazy person a lot of the time and ate a goodly number of "frozen, pre-packaged convenience foods;" my mother, who has told everyone she knows to buy the book; my Aunt Edna, who gave me a slow cooker and thereby spared my family from having to eat even more "frozen, pre-packaged convenience foods;" the other Lynn, who had lots of good stuff and was willing to share; Beck and Randy, who gave me quality time when I needed it; Peg, who told me I could when I said I couldn't; Joan, who always has been there for me and hasn't complained because I haven't been there for her much lately; Nancy, who kept my mind aerobically fit, even when my body wasn't and Mary, who encouraged me to make my fantasies become realities.

ALABAMA
STATE PARKS

CAMPERS WILL ENJOY
ALABAMA STATE PARKS

2,450 IMPROVED CAMPSITES!!!!!

STATE PARK	IMPROVED CAMPSITES	CITY	PHONE
Blue Springs	50	Clio	397-4875
Buck's Pocket	45	Grove Oak	659-2000
Cheaha	73	Lineville	488-5115
Chewacla	36	Auburn	887-5621
DeSoto	78	Fort Payne	845-5075
Florala	30	Florala	858-6425
Gulf	468	Gulf Shores	948-6353
Joe Wheeler	116	Rogersville	247-1184
Lake Guntersville	322	Guntersville	582-8418
Lake Lurleen	86	Coker	339-1558
Lakepoint Resort	244	Eufaula	687-6676
Monte Sano	89	Huntsville	534-6589
Oak Mountain	91	Pelham	663-3061
Roland Cooper	41	Camden	682-4838
Rickwood Caverns	20	Warrior	647-9692
Wind Creek	669	Alexander City	329-0845

ALABAMA STATE PARKS
CENTRAL RESERVATION SERVICE
FOR CAMPSITES, CABINS, CHALETS AND LODGES
CALL TOLL FREE
1-800-ALA-PARK (Nationwide)
Monday-Friday — 8:00 A.M. - 5:00 P.M. — Except Holidays

MASTER CARD
and VISA Accepted
in Major Park facilities

April, 1990

Call (205) 242-3333
IN MONTGOMERY, ALABAMA
Alabama Department of
Conservation & Natural Resources
DIVISION OF STATE PARKS
64 North Union Street
Montgomery, Alabama 36130

Printed in U.S.A.

Alabama's State Parks 229

ALABAMA STATE PARKS

STATE PARK	ACRES	Improved Campsites/with facilities	Primitive Camping	Campstore	Comfort Stations	Family Cottage (Units)	Motel (Units)	Restaurant	Convention, Meeting Room Facilities	Gift Shop	Group Lodge	Golf Course (Size)	Marina	Picnic Area	Play Area	Refreshments	Swimming	Boating	Fishing	Hiking	Tennis	Bicycle Rentals	Horse Stables & Trails	Fishing Pier	Group Pavilions
Cheaha	2,179	73	A	A	A	15	30	A	A	A	A			A	A	A	A		A	A					A
DeSoto	5,067	78	A	A	A	21	25	A	A	A				A	A	A		A	A	A					A
Gulf	6,000	468		A	A	21	144	A	A	A	A	18	A	A	A	A	A	A	A	A	A	A			A	A
Joe Wheeler	2,550	116	A	A	A	23	74	A	A	A	A	18	A	A	A	A	A	A	A	A					A
Lake Guntersville	5,909	322	A	A	A	34	100	A	A	A		18		A	A	A	A	A	A	A				A	A
Lake Lurleen	1,625	86		A	A								A	A	A	A	A	A	A	A				A	A
Lakepoint Resort	1,220	244		A	A	29	101	A	A	A		18	A	A	A	A	A	A	A	A	A	A		A	A
Oak Mountain	9,940	49		A	A	10			A			18	A	A	A	A	A	A	A	A	A		A		A
Roland Cooper	200	41		A	A	5						9		A	A	A		A	A						A
Wind Creek	1,445	669		A	A								A	A	A	A	A	A	A	A				A	A
Bladon Springs	357													A	A										A
Blue Springs	103	50	A		A									A	A	A	A	A	A		A				A
Buck's Pocket	2,000	45	A	A	A									A				A	A	A					
Chattahoochee	596		A		A									A	A										
Chewacla	696	36	A		A	5								A	A	A	A	A	A	A					A
Chickasaw	40		A		A									A	A					A					A
Florala	40	C	P		A									A	A	A	A	A							A
Claude D. Kelley	960		A		A	2								A	A		A	A	A	P					A
Monte Sano	2,140	89	A	A	A	14								A	A	A				A					A
Paul M. Grist	1,080		A		A									A	A		A	A	A	A					A
Rickwood Caverns	380	20	A		A					A				A	A	A	A			A					A
Cathedral Caverns	100	P			P	P		P	P					P	P	P									
Frank Jackson	2,050	P	P		P									P	P			P	P	P				P	P
Meaher	1,327	P			P									P	P									P	

A — Available
C — Under Construction
P — Planned Construction

Some facilities are seasonal
No PETS allowed In State Parks Lodging Facilities, Including motel rooms, cabins, cottages and chalets.

CAMPGROUND REGULATIONS

Only one camping unit per site. "Doubling up" is not allowed.

Maximum occupancy per site: 8 persons, 2 motor vehicles. Occupancy limited to 14 days: April 1 through October 31. Pets must be kept on a leash. They are not allowed on beaches or in buildings, (except seeing eye dogs.)

Minors under age 18 must be accompanied by a responsible adult.

No open fires are permitted, except in the grills provided at each campsite, or in areas specifically designated by Park Manager.

Drainage of water, soap, grease or any other waste product onto the ground or into anything other than an approved holding tank or the sewage receptacles and dump stations provided is a violation of State Law. Use a suitable holding fixture for **ALL** waste water and dispose of properly.

Quiet hours are enforced from 10:00 p.m. until 6:00 a.m.

Complete Parks Regulations are posted in conspicuous locations. Please be familiar with and observe these regulations.

Tent or RV must occupy campsite immediately after registering.

ALABAMA STATE PARKS CENTRAL RESERVATION.SERVICE CALL TOLL FREE 1-800-ALA-PARK NATIONWIDE

IN MONTGOMERY, ALABAMA CALL 261-3333

The Alabama State Parks Central Reservation service is open Monday through Friday from 8:00 A.M. until 5:00 P.M. (except holidays).

CAMPGROUND RESERVATION PROCEDURES

A non-refundable deposit equal to one night rental will be required in order to reserve a campsite. Campsites may be reserved by telephoning directly the park of your choice, or to the Central Reservation Center. **Collect calls will not be accepted.** Reservations will be taken at each park between 9:00 a.m. and 5:00 p.m., Monday through Friday, and at the Central Reservation Center between 8:00 a.m. and 5:00 p.m., Monday through Friday. Reservations will not be taken during weekends or holidays.

Reservations will be accepted for anyone who wishes to reserve a campsite for one week or more up to 12 months prior to arrival date. Anyone who wishes to reserve a campsite for less than a week may reserve no more than 60 days prior to the day of arrival.

2-Nights rental is required on weekend reservations.

3-Nights rental is required on the following weekends: Memorial Day, Independence Day, and Labor Day.

No camping group or club reservations will be made for Memorial Day, July 4, and Labor Day weekends.

Reservations will be accepted for improved campsites, in most parks. Specific campsites will not be reserved. No reservations required for primitive campsites.

Method of Prepayment: Bank Americard (VISA) and Master Card will be accepted by phone. Postal money orders or certified checks will be accepted if received 10 days from the date the reservation is taken. Prepayments subject to Bank approval. Note: **Personal Checks Not Accepted.**

CHECK-IN TIME — 4:00 P.M. IN MOST PARKS
CHECK-OUT TIME — 11:00 A.M. IN MOST PARKS

NOTE: Campers who are staying in the campground and decide to stay an extra day past their reservations must renew their permit prior to 11:00 A.M. on check out date in order to keep their site, providing it has not been reserved and is still available.

Traveler's Notes

ABOUT THE AUTHOR

LYNN EDGE started her writing career as a general assignment reporter for The Birmingham News. For the last 18 years, she has been a freelance writer, contributing to newspapers and magazines throughout the United States.

While "Shoals to Sand Dunes" is her first book, her second - a Guide/Cookbook on the Bed and Breakfasts of Alabama - already is in the works.

Ms. Edge is married and has two children. She and her family live in Birmingham.